MICHAEL MORBIUS was born with a rare blood disorder. Seeking a cure, he devoted his life to medicine and became a Nobel Prize-winning researcher.

As his efforts to find a cure proved fruitless, Morbius grew impatient. He developed a new treatment using vampire bat DNA and electroshock therapy…with himself as the test subject!

The experiment successfully changed his genetics but at a terrible price. Michael gained the ability to fly, a regenerative healing factor and a unique hypnotic stare, but, in turn, he's grown fangs, becomes weaker when in sunlight and walks the Earth with an unrelenting bloodlust as…

Morbius
THE LIVING VAMPIRE

VITA AYALA
writer

MARCELO FERREIRA
with PAULO SIQUEIRA *(#4)*
& FRANCESCO MOBILI *(#5)*
pencilers

ROBERTO POGGI
with SCOTT HANNA *(#2, #4)*
& JP MAYER *(#5)*
inkers

DONO SÁNCHEZ-ALMARA
color artist

VC's CLAYTON COWLES
letterer

DANNY KHAZEM
assistant editor

DEVIN LEWIS
editor

collection editor JENNIFER GRÜNWALD † assistant managing editor MAIA LOY

assistant managing editor LISA MONTALBANO † editor, special projects MARK D. BEAZLEY

vp production & special projects JEFF YOUNGQUIST † book designer JAY BOWEN with ANTHONY GAMBINO

svp print, sales & marketing DAVID GABRIEL † editor in chief C.B. CEBULSKI

MORBIUS VOL. 1: OLD WOUNDS. Contains material originally published in magazine form as MORBIUS (2019) #1-5. First printing 2020. ISBN 978-1-302-92099-9. Published by MARVEL WORLDWIDE, INC., a subsidiary of MARVEL ENTERTAINMENT, LLC. OFFICE OF PUBLICATION: 1290 Avenue of the Americas, New York, NY 10104. © 2020 MARVEL No similarity between any of the names, characters, persons, and/or institutions in this magazine with those of any living or dead person or institution is intended, and any such similarity which may exist is purely coincidental. Printed in Canada. KEVIN FEIGE, Chief Creative Officer; DAN BUCKLEY, President, Marvel Entertainment; JOHN NEE, Publisher; JOE QUESADA, EVP & Creative Director; TOM BREVOORT, SVP of Publishing; DAVID BOGART, Associate Publisher & SVP of Talent Affairs; Publishing & Partnership; DAVID GABRIEL, VP of Print & Digital Publishing; JEFF YOUNGQUIST, VP of Production & Special Projects; DAN CARR, Executive Director of Publishing Technology; ALEX MORALES, Director of Publishing Operations; DAN EDINGTON, Managing Editor; SUSAN CRESPI, Production Manager; STAN LEE, Chairman Emeritus. For information regarding advertising in Marvel Comics or on Marvel.com, please contact Vit DeBellis, Custom Solutions & Integrated Advertising Manager, at vdebellis@marvel.com. For Marvel subscription inquiries, please call 888-511-5480. Manufactured between 3/6/2020 and 4/7/2020 by SOLISCO PRINTERS, SCOTT, QC, CANADA.

10 9 8 7 6 5 4 3 2 1

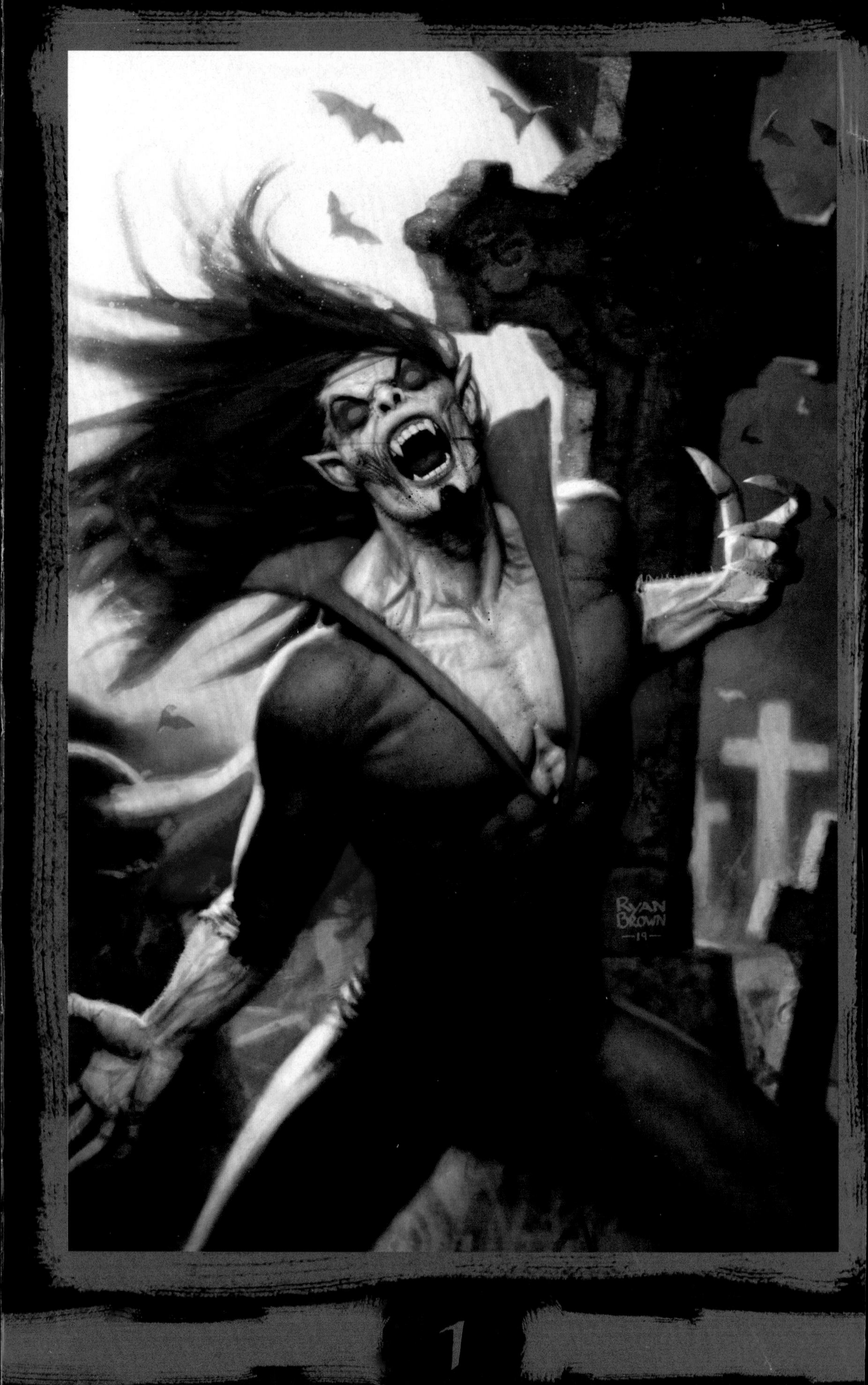
RYAN
BROWN
-19-

1

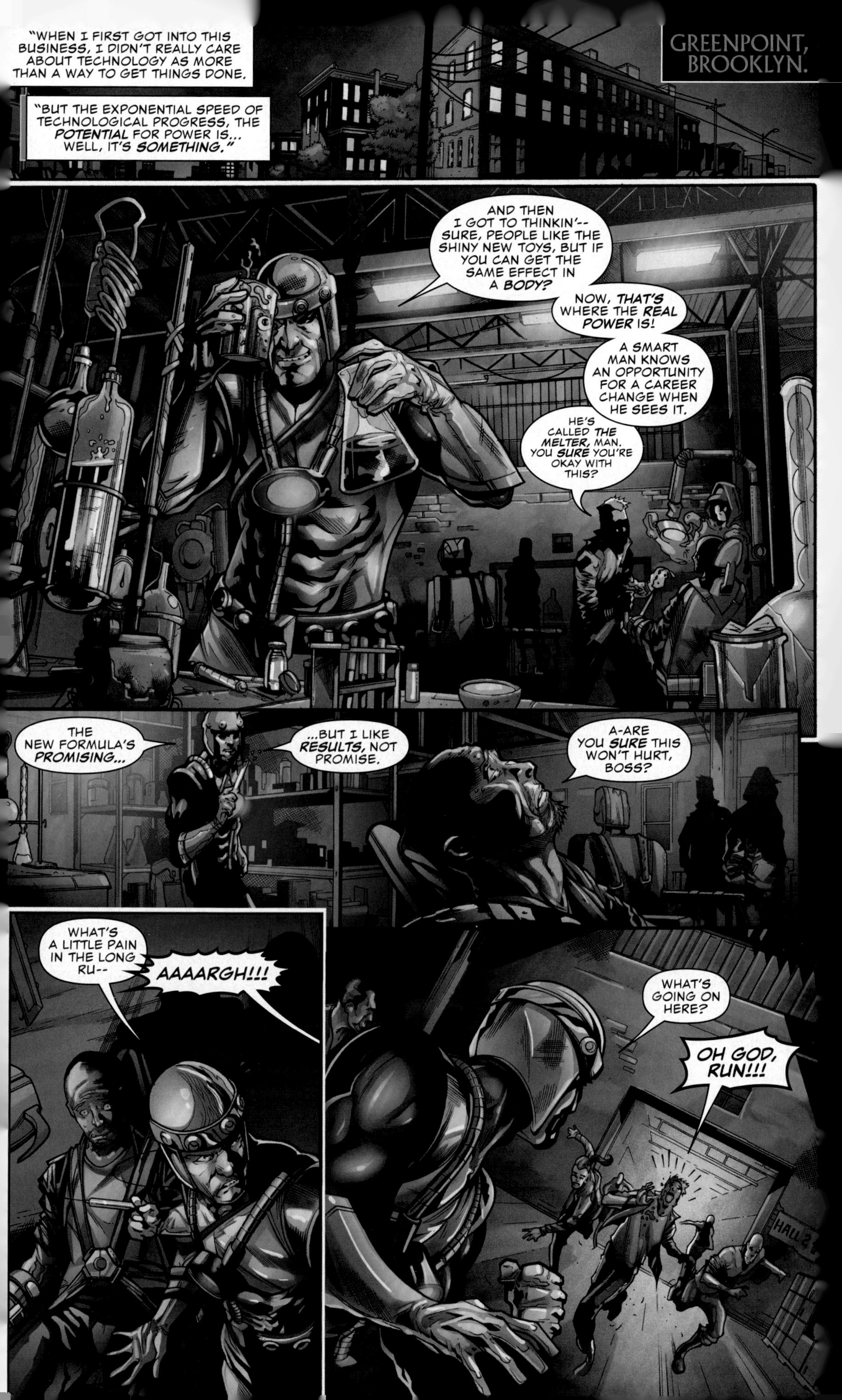

GREENPOINT, BROOKLYN.
"WHEN I FIRST GOT INTO THIS BUSINESS, I DIDN'T REALLY CARE ABOUT TECHNOLOGY AS MORE THAN A WAY TO GET THINGS DONE.
"BUT THE EXPONENTIAL SPEED OF TECHNOLOGICAL PROGRESS, THE POTENTIAL FOR POWER IS... WELL, IT'S SOMETHING."
AND THEN I GOT TO THINKIN'-- SURE, PEOPLE LIKE THE SHINY NEW TOYS, BUT IF YOU CAN GET THE SAME EFFECT IN A BODY?
NOW, THAT'S WHERE THE REAL POWER IS!
A SMART MAN KNOWS AN OPPORTUNITY FOR A CAREER CHANGE WHEN HE SEES IT.
HE'S CALLED THE MELTER, MAN. YOU SURE YOU'RE OKAY WITH THIS?
THE NEW FORMULA'S PROMISING...
...BUT I LIKE RESULTS, NOT PROMISE.
A-ARE YOU SURE THIS WON'T HURT, BOSS?
WHAT'S A LITTLE PAIN IN THE LONG RU--
AAAARGH!!!
WHAT'S GOING ON HERE?
OH GOD, RUN!!!

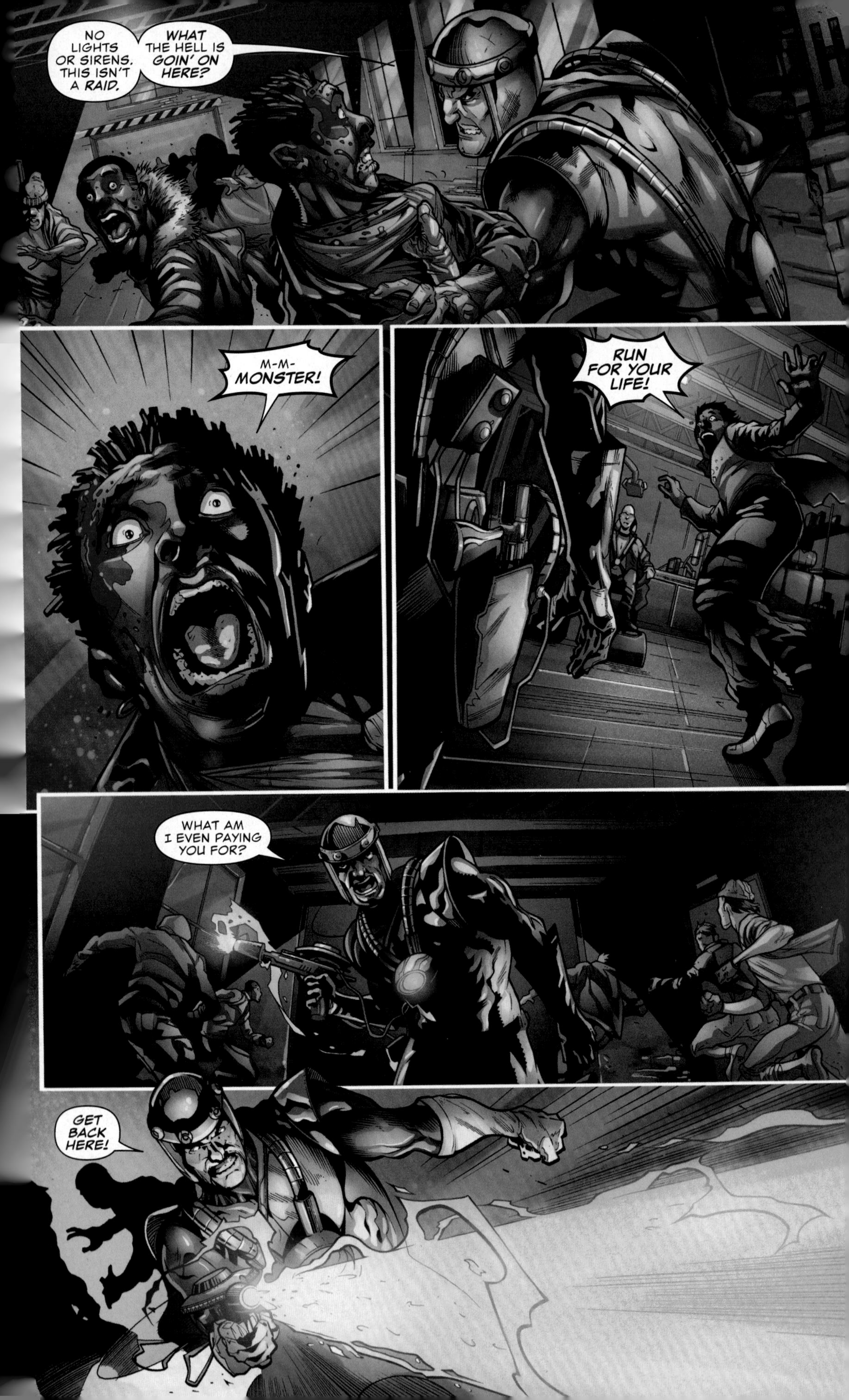
NO LIGHTS OR SIRENS. THIS ISN'T A RAID.
WHAT THE HELL IS GOIN' ON HERE?
M-M-MONSTER!
RUN FOR YOUR LIFE!
WHAT AM I EVEN PAYING YOU FOR?
GET BACK HERE!

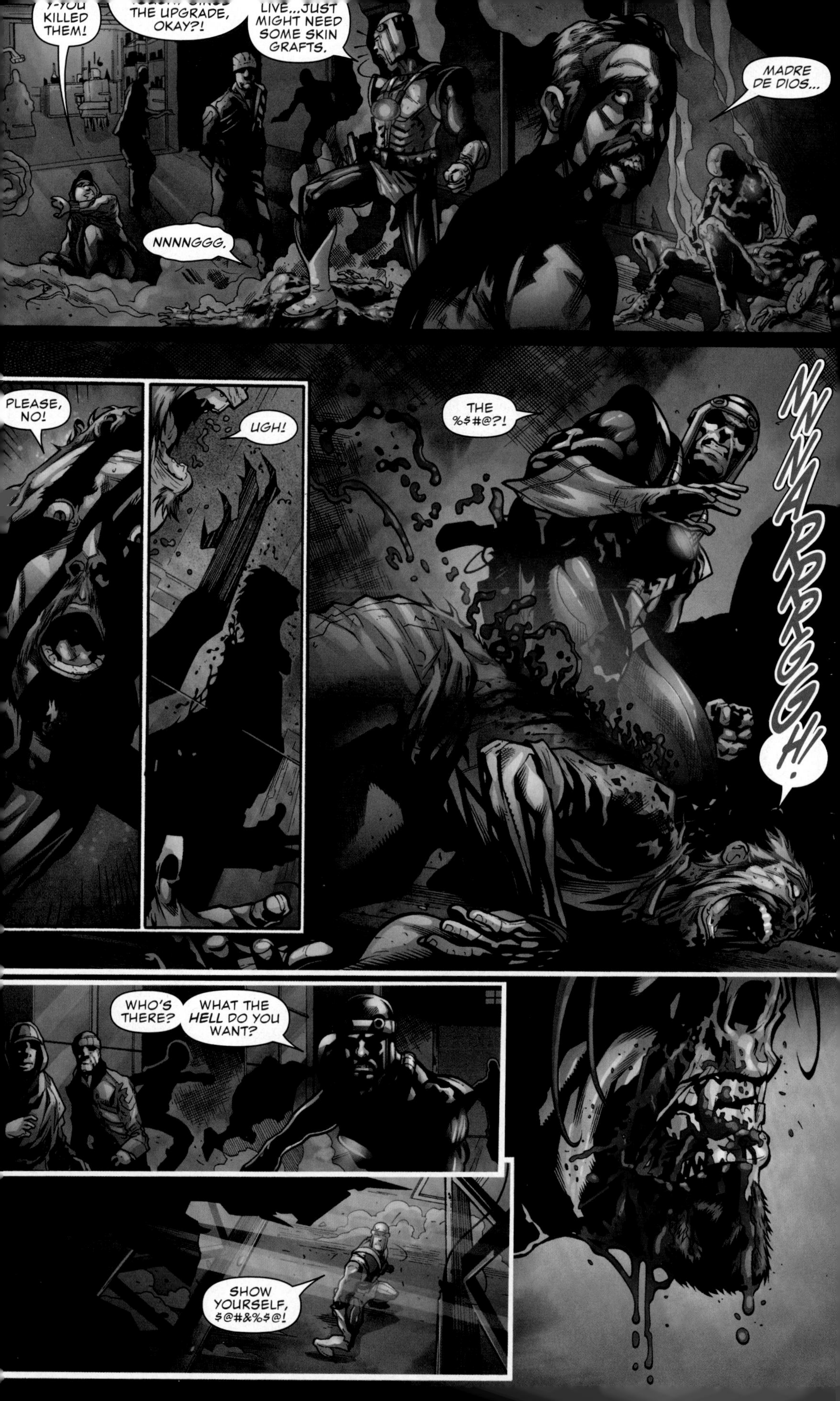

KILLED THEM!
THE UPGRADE, OKAY?!
LIVE...JUST MIGHT NEED SOME SKIN GRAFTS.
MADRE DE DIOS...
NNNNGGG.
PLEASE, NO!
UGH!
THE %$#@?!
NNNARRRGGH!
WHO'S THERE?
WHAT THE HELL DO YOU WANT?
SHOW YOURSELF, $@#&%$@!

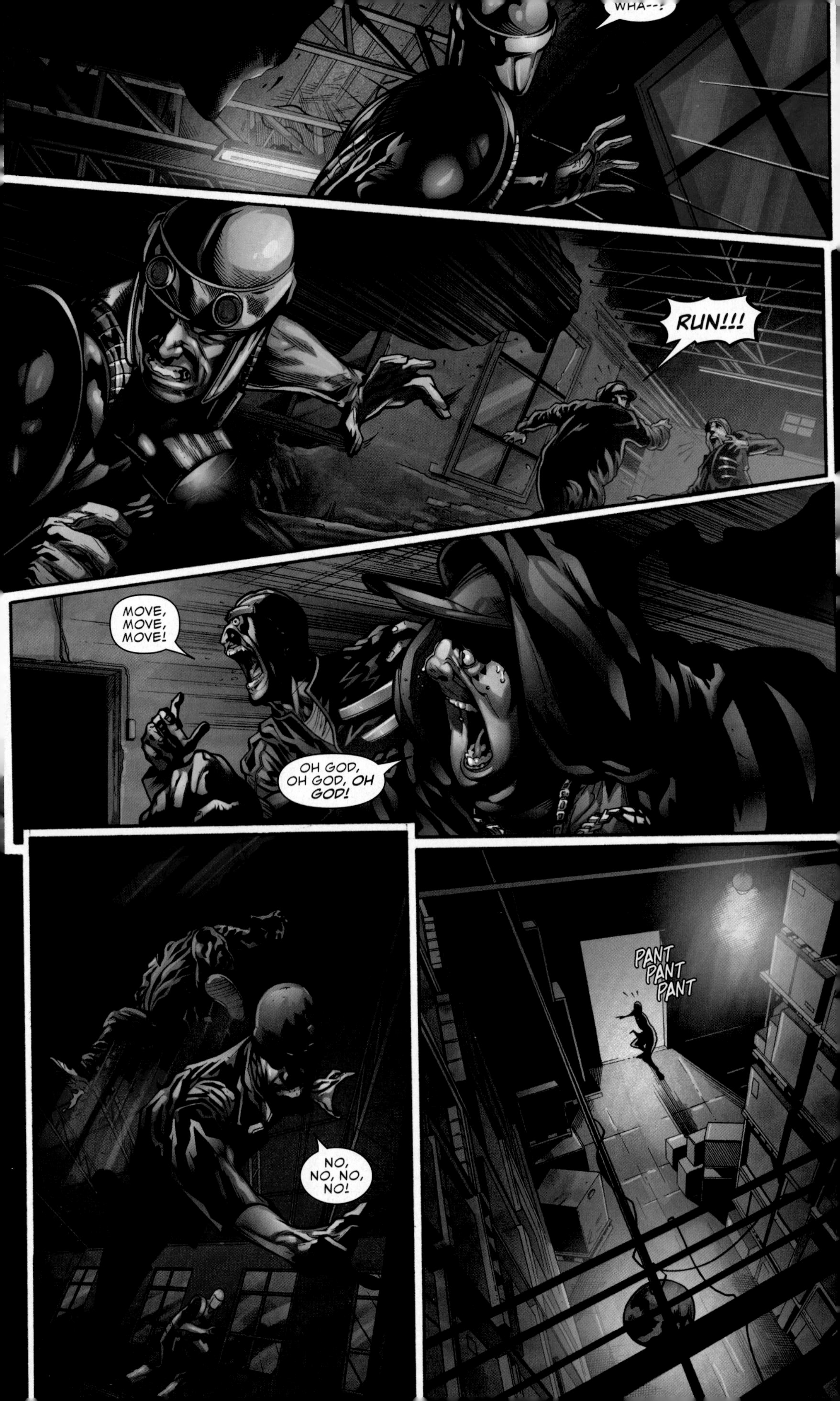
WHA--?
RUN!!!
MOVE, MOVE, MOVE!
OH GOD, OH GOD, OH GOD!
NO, NO, NO, NO!
PANT PANT PANT

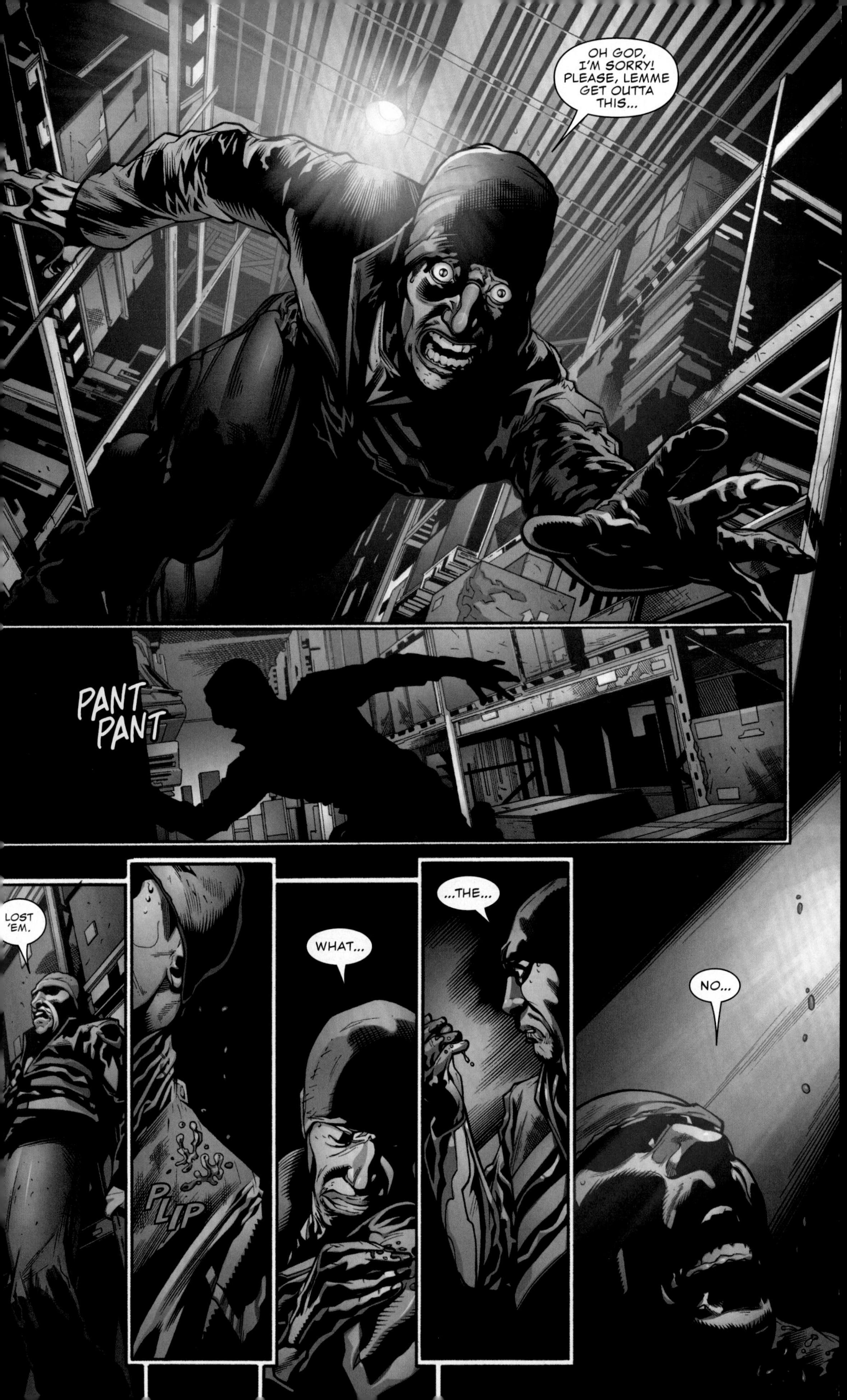
OH GOD, I'M SORRY! PLEASE, LEMME GET OUTTA THIS...
PANT PANT
LOST 'EM.
PLIP
WHAT...
...THE...
NO...

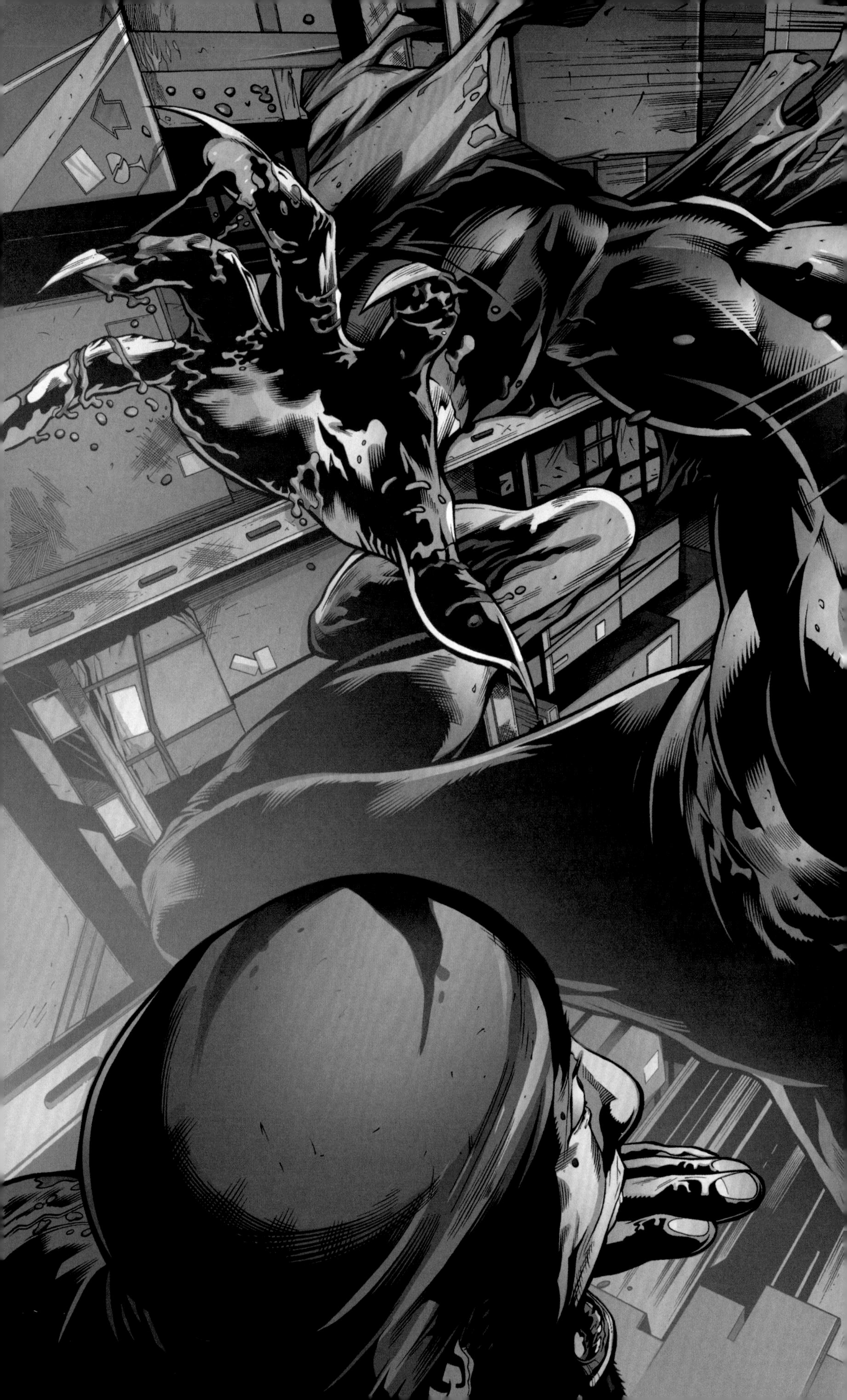

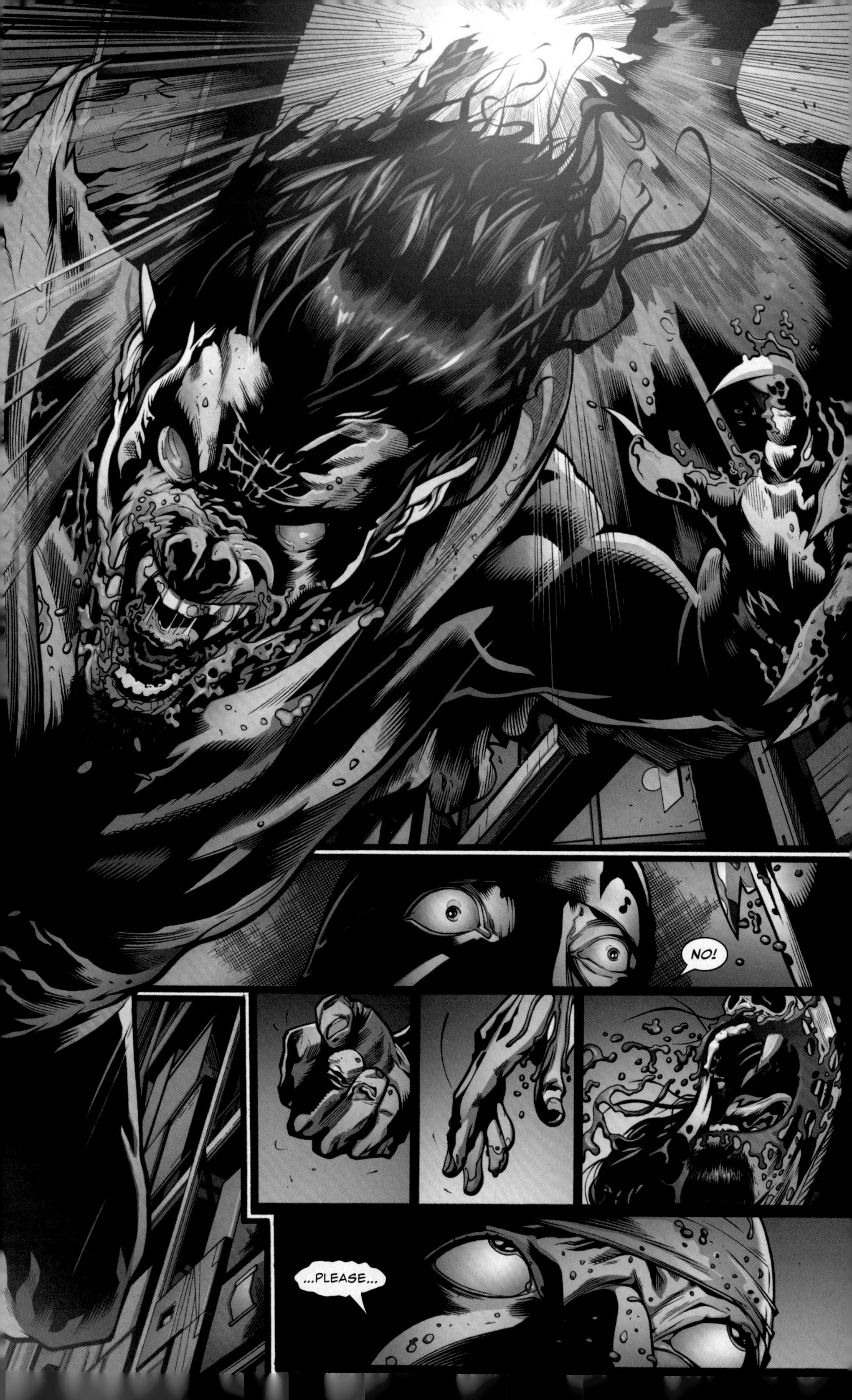
NO!
...PLEASE...

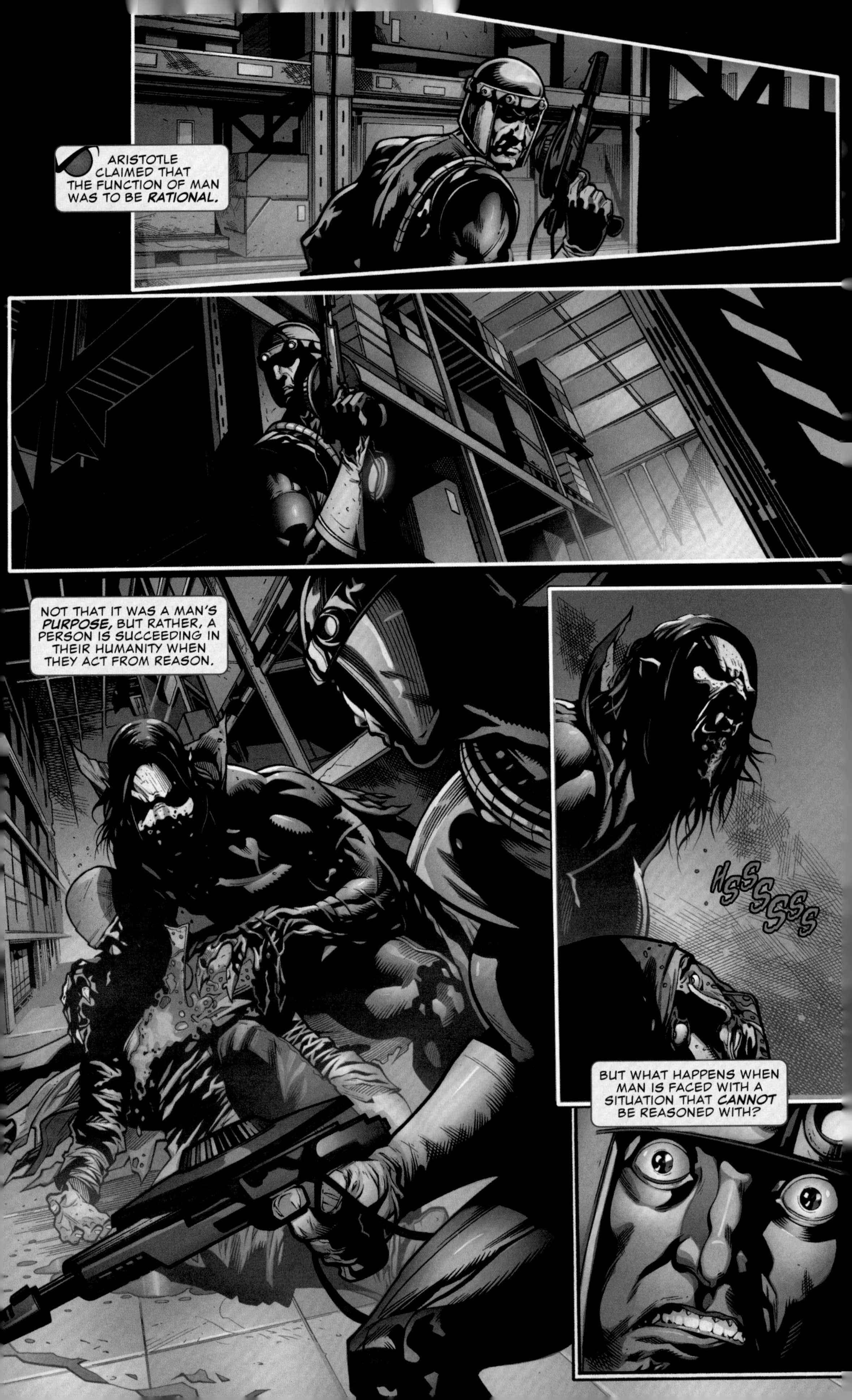
ARISTOTLE CLAIMED THAT THE FUNCTION OF MAN WAS TO BE RATIONAL.
NOT THAT IT WAS A MAN'S PURPOSE, BUT RATHER, A PERSON IS SUCCEEDING IN THEIR HUMANITY WHEN THEY ACT FROM REASON.
HSSSSSS
BUT WHAT HAPPENS WHEN MAN IS FACED WITH A SITUATION THAT CANNOT BE REASONED WITH?

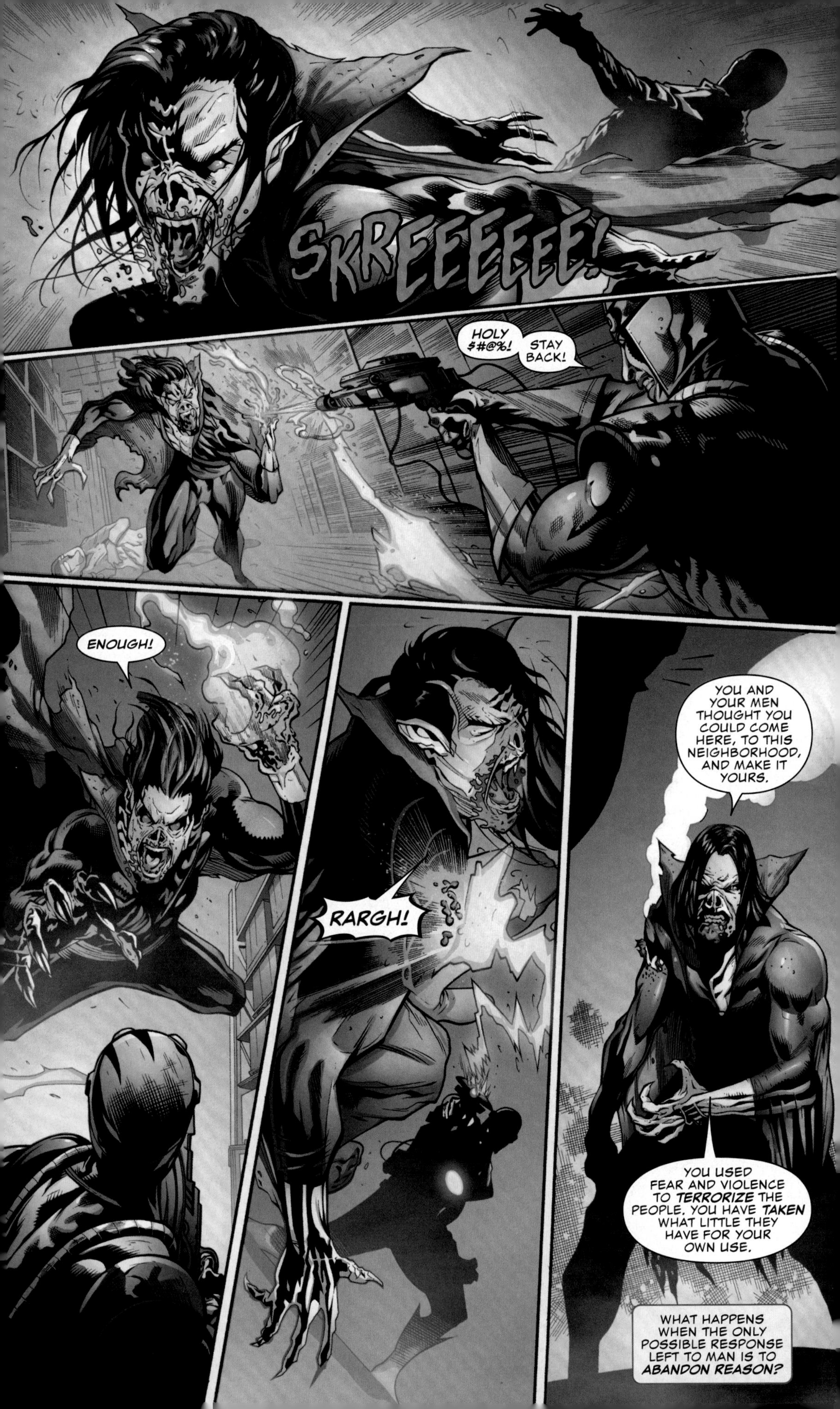

SKREEEEEEE!
HOLY $#@%!
STAY BACK!
ENOUGH!
RARGH!
YOU AND YOUR MEN THOUGHT YOU COULD COME HERE, TO THIS NEIGHBORHOOD, AND MAKE IT YOURS.
YOU USED FEAR AND VIOLENCE TO TERRORIZE THE PEOPLE. YOU HAVE TAKEN WHAT LITTLE THEY HAVE FOR YOUR OWN USE.
WHAT HAPPENS WHEN THE ONLY POSSIBLE RESPONSE LEFT TO MAN IS TO ABANDON REASON?

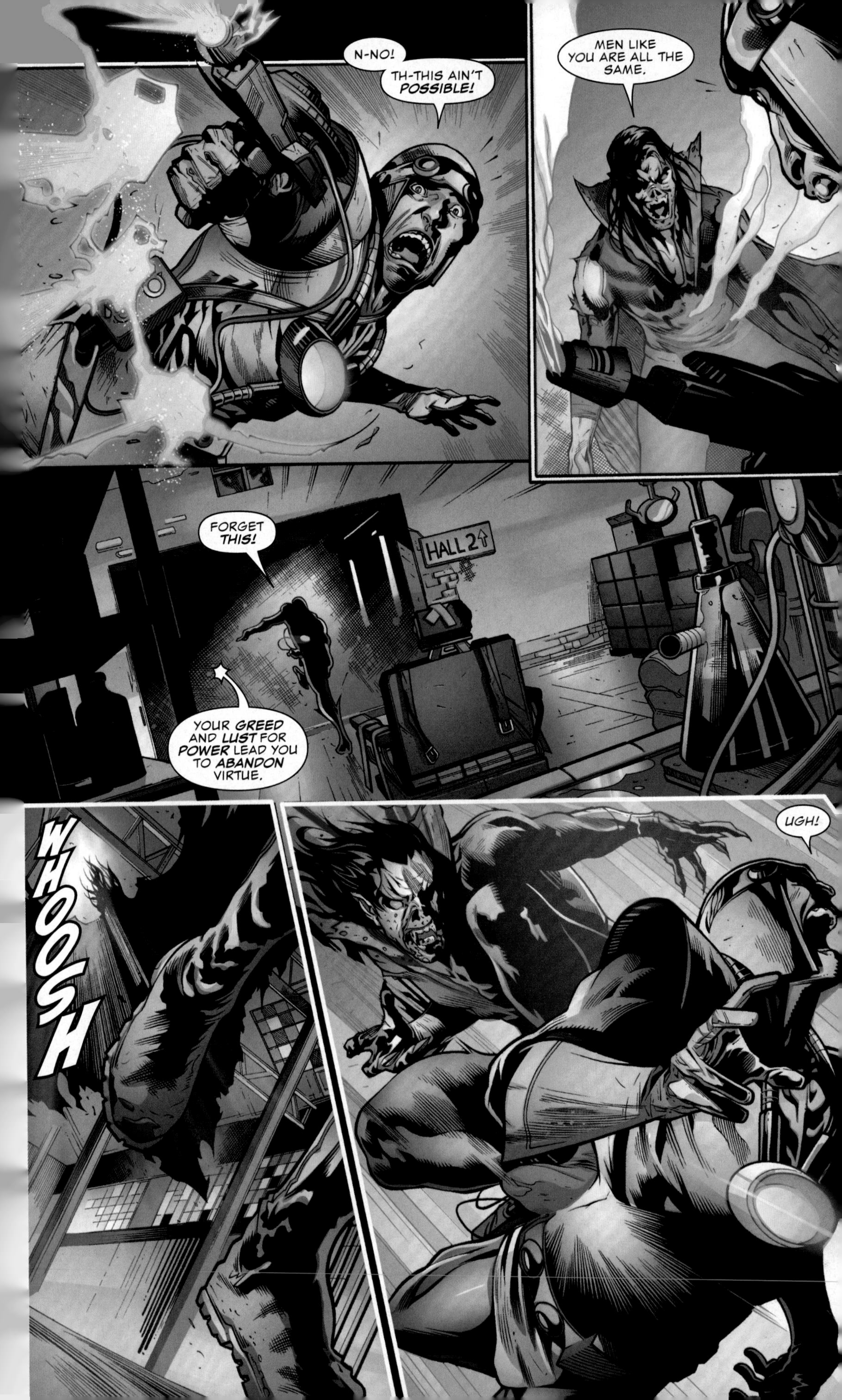
N-NO!
TH-THIS AIN'T POSSIBLE!
MEN LIKE YOU ARE ALL THE SAME.
FORGET THIS!
HALL 2
YOUR GREED AND LUST FOR POWER LEAD YOU TO ABANDON VIRTUE.
WHOOOSH
UGH!

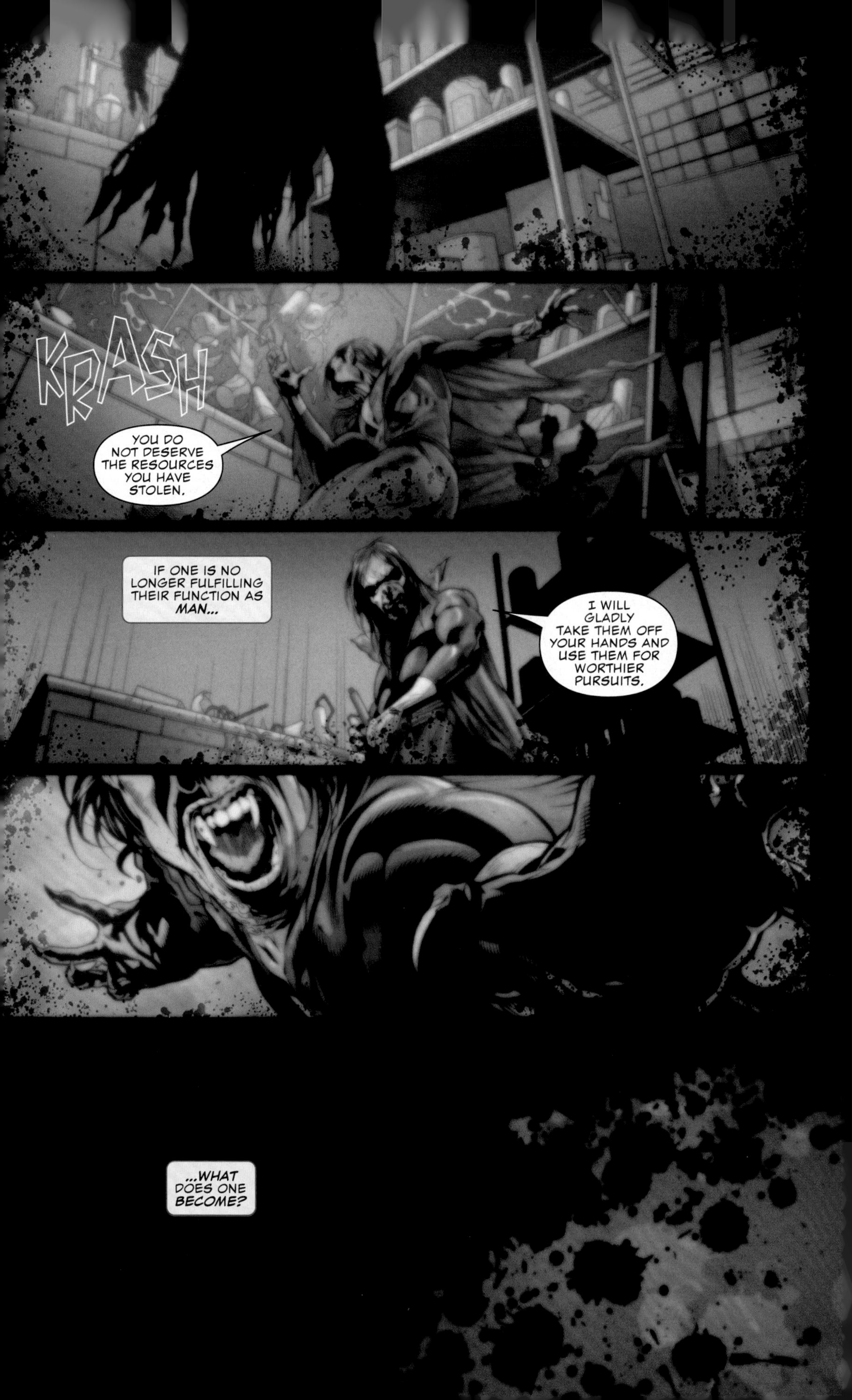
KRASH
YOU DO NOT DESERVE THE RESOURCES YOU HAVE STOLEN.
IF ONE IS NO LONGER FULFILLING THEIR FUNCTION AS MAN...
I WILL GLADLY TAKE THEM OFF YOUR HANDS AND USE THEM FOR WORTHIER PURSUITS.
...WHAT DOES ONE BECOME?

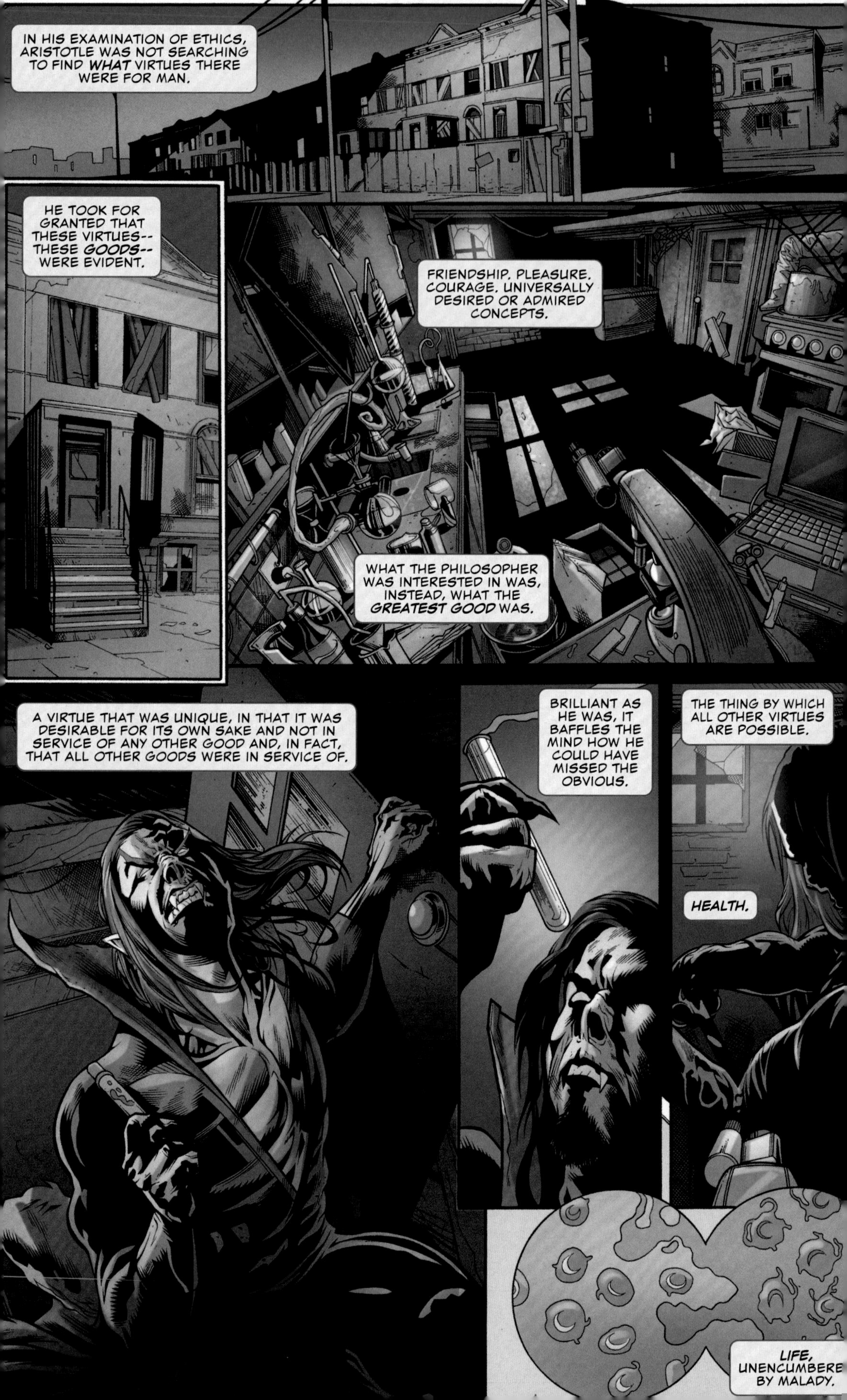
IN HIS EXAMINATION OF ETHICS, ARISTOTLE WAS NOT SEARCHING TO FIND *WHAT* VIRTUES THERE WERE FOR MAN.
HE TOOK FOR GRANTED THAT THESE VIRTUES-- THESE *GOODS*-- WERE EVIDENT.
FRIENDSHIP. PLEASURE. COURAGE. UNIVERSALLY DESIRED OR ADMIRED CONCEPTS.
WHAT THE PHILOSOPHER WAS INTERESTED IN WAS, INSTEAD, WHAT THE *GREATEST GOOD* WAS.
A VIRTUE THAT WAS UNIQUE, IN THAT IT WAS DESIRABLE FOR ITS OWN SAKE AND NOT IN SERVICE OF ANY OTHER GOOD AND, IN FACT, THAT ALL OTHER GOODS WERE IN SERVICE OF.
BRILLIANT AS HE WAS, IT BAFFLES THE MIND HOW HE COULD HAVE MISSED THE OBVIOUS.
THE THING BY WHICH ALL OTHER VIRTUES ARE POSSIBLE.
HEALTH.
LIFE, UNENCUMBERE BY MALADY.

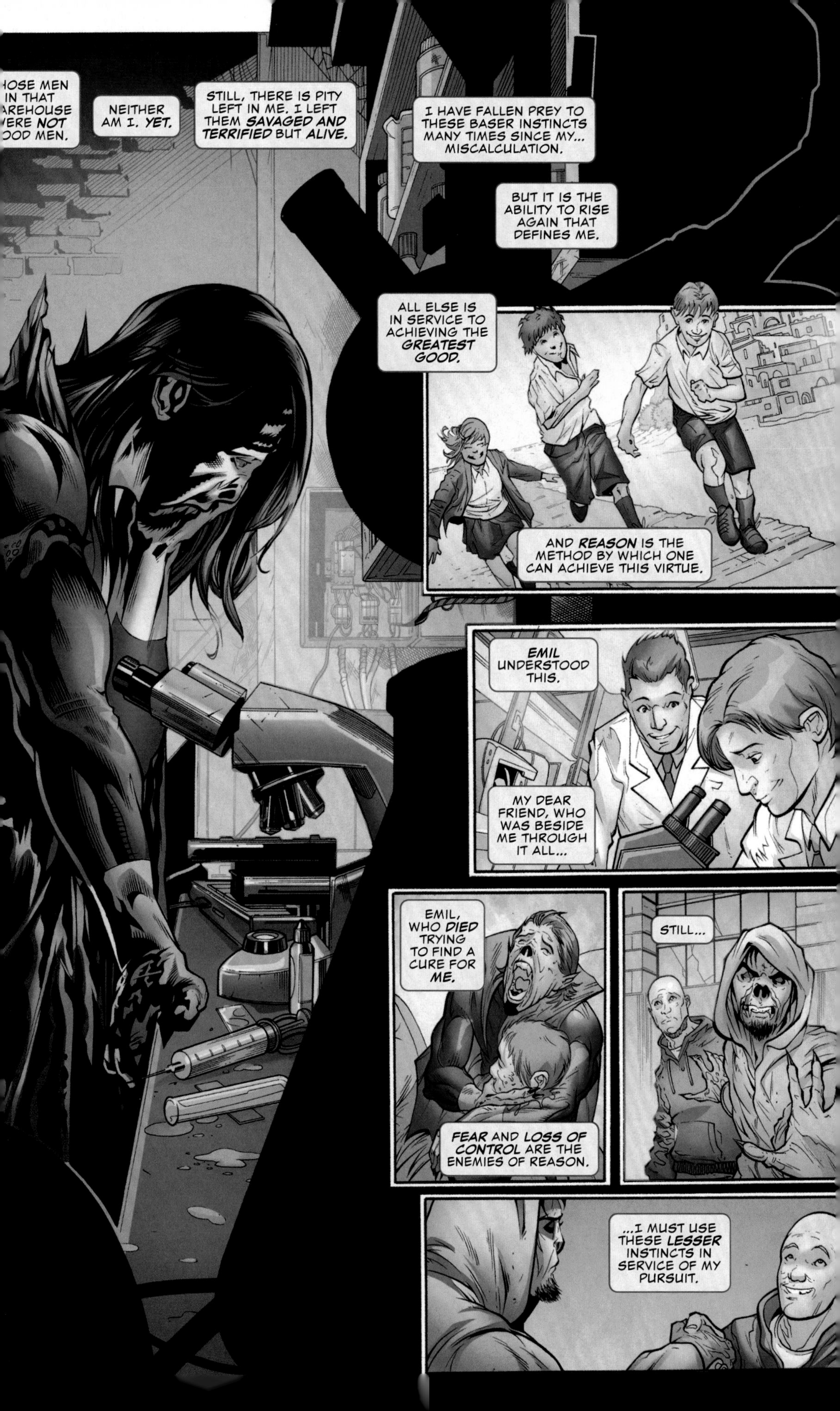
HOSE MEN IN THAT AREHOUSE VERE NOT OOD MEN.
NEITHER AM I. YET.
STILL, THERE IS PITY LEFT IN ME. I LEFT THEM SAVAGED AND TERRIFIED BUT ALIVE.
I HAVE FALLEN PREY TO THESE BASER INSTINCTS MANY TIMES SINCE MY... MISCALCULATION.
BUT IT IS THE ABILITY TO RISE AGAIN THAT DEFINES ME.
ALL ELSE IS IN SERVICE TO ACHIEVING THE GREATEST GOOD.
AND REASON IS THE METHOD BY WHICH ONE CAN ACHIEVE THIS VIRTUE.
EMIL UNDERSTOOD THIS.
MY DEAR FRIEND, WHO WAS BESIDE ME THROUGH IT ALL...
EMIL, WHO DIED TRYING TO FIND A CURE FOR ME.
FEAR AND LOSS OF CONTROL ARE THE ENEMIES OF REASON.
STILL...
...I MUST USE THESE LESSER INSTINCTS IN SERVICE OF MY PURSUIT.

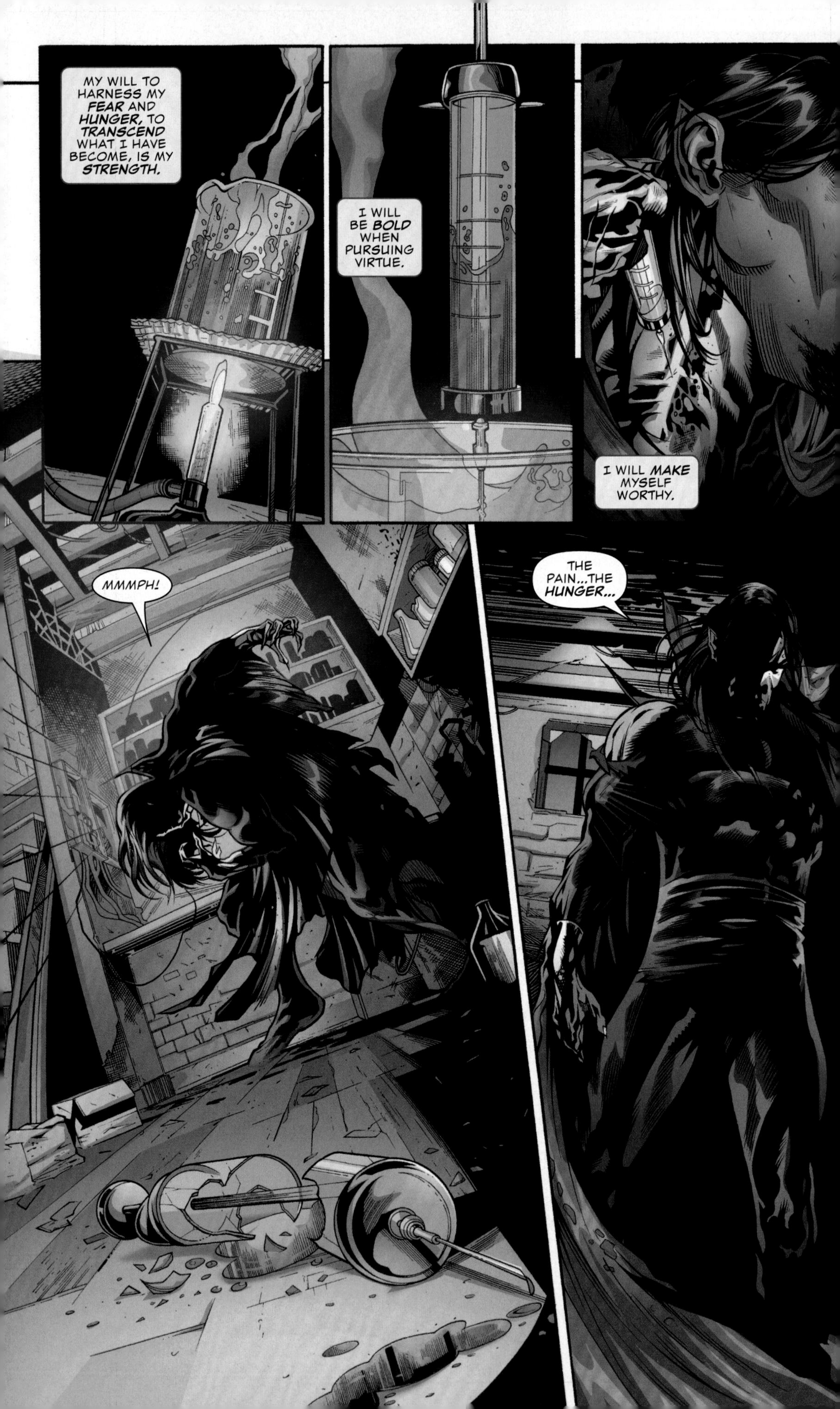

MY WILL TO HARNESS MY FEAR AND HUNGER, TO TRANSCEND WHAT I HAVE BECOME, IS MY STRENGTH.
I WILL BE BOLD WHEN PURSUING VIRTUE.
I WILL MAKE MYSELF WORTHY.
MMMPH!
THE PAIN...THE HUNGER...

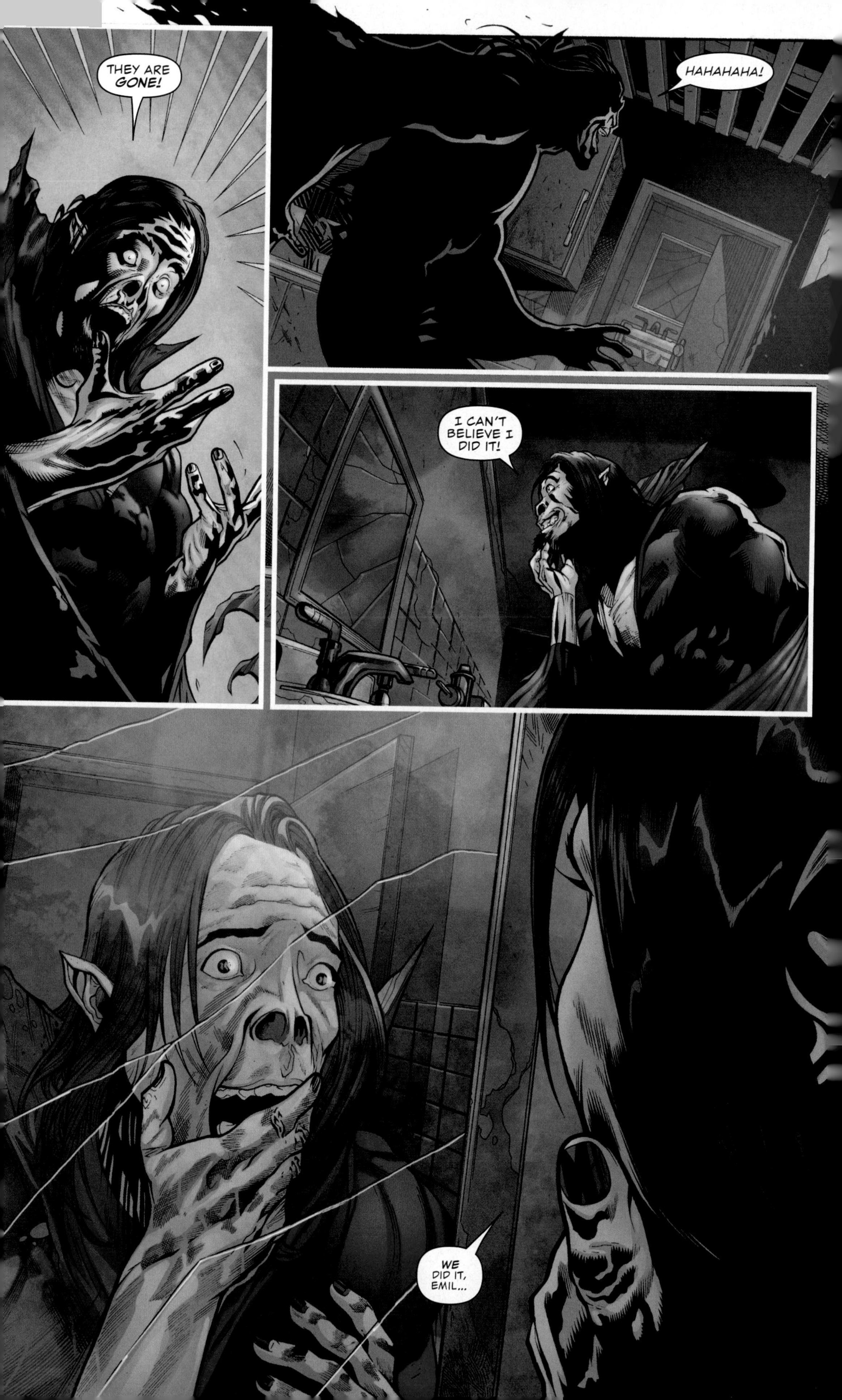

THEY ARE GONE!
HAHAHAHA!
I CAN'T BELIEVE I DID IT!
WE DID IT, EMIL...

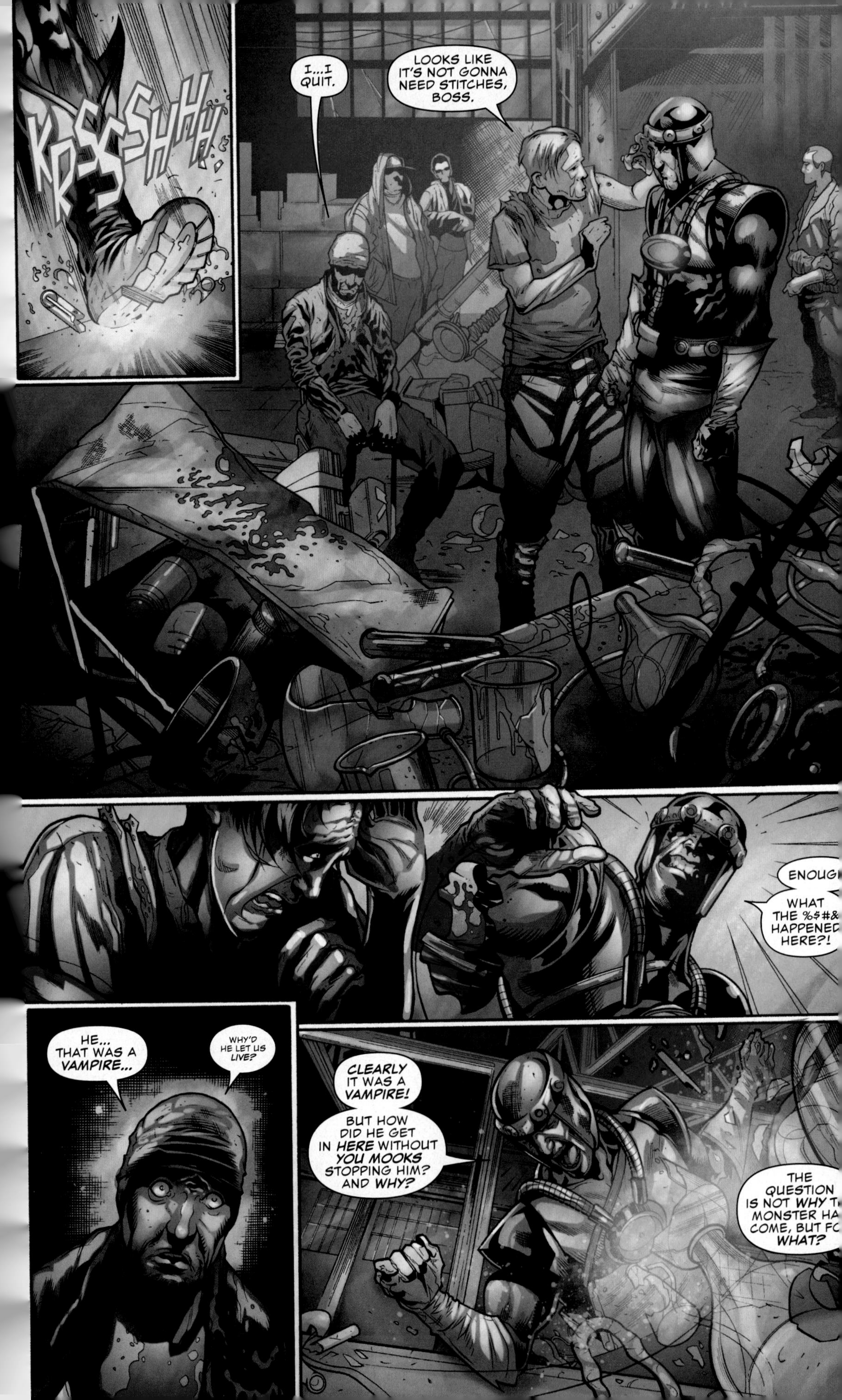

KRSSHHH!
I...I QUIT.
LOOKS LIKE IT'S NOT GONNA NEED STITCHES, BOSS.
ENOUG
WHAT THE %$#& HAPPENED HERE?!
HE... THAT WAS A VAMPIRE...
WHY'D HE LET US LIVE?
CLEARLY IT WAS A VAMPIRE!
BUT HOW DID HE GET IN HERE WITHOUT YOU MOOKS STOPPING HIM? AND WHY?
THE QUESTION IS NOT WHY T MONSTER HA COME, BUT FO WHAT?

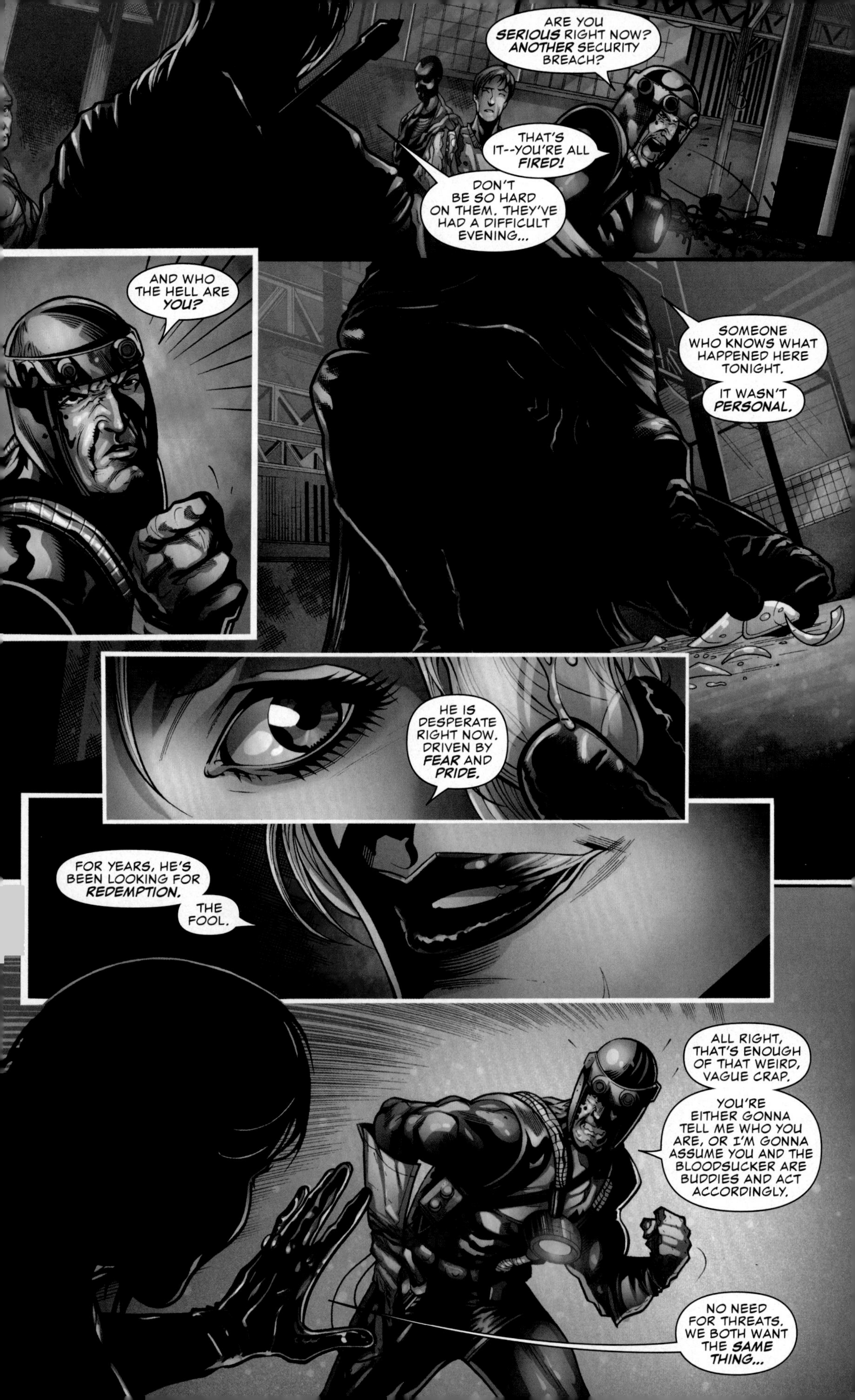
ARE YOU SERIOUS RIGHT NOW? ANOTHER SECURITY BREACH?
THAT'S IT--YOU'RE ALL FIRED!
DON'T BE SO HARD ON THEM. THEY'VE HAD A DIFFICULT EVENING...
AND WHO THE HELL ARE YOU?
SOMEONE WHO KNOWS WHAT HAPPENED HERE TONIGHT.
IT WASN'T PERSONAL.
HE IS DESPERATE RIGHT NOW. DRIVEN BY FEAR AND PRIDE.
FOR YEARS, HE'S BEEN LOOKING FOR REDEMPTION.
THE FOOL.
ALL RIGHT, THAT'S ENOUGH OF THAT WEIRD, VAGUE CRAP.
YOU'RE EITHER GONNA TELL ME WHO YOU ARE, OR I'M GONNA ASSUME YOU AND THE BLOODSUCKER ARE BUDDIES AND ACT ACCORDINGLY.
NO NEED FOR THREATS. WE BOTH WANT THE SAME THING...

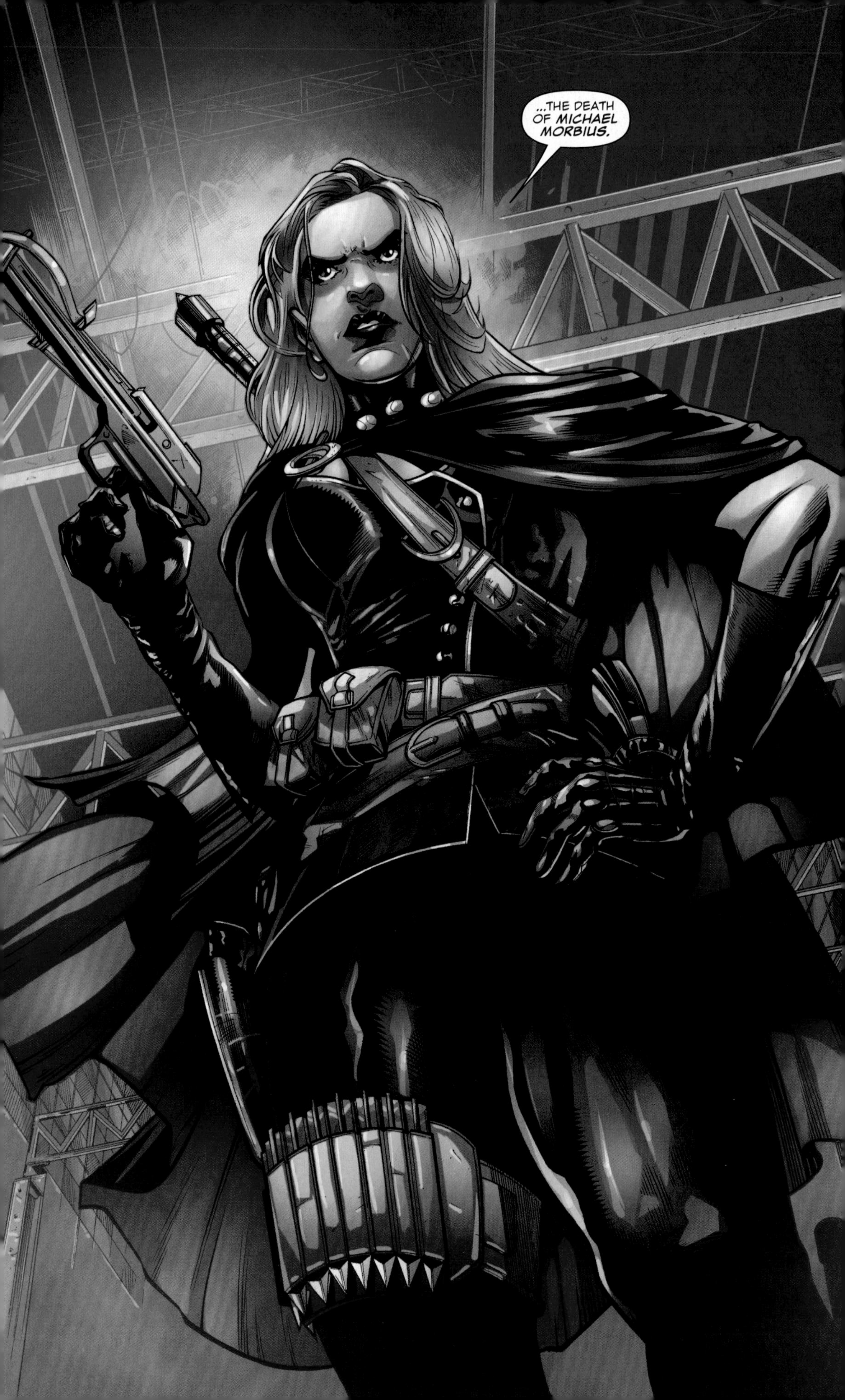

...THE DEATH OF MICHAEL MORBIUS.

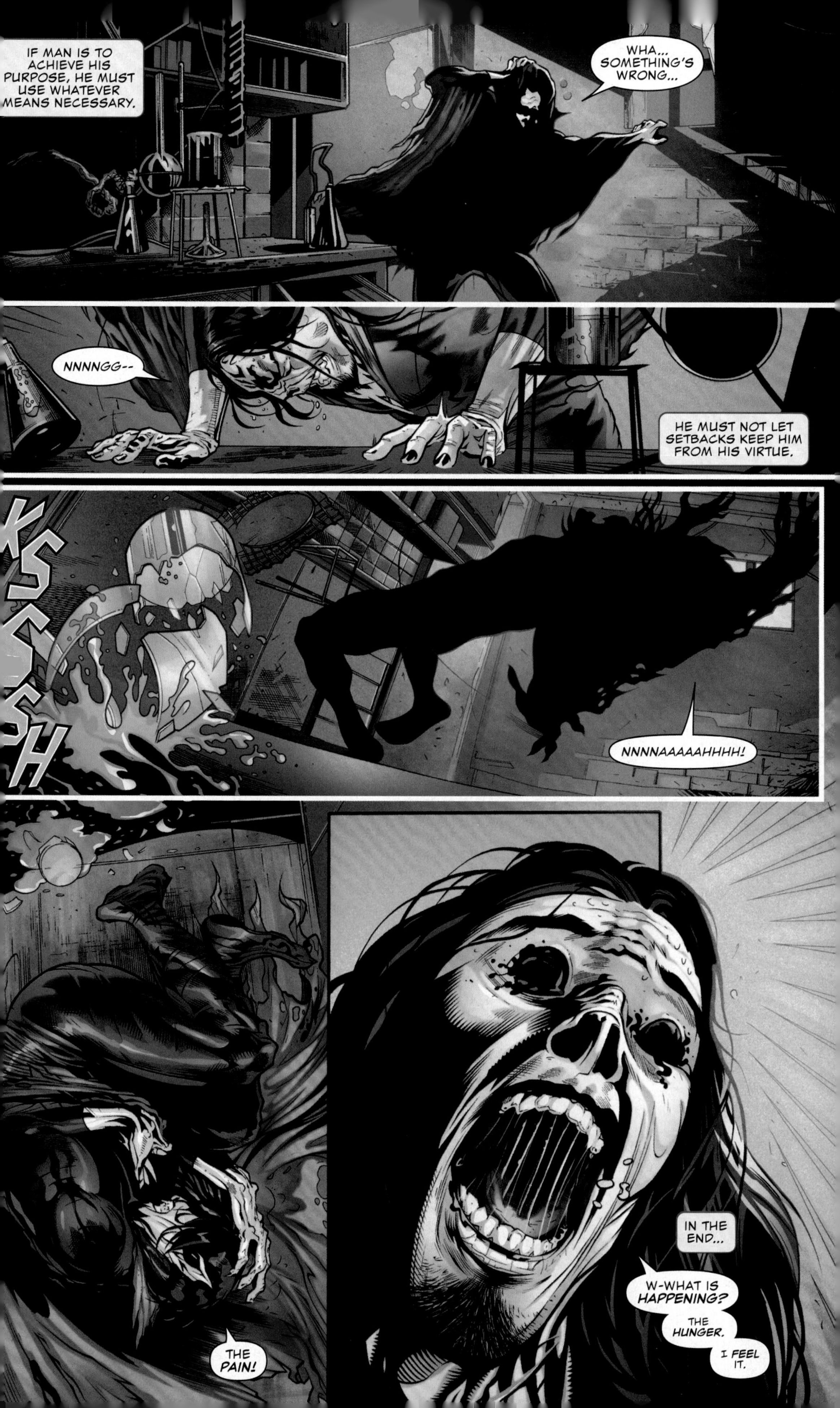
IF MAN IS TO ACHIEVE HIS PURPOSE, HE MUST USE WHATEVER MEANS NECESSARY.
WHA... SOMETHING'S WRONG...
NNNNGG--
HE MUST NOT LET SETBACKS KEEP HIM FROM HIS VIRTUE.
KSSSH
NNNNAAAAAHHHH!
THE PAIN!
IN THE END...
W-WHAT IS HAPPENING?
THE HUNGER.
I FEEL IT.

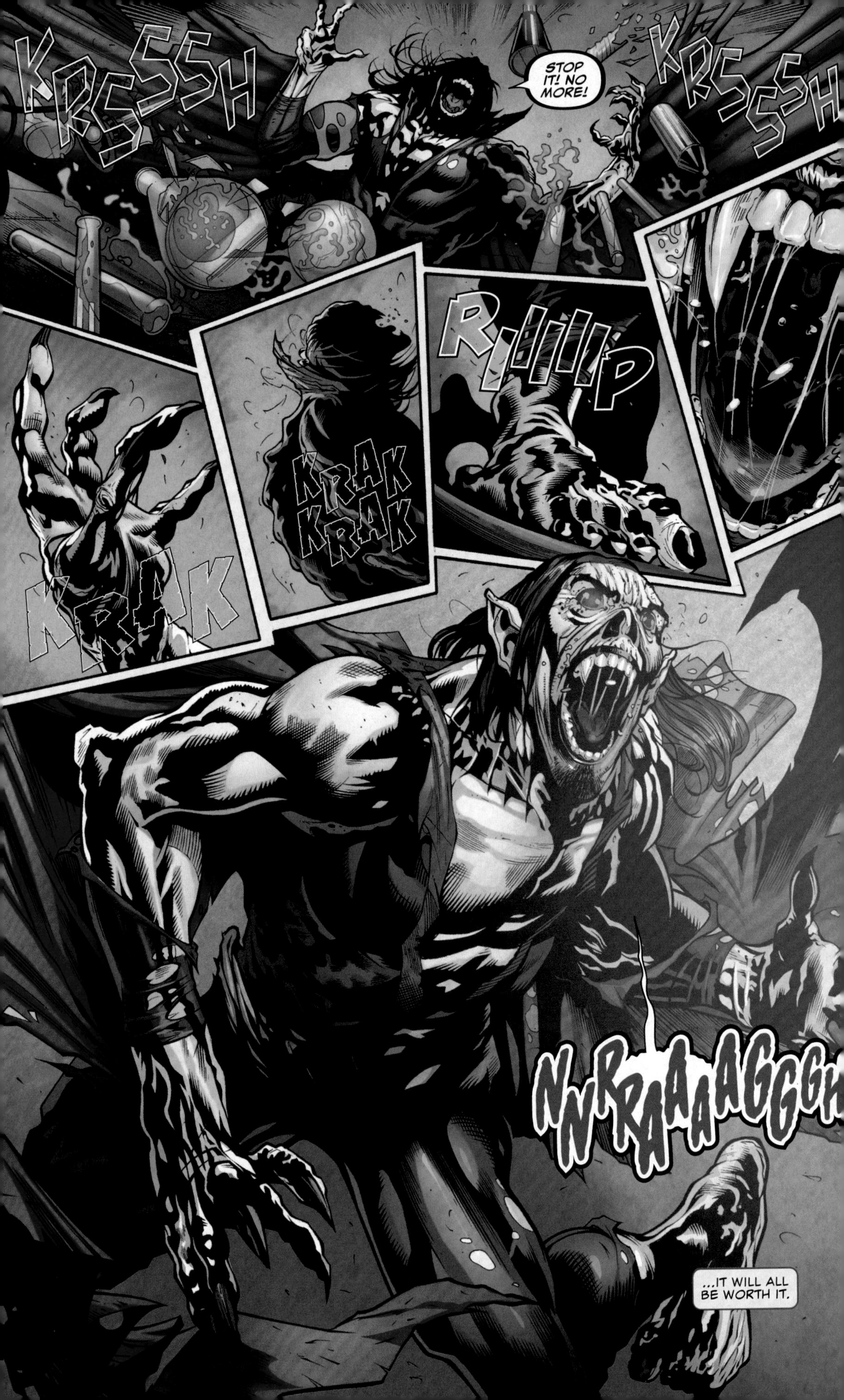
KRSSSH
STOP IT! NO MORE!
KRSSSH
KRAK
KRAK KRAK
RIIIIIP
NNRAAAAGGGH
...IT WILL ALL BE WORTH IT.

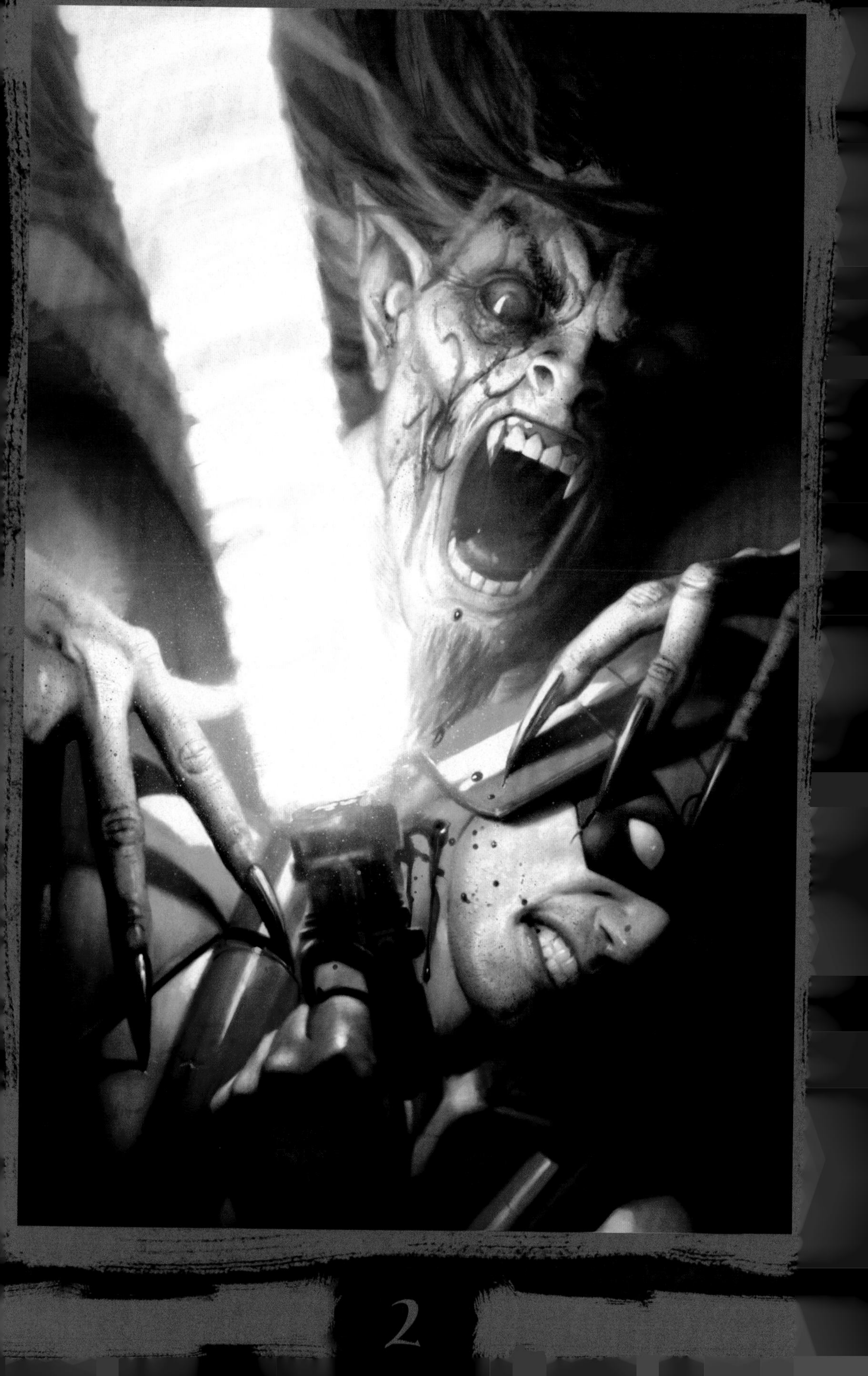

2

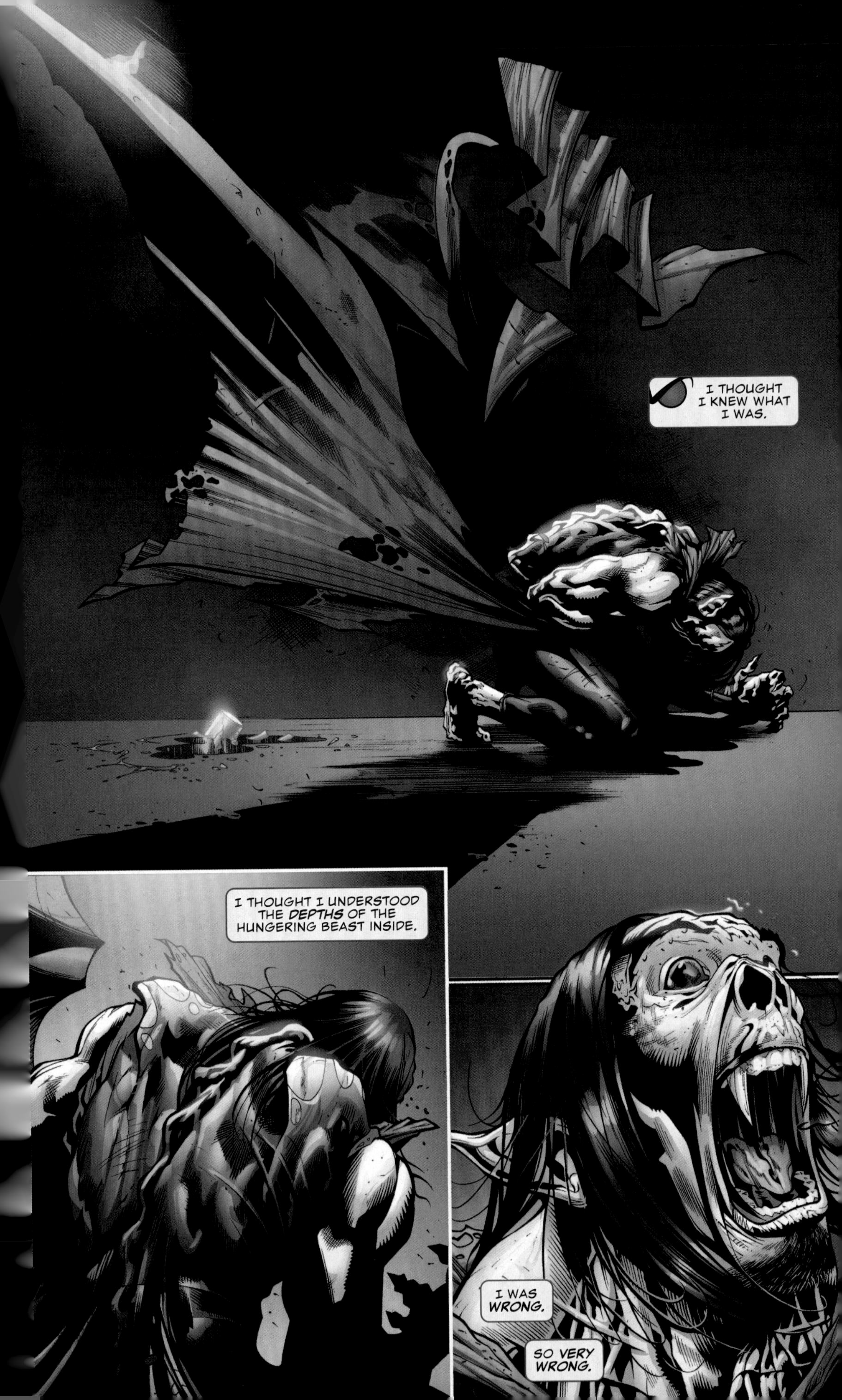
I THOUGHT I KNEW WHAT I WAS.
I THOUGHT I UNDERSTOOD THE *DEPTHS* OF THE HUNGERING BEAST INSIDE.
I WAS **WRONG.**
SO VERY **WRONG.**

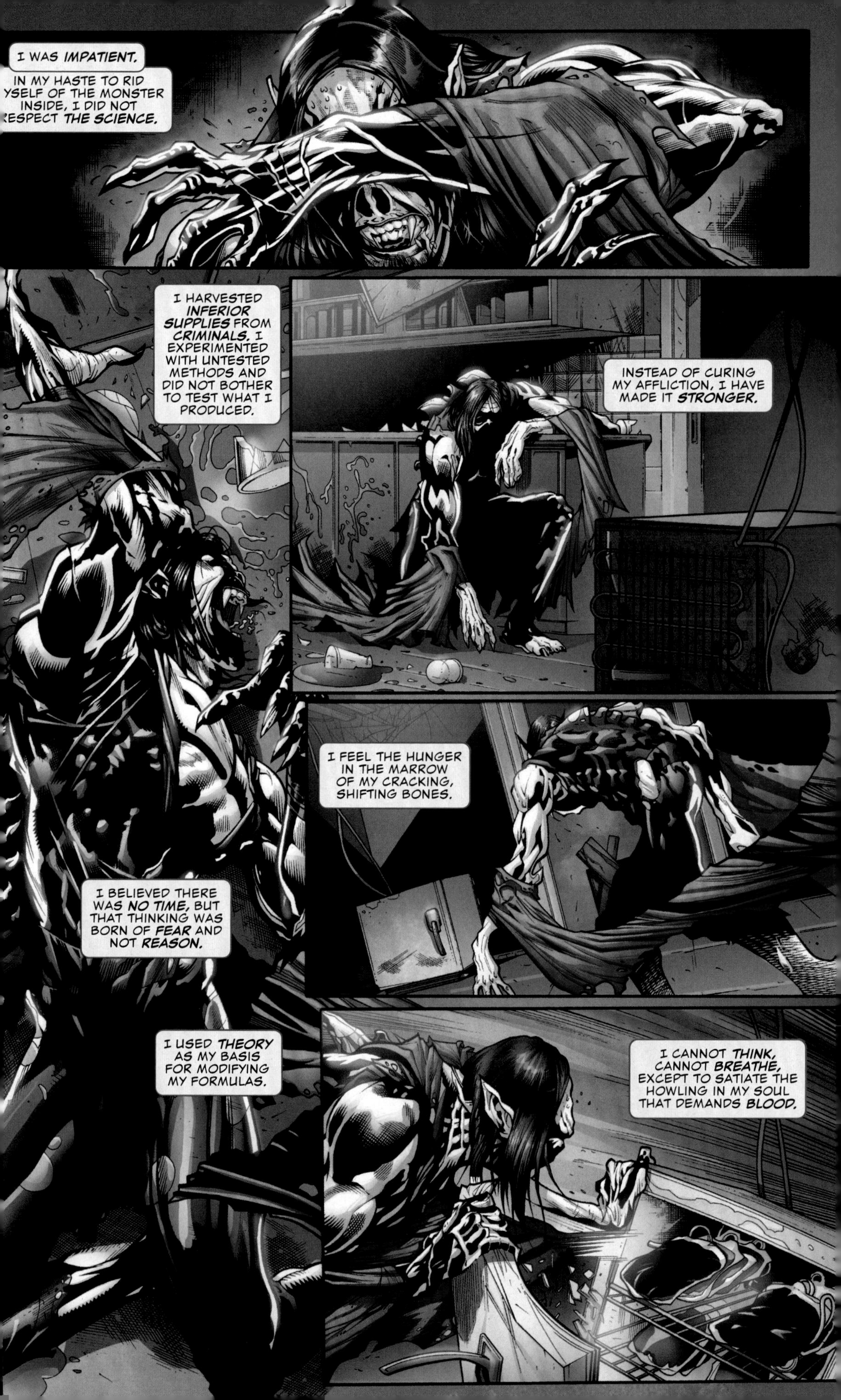

I WAS IMPATIENT.
IN MY HASTE TO RID YSELF OF THE MONSTER INSIDE, I DID NOT RESPECT THE SCIENCE.
I HARVESTED INFERIOR SUPPLIES FROM CRIMINALS. I EXPERIMENTED WITH UNTESTED METHODS AND DID NOT BOTHER TO TEST WHAT I PRODUCED.
INSTEAD OF CURING MY AFFLICTION, I HAVE MADE IT STRONGER.
I FEEL THE HUNGER IN THE MARROW OF MY CRACKING, SHIFTING BONES.
I BELIEVED THERE WAS NO TIME, BUT THAT THINKING WAS BORN OF FEAR AND NOT REASON.
I USED THEORY AS MY BASIS FOR MODIFYING MY FORMULAS.
I CANNOT THINK, CANNOT BREATHE, EXCEPT TO SATIATE THE HOWLING IN MY SOUL THAT DEMANDS BLOOD.

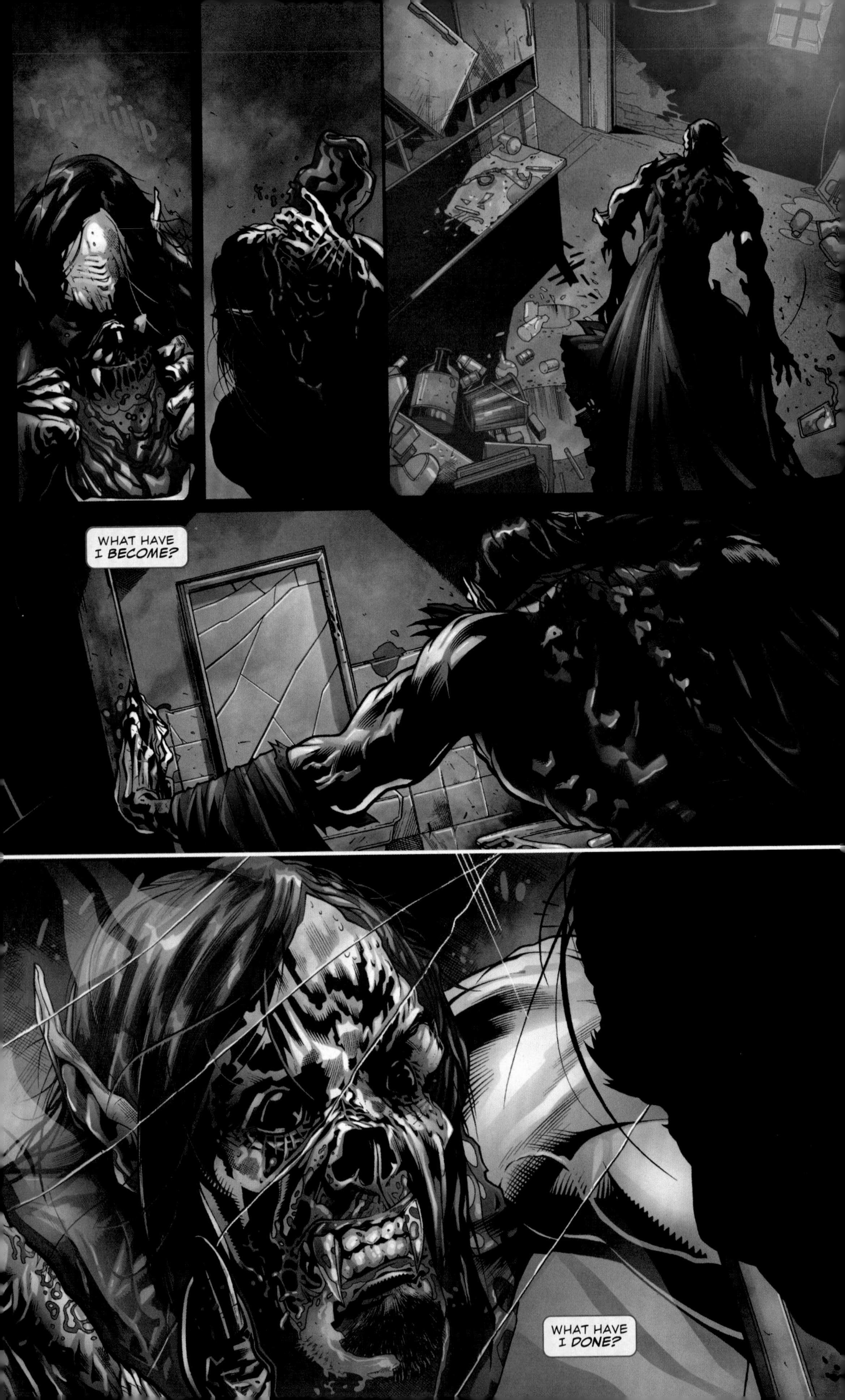
WHAT HAVE I BECOME?
WHAT HAVE I DONE?

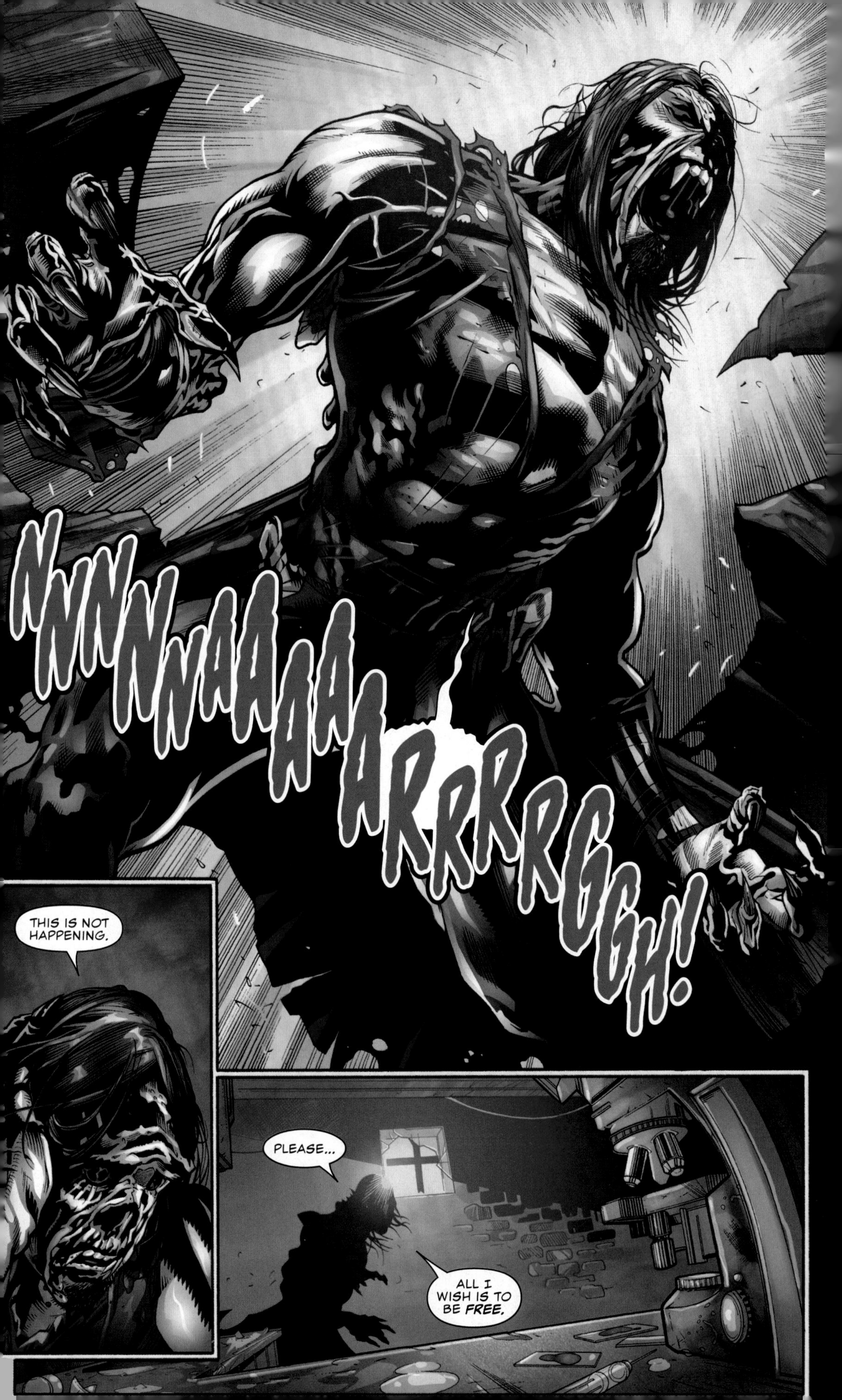

NNNNNAAAAAARRRRGGH!
THIS IS NOT HAPPENING.
PLEASE...
ALL I WISH IS TO BE FREE.

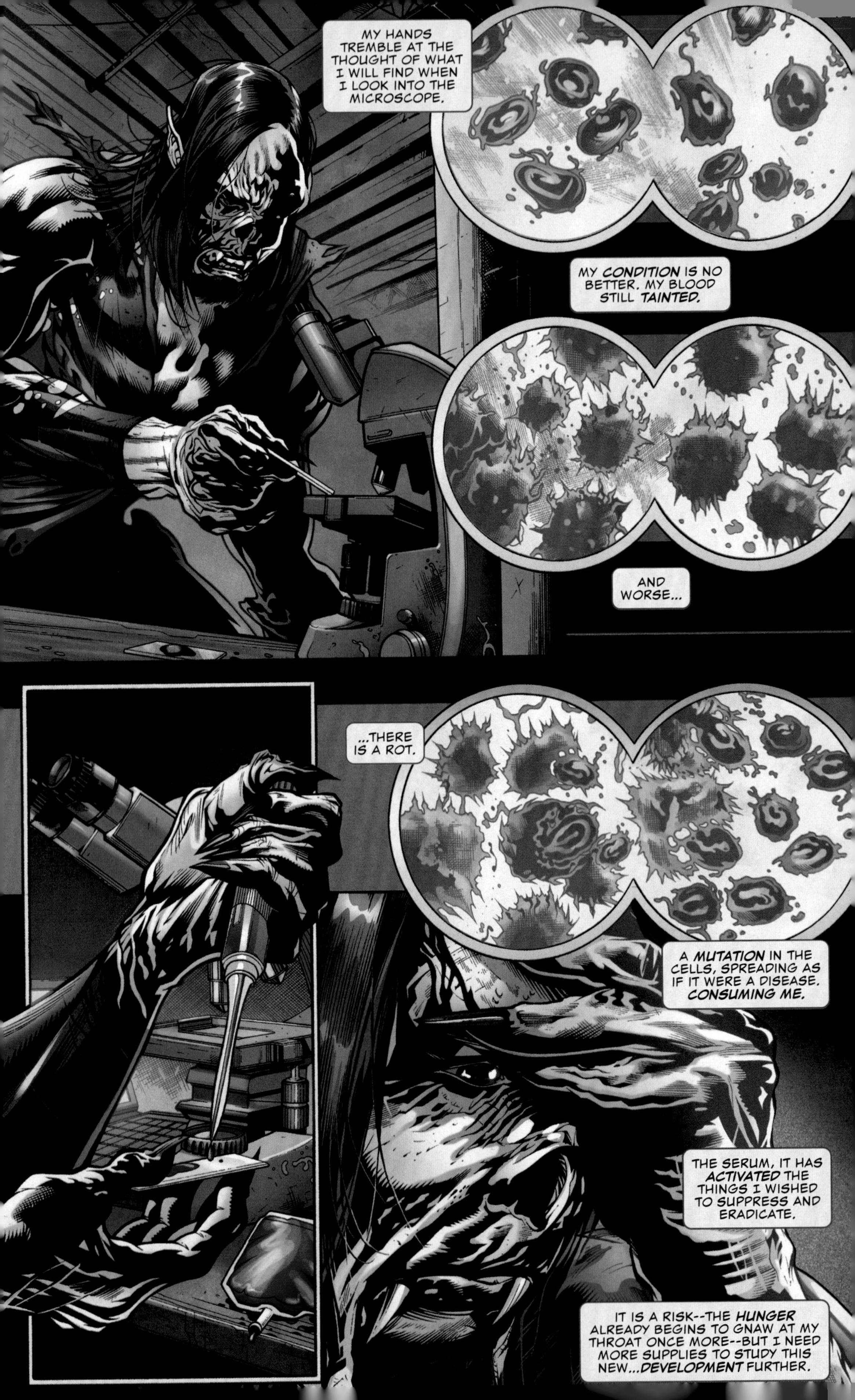
MY HANDS TREMBLE AT THE THOUGHT OF WHAT I WILL FIND WHEN I LOOK INTO THE MICROSCOPE.
MY CONDITION IS NO BETTER. MY BLOOD STILL TAINTED.
AND WORSE...
...THERE IS A ROT.
A MUTATION IN THE CELLS, SPREADING AS IF IT WERE A DISEASE. CONSUMING ME.
THE SERUM, IT HAS ACTIVATED THE THINGS I WISHED TO SUPPRESS AND ERADICATE.
IT IS A RISK--THE HUNGER ALREADY BEGINS TO GNAW AT MY THROAT ONCE MORE--BUT I NEED MORE SUPPLIES TO STUDY THIS NEW...DEVELOPMENT FURTHER.

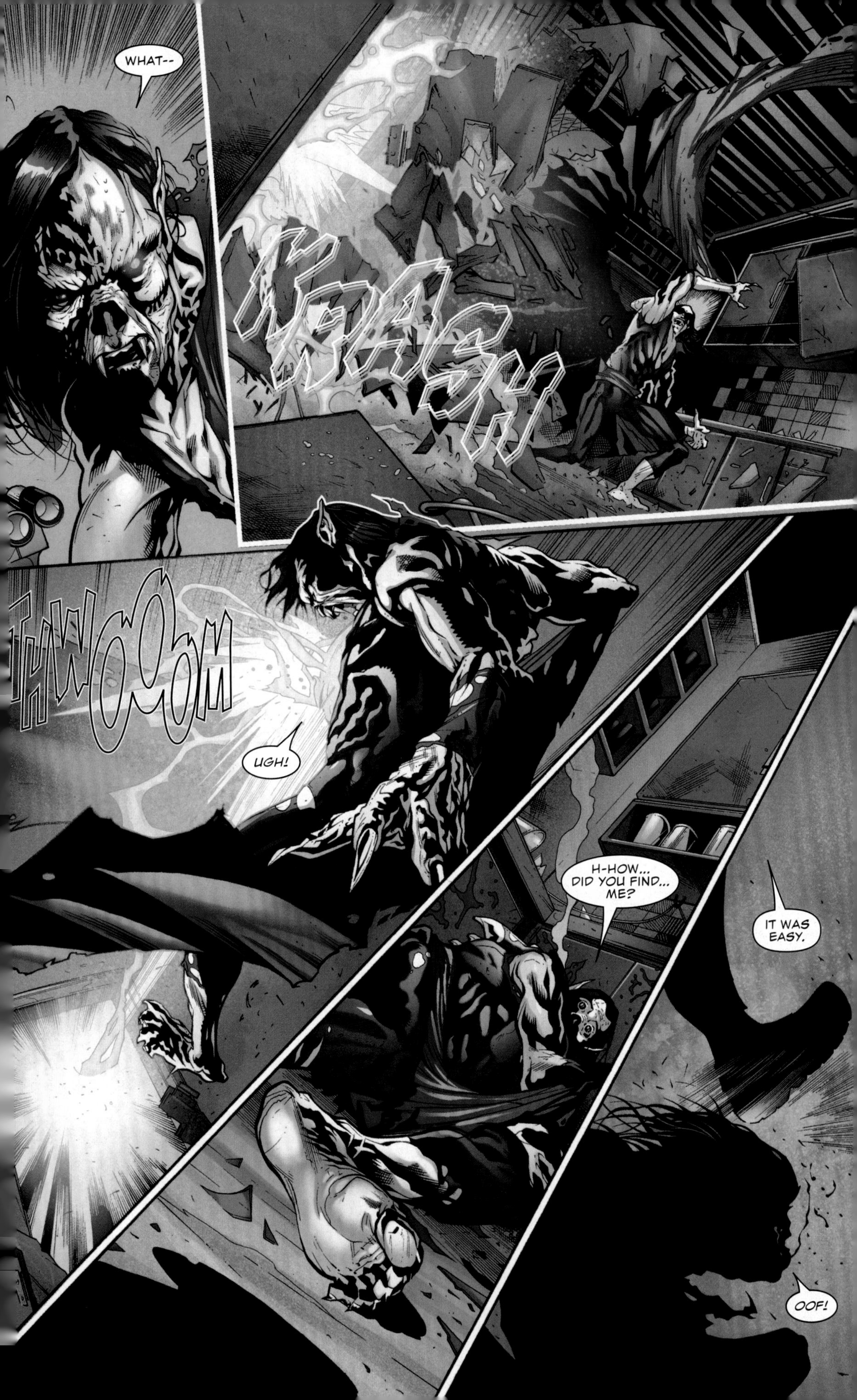
WHAT--
KRASH
THWOOOM
UGH!
H-HOW... DID YOU FIND... ME?
IT WAS EASY.
OOF!

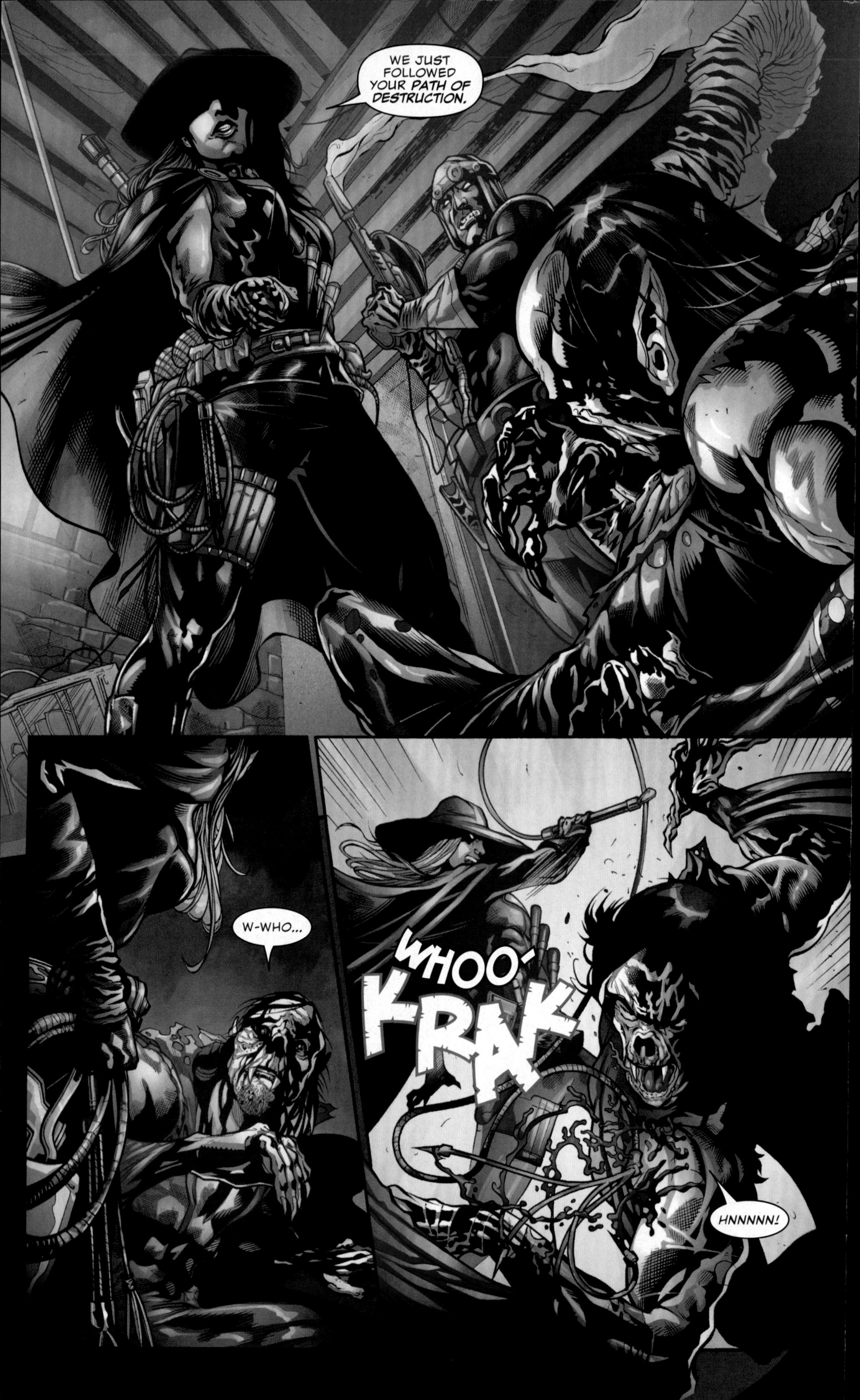
WE JUST FOLLOWED YOUR PATH OF DESTRUCTION.
W-WHO...
WHOO-KRAK
HNNNNN!

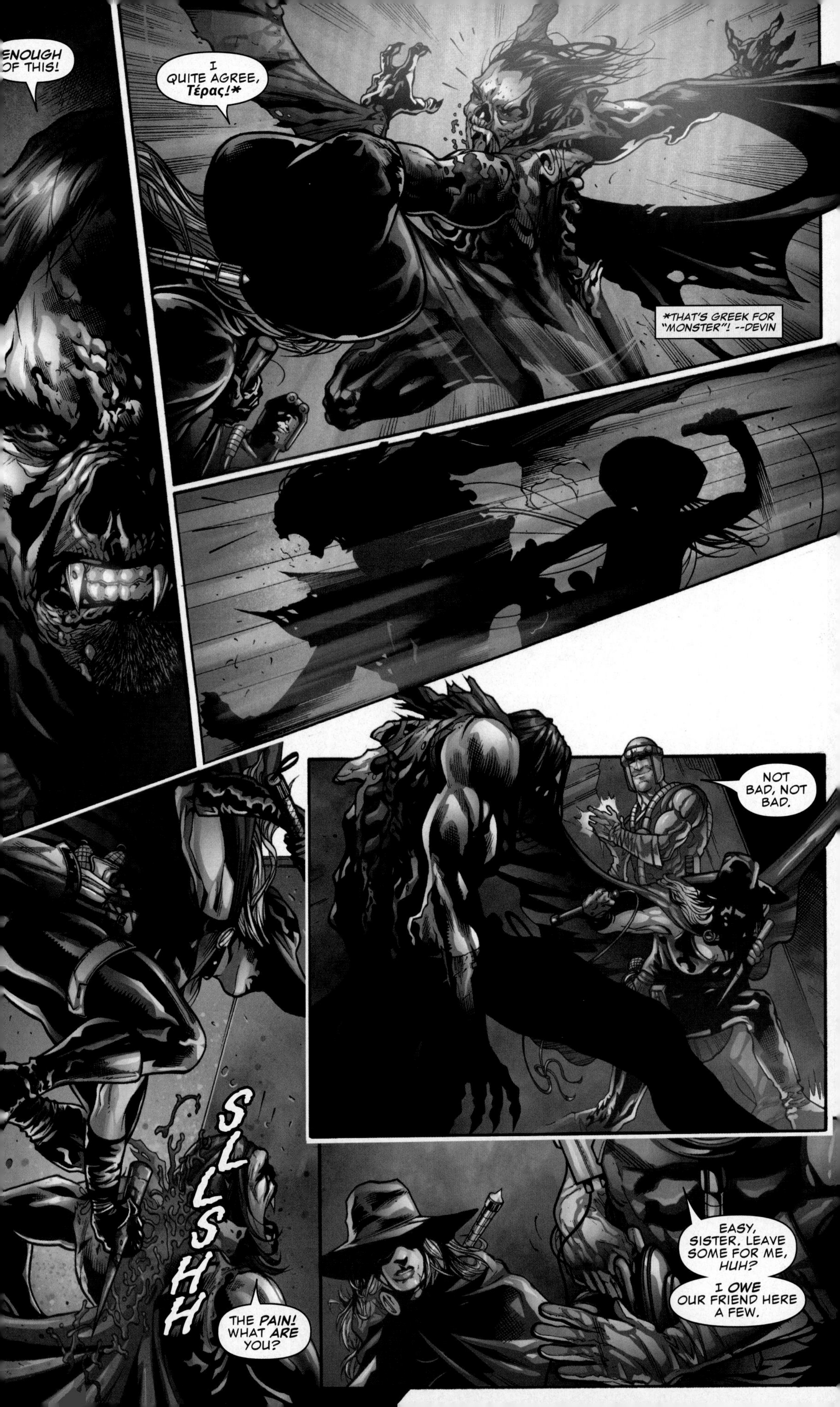

ENOUGH OF THIS!
I QUITE AGREE, Τέρας!*
*THAT'S GREEK FOR "MONSTER"! --DEVIN
NOT BAD, NOT BAD.
SLLSHH
THE PAIN! WHAT ARE YOU?
EASY, SISTER. LEAVE SOME FOR ME, HUH?
I OWE OUR FRIEND HERE A FEW.

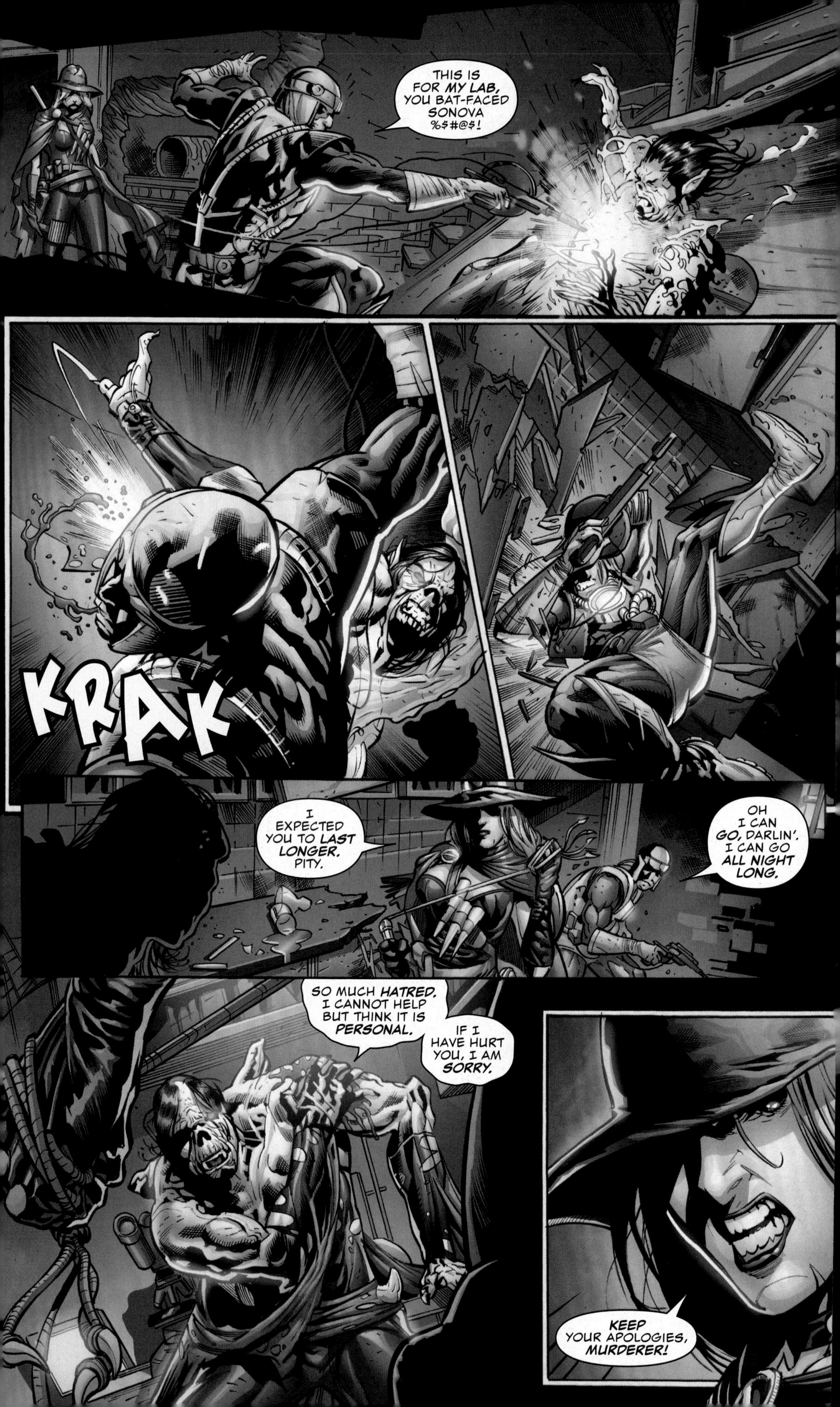

THIS IS FOR MY LAB, YOU BAT-FACED SONOVA %$#@$!
KRAK
I EXPECTED YOU TO LAST LONGER. PITY.
OH I CAN GO, DARLIN'. I CAN GO ALL NIGHT LONG.
SO MUCH HATRED. I CANNOT HELP BUT THINK IT IS PERSONAL.
IF I HAVE HURT YOU, I AM SORRY.
KEEP YOUR APOLOGIES, MURDERER!

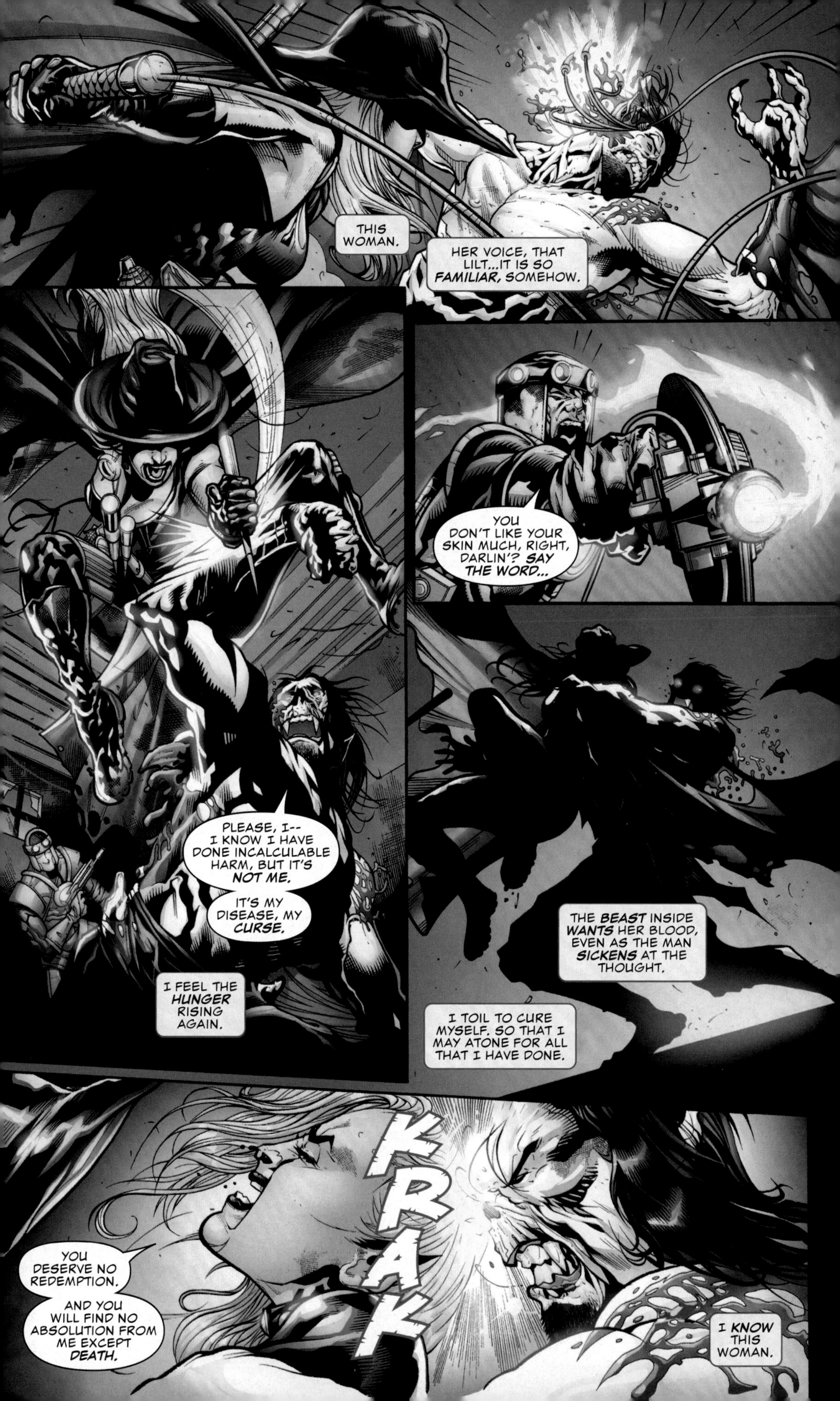
THIS WOMAN.
HER VOICE, THAT LILT...IT IS SO FAMILIAR, SOMEHOW.
PLEASE, I-- I KNOW I HAVE DONE INCALCULABLE HARM, BUT IT'S NOT ME.
IT'S MY DISEASE, MY CURSE.
I FEEL THE HUNGER RISING AGAIN.
YOU DON'T LIKE YOUR SKIN MUCH, RIGHT, DARLIN'? SAY THE WORD...
THE BEAST INSIDE WANTS HER BLOOD, EVEN AS THE MAN SICKENS AT THE THOUGHT.
I TOIL TO CURE MYSELF. SO THAT I MAY ATONE FOR ALL THAT I HAVE DONE.
KRAK
YOU DESERVE NO REDEMPTION.
AND YOU WILL FIND NO ABSOLUTION FROM ME EXCEPT DEATH.
I KNOW THIS WOMAN.

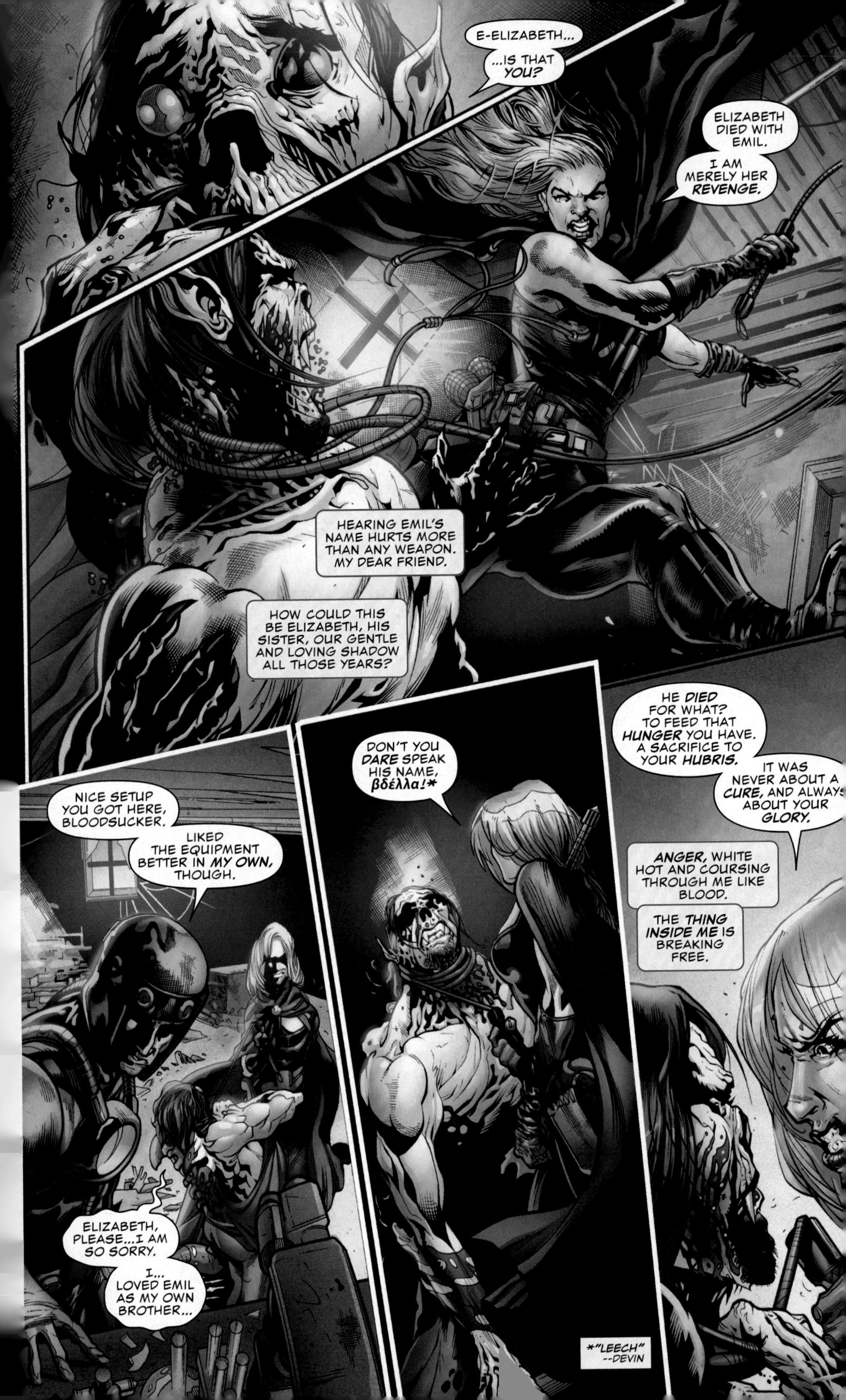
E-ELIZABETH...
...IS THAT YOU?
ELIZABETH DIED WITH EMIL.
I AM MERELY HER REVENGE.
HEARING EMIL'S NAME HURTS MORE THAN ANY WEAPON. MY DEAR FRIEND.
HOW COULD THIS BE ELIZABETH, HIS SISTER, OUR GENTLE AND LOVING SHADOW ALL THOSE YEARS?
NICE SETUP YOU GOT HERE, BLOODSUCKER.
LIKED THE EQUIPMENT BETTER IN MY OWN, THOUGH.
ELIZABETH, PLEASE...I AM SO SORRY.
I... LOVED EMIL AS MY OWN BROTHER...
DON'T YOU DARE SPEAK HIS NAME, βδέλλα!*
HE DIED FOR WHAT? TO FEED THAT HUNGER YOU HAVE. A SACRIFICE TO YOUR HUBRIS.
IT WAS NEVER ABOUT A CURE, AND ALWAYS ABOUT YOUR GLORY.
ANGER, WHITE HOT AND COURSING THROUGH ME LIKE BLOOD.
THE THING INSIDE ME IS BREAKING FREE.
*"LEECH" --DEVIN

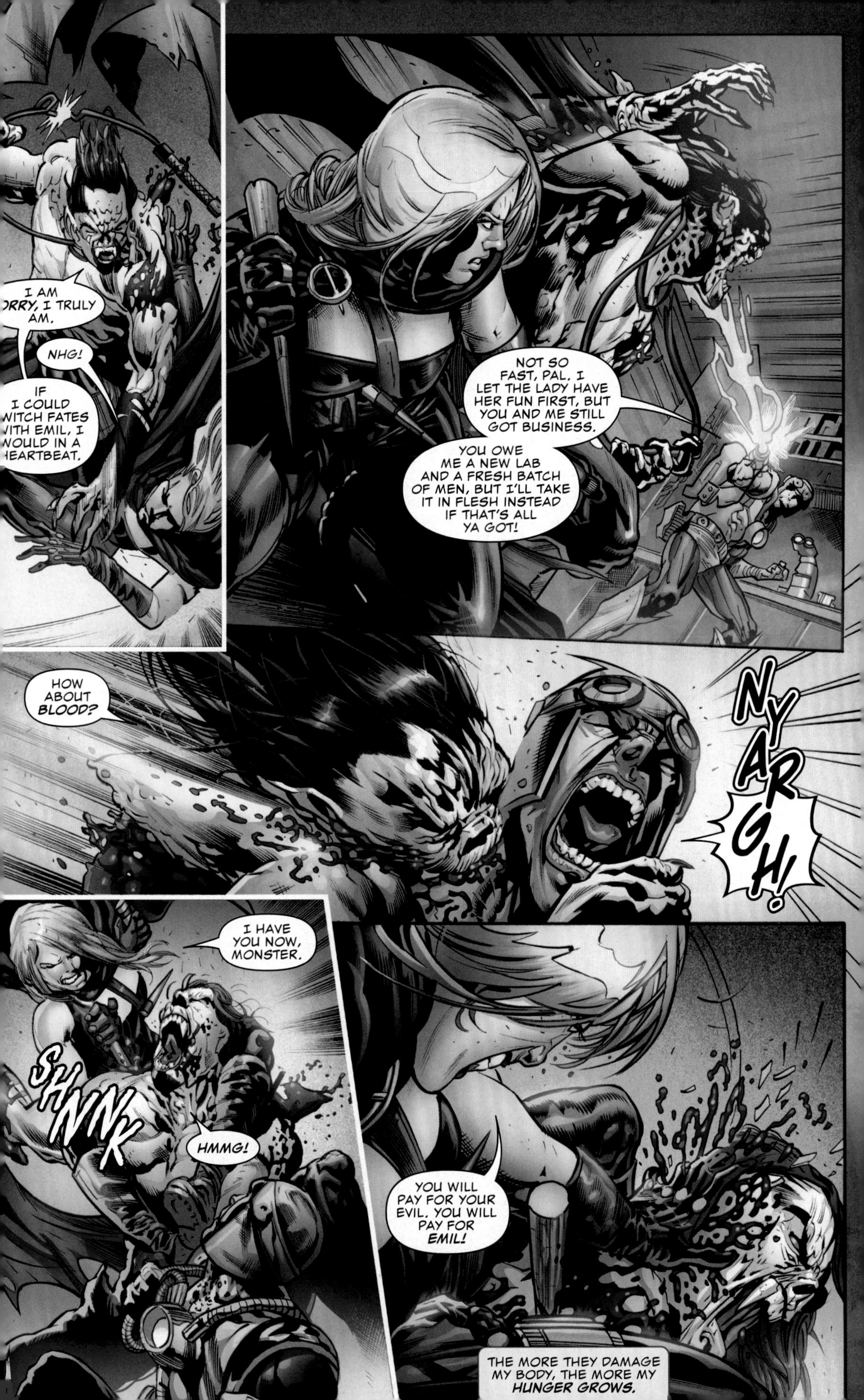

I AM
ORRY, I TRULY
AM.
NHG!
IF
I COULD
WITCH FATES
WITH EMIL, I
WOULD IN A
HEARTBEAT.
NOT SO FAST, PAL. I LET THE LADY HAVE HER FUN FIRST, BUT YOU AND ME STILL GOT BUSINESS.
YOU OWE ME A NEW LAB AND A FRESH BATCH OF MEN, BUT I'LL TAKE IT IN FLESH INSTEAD IF THAT'S ALL YA GOT!
HOW ABOUT BLOOD?
NYARGH!
I HAVE YOU NOW, MONSTER.
SHNNK
HMMG!
YOU WILL PAY FOR YOUR EVIL. YOU WILL PAY FOR EMIL!
THE MORE THEY DAMAGE MY BODY, THE MORE MY HUNGER GROWS.

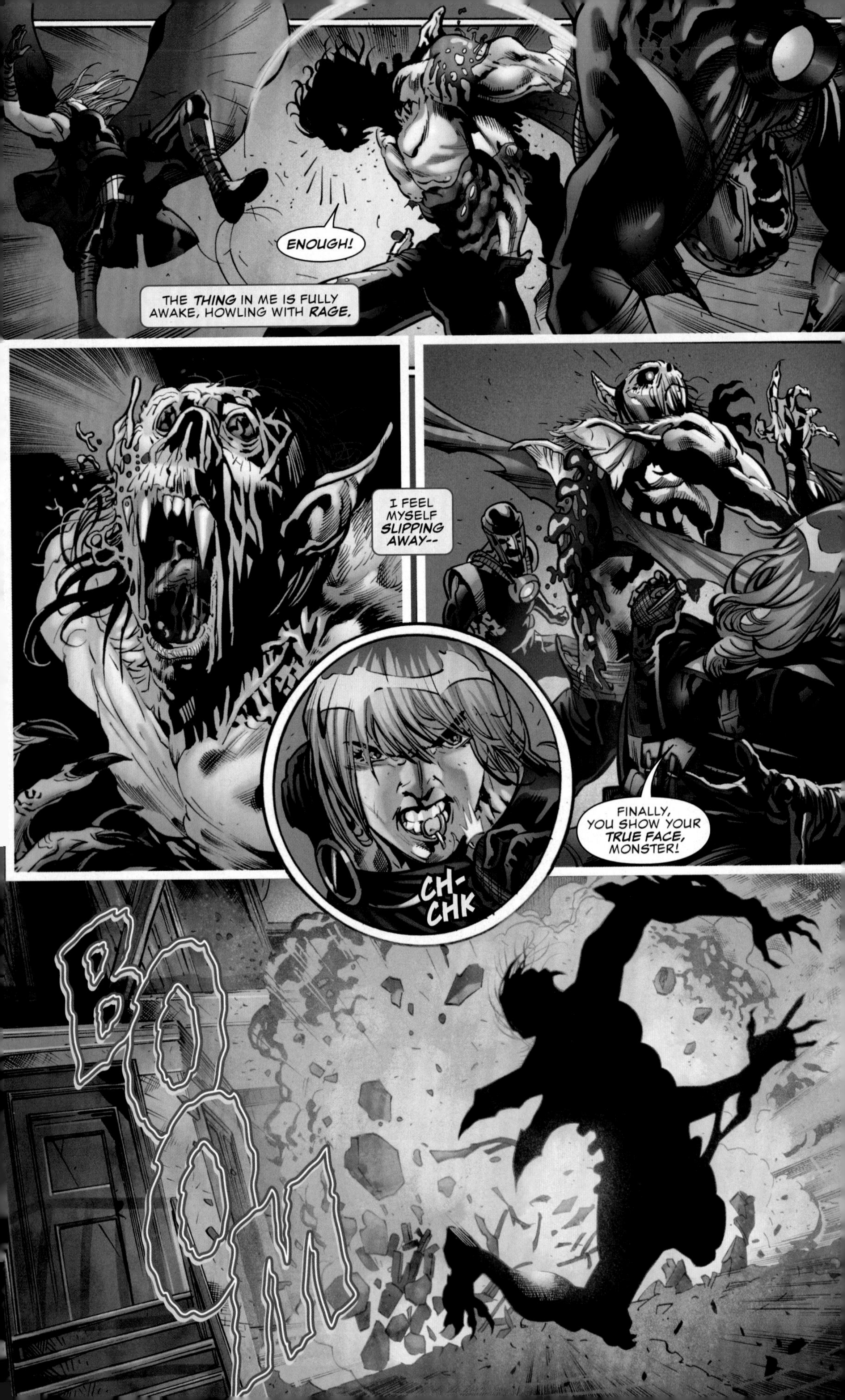
ENOUGH!
THE THING IN ME IS FULLY AWAKE, HOWLING WITH RAGE.
I FEEL MYSELF SLIPPING AWAY--
FINALLY, YOU SHOW YOUR TRUE FACE, MONSTER!
CH-CHK
BOOM

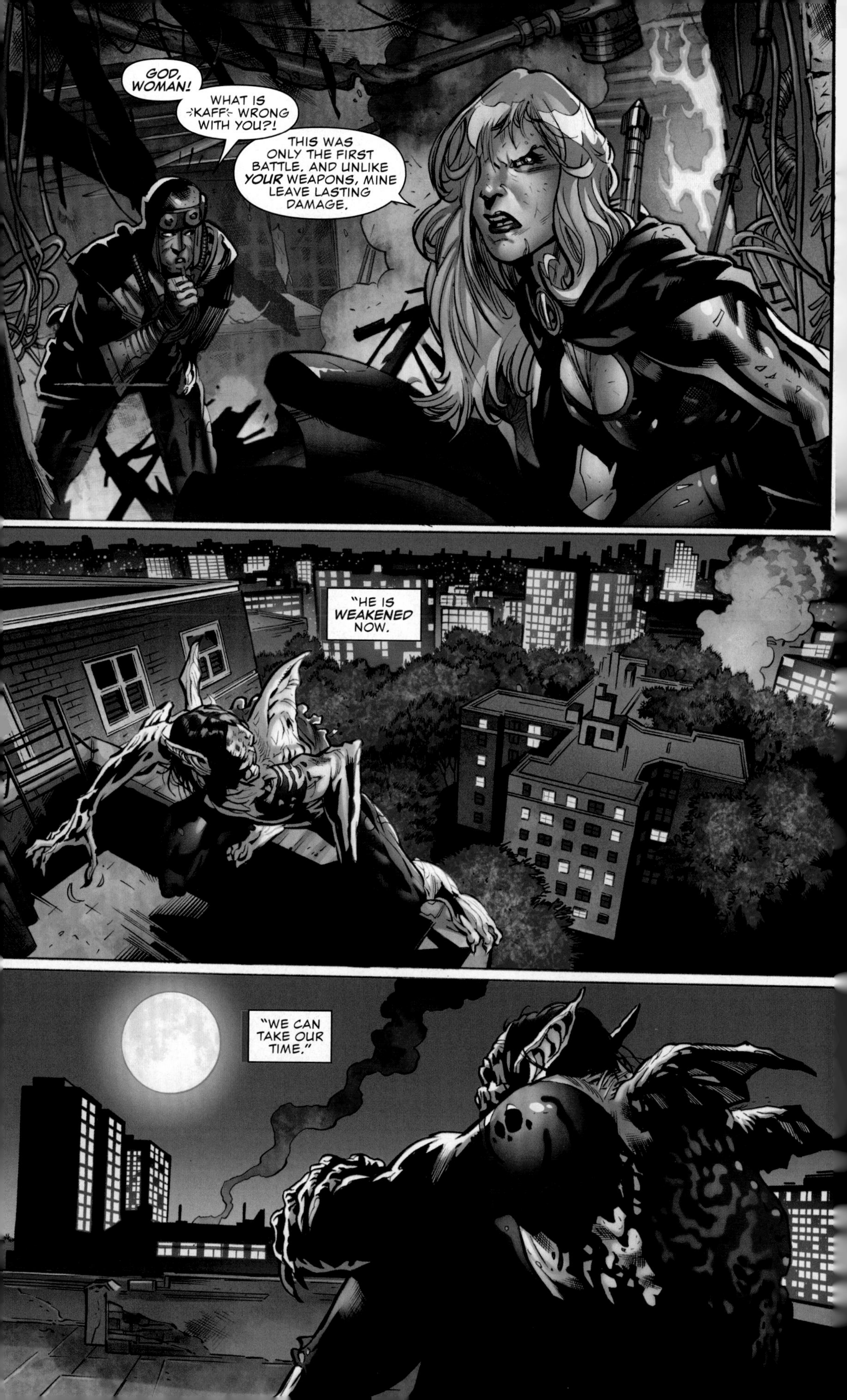
GOD, WOMAN!
WHAT IS -KAFF- WRONG WITH YOU?!
THIS WAS ONLY THE FIRST BATTLE, AND UNLIKE YOUR WEAPONS, MINE LEAVE LASTING DAMAGE.
"HE IS WEAKENED NOW.
"WE CAN TAKE OUR TIME."

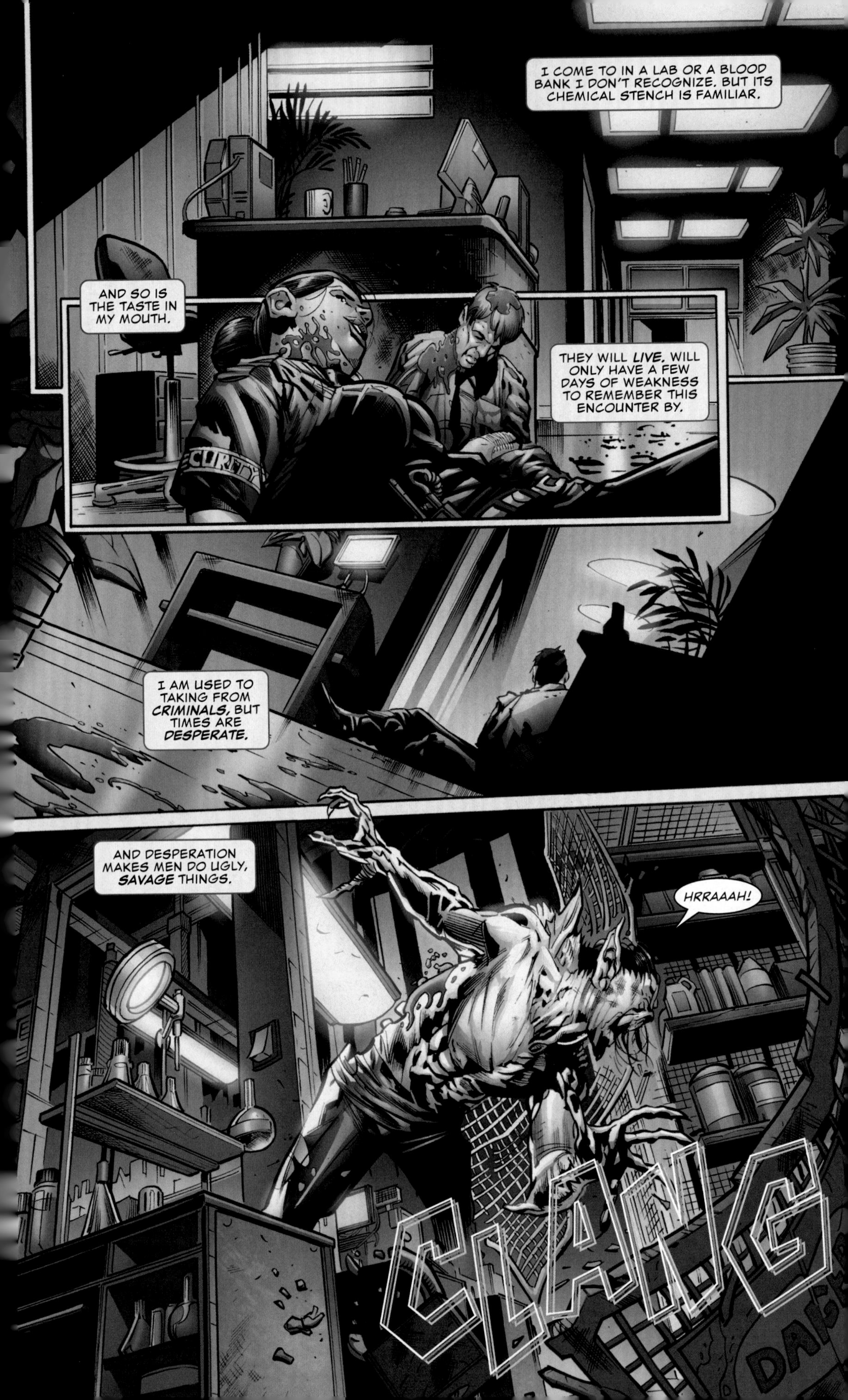
I COME TO IN A LAB OR A BLOOD BANK I DON'T RECOGNIZE. BUT ITS CHEMICAL STENCH IS FAMILIAR.
AND SO IS THE TASTE IN MY MOUTH.
THEY WILL *LIVE.* WILL ONLY HAVE A FEW DAYS OF WEAKNESS TO REMEMBER THIS ENCOUNTER BY.
I AM USED TO TAKING FROM *CRIMINALS,* BUT TIMES ARE *DESPERATE.*
AND DESPERATION MAKES MEN DO UGLY, *SAVAGE* THINGS.
HRRAAAH!
CLANG

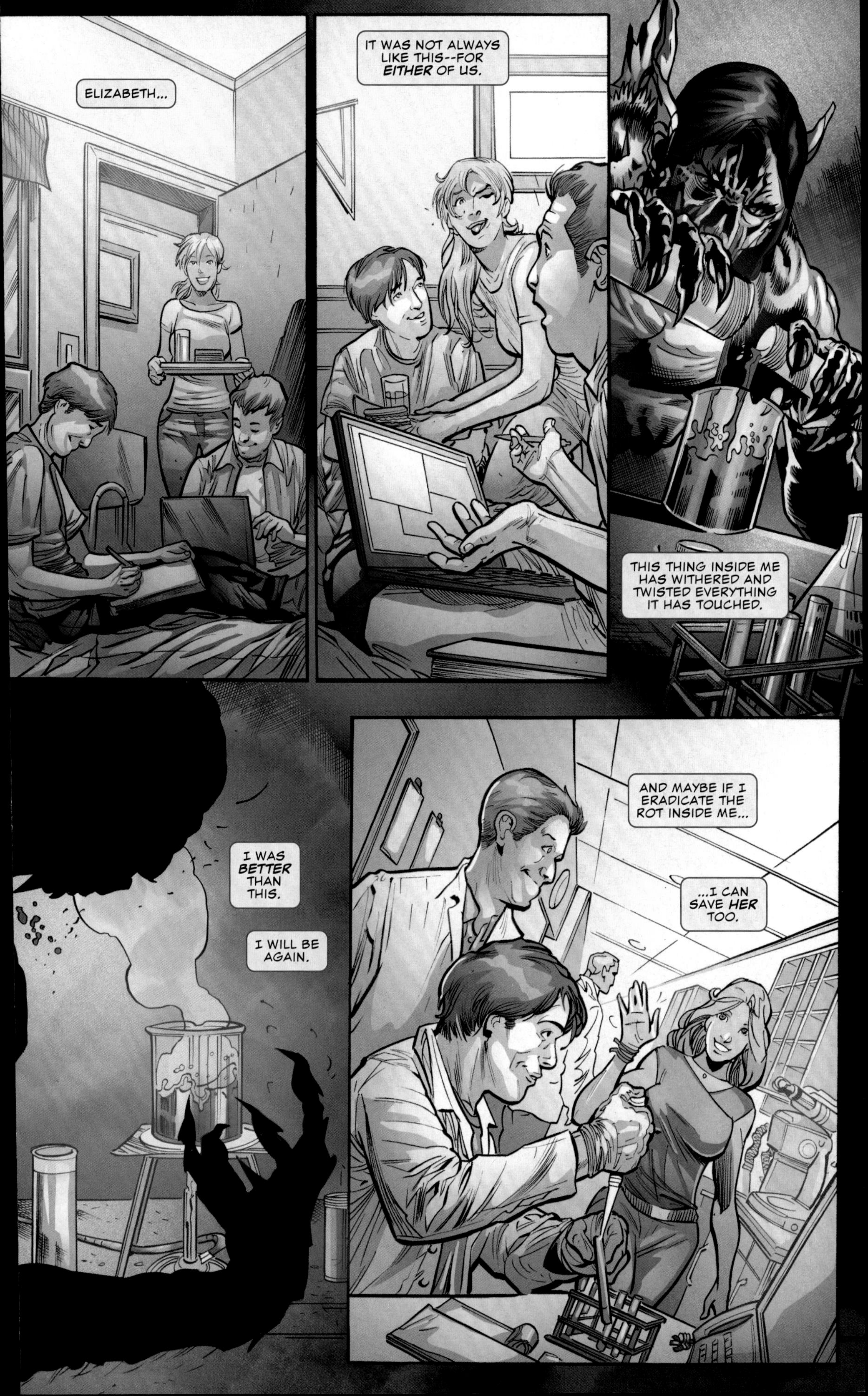
ELIZABETH...
IT WAS NOT ALWAYS LIKE THIS--FOR EITHER OF US.
THIS THING INSIDE ME HAS WITHERED AND TWISTED EVERYTHING IT HAS TOUCHED.
I WAS BETTER THAN THIS.
I WILL BE AGAIN.
AND MAYBE IF I ERADICATE THE ROT INSIDE ME...
...I CAN SAVE HER TOO.

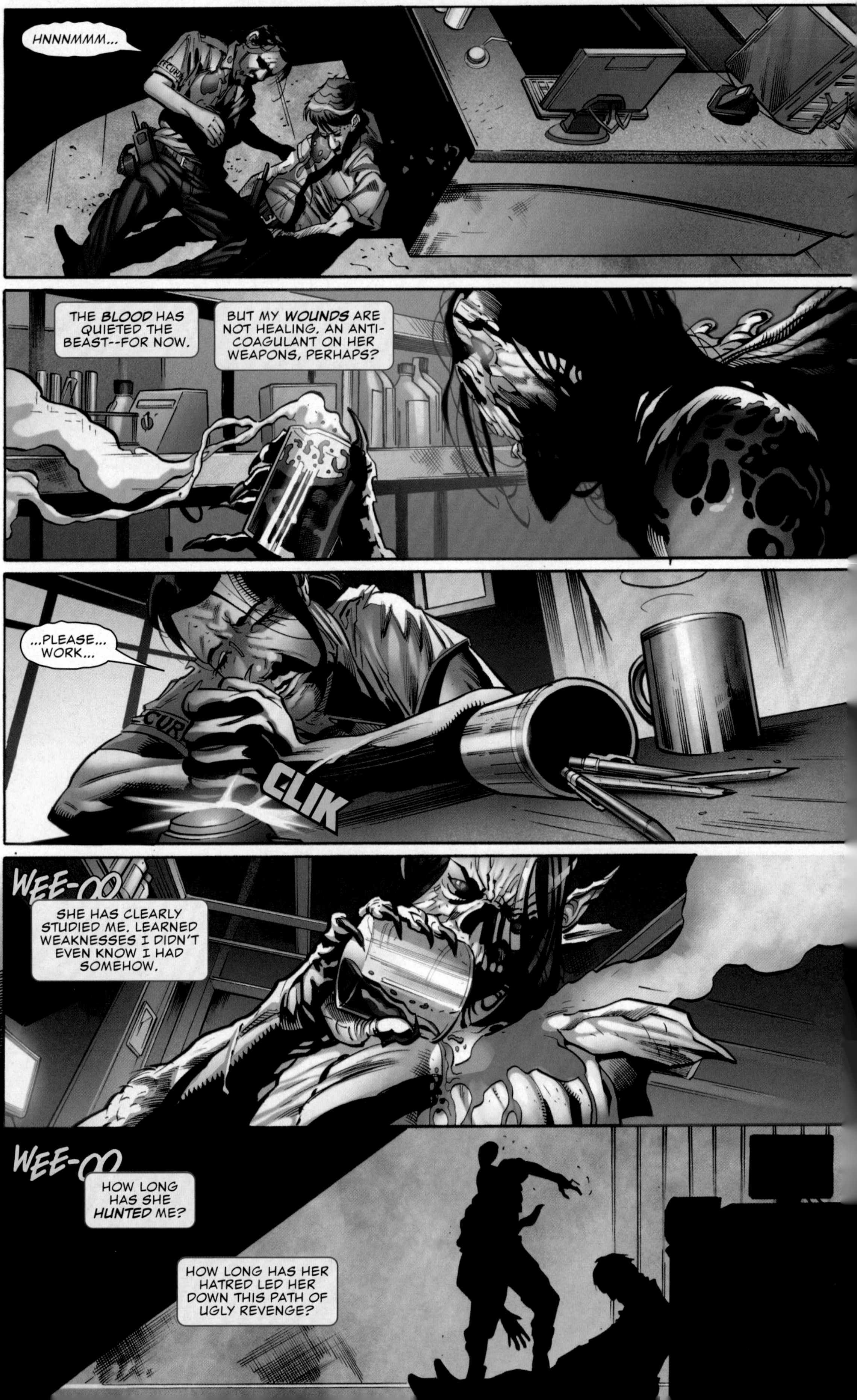
HNNNMMM...
THE BLOOD HAS QUIETED THE BEAST--FOR NOW.
BUT MY WOUNDS ARE NOT HEALING. AN ANTI-COAGULANT ON HER WEAPONS, PERHAPS?
...PLEASE... WORK...
CLIK
WEE-OO
SHE HAS CLEARLY STUDIED ME. LEARNED WEAKNESSES I DIDN'T EVEN KNOW I HAD SOMEHOW.
WEE-OO
HOW LONG HAS SHE HUNTED ME?
HOW LONG HAS HER HATRED LED HER DOWN THIS PATH OF UGLY REVENGE?

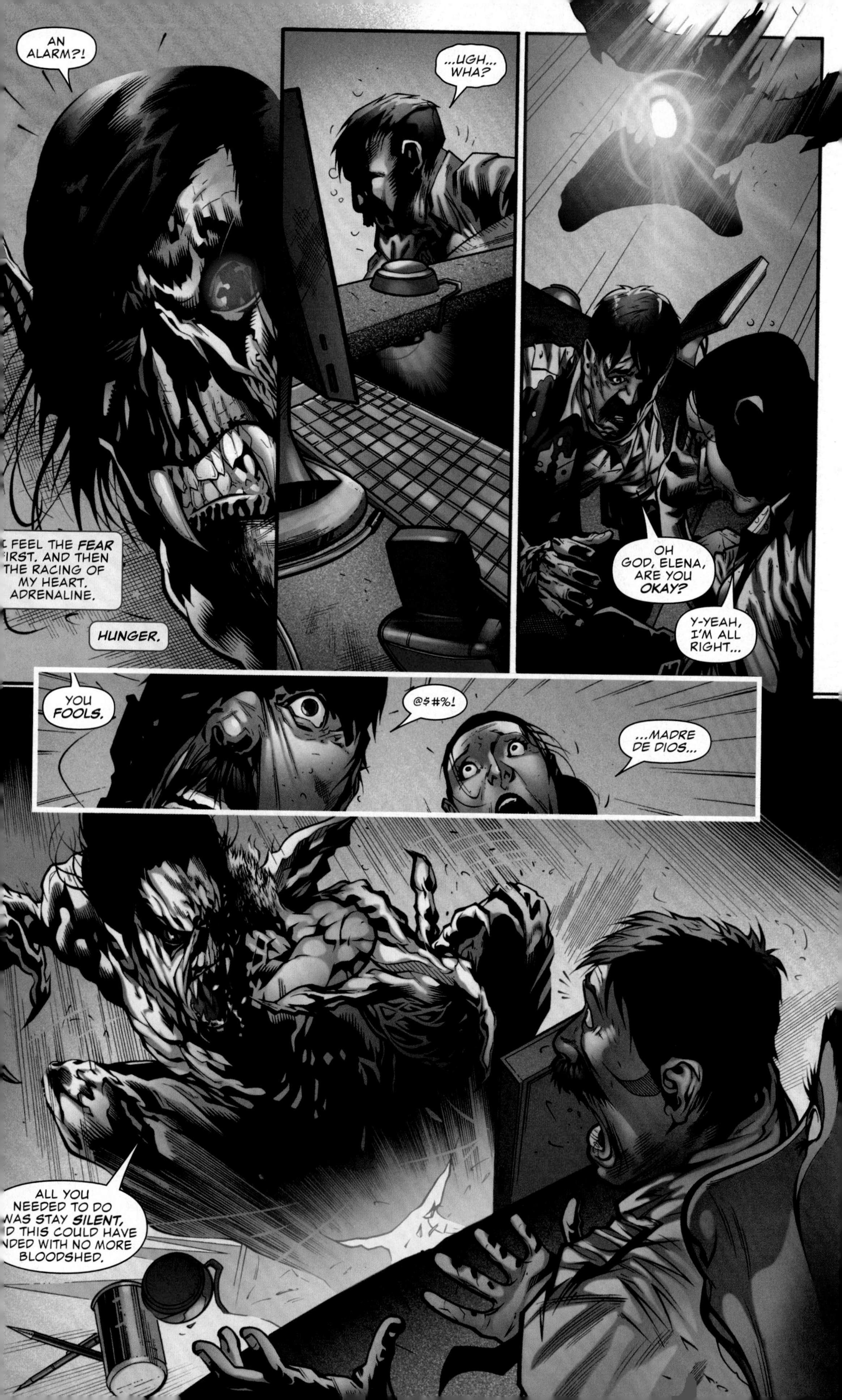

AN ALARM?!
...UGH... WHA?
I FEEL THE FEAR FIRST. AND THEN THE RACING OF MY HEART. ADRENALINE.
HUNGER.
OH GOD, ELENA, ARE YOU OKAY?
Y-YEAH, I'M ALL RIGHT...
YOU FOOLS.
@$#%!
...MADRE DE DIOS...
ALL YOU NEEDED TO DO WAS STAY SILENT, AND THIS COULD HAVE ENDED WITH NO MORE BLOODSHED.

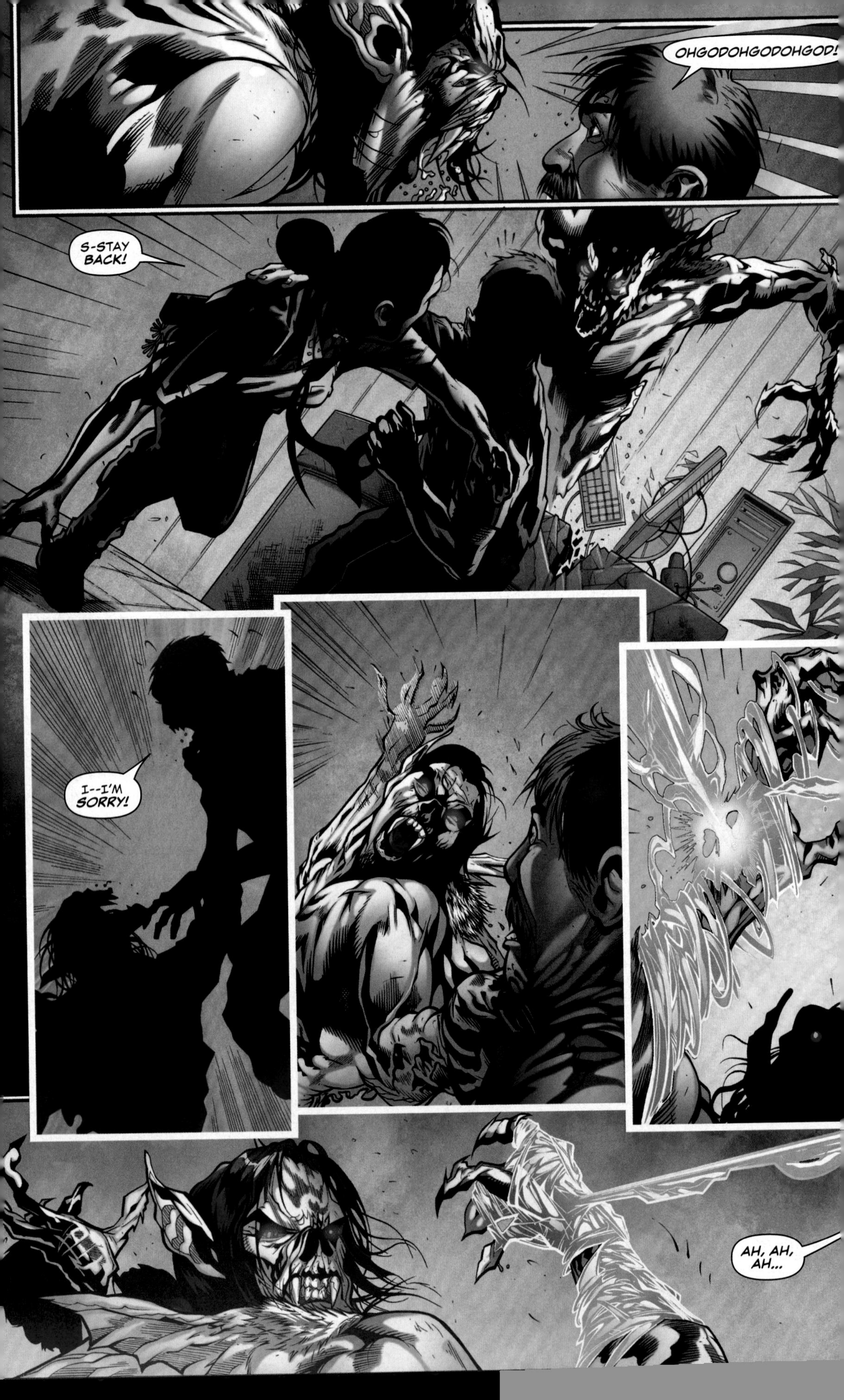
OHGODOHGODOHGOD!
S-STAY BACK!
I--I'M SORRY!
AH, AH, AH...

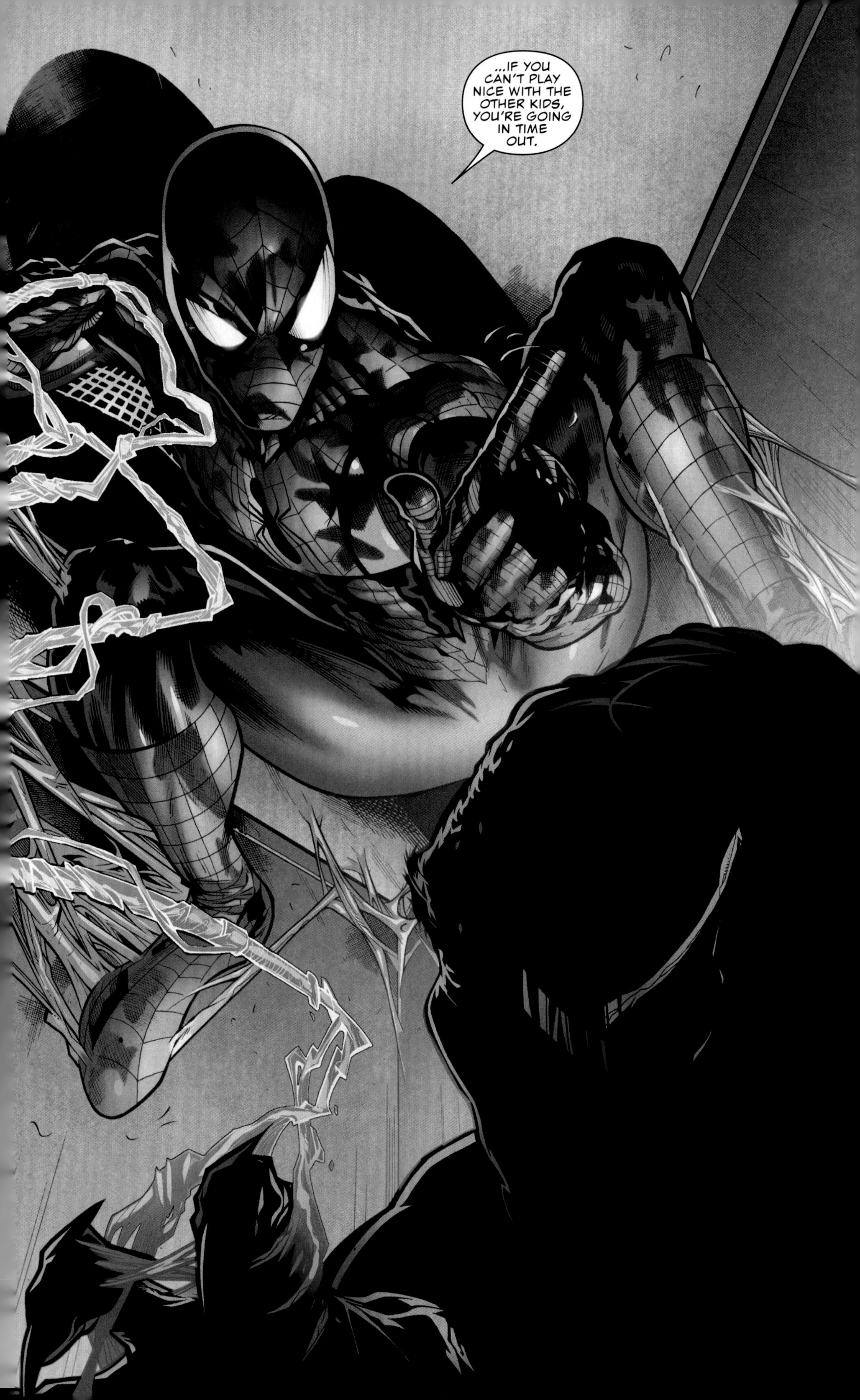
...IF YOU CAN'T PLAY NICE WITH THE OTHER KIDS, YOU'RE GOING IN TIME OUT.

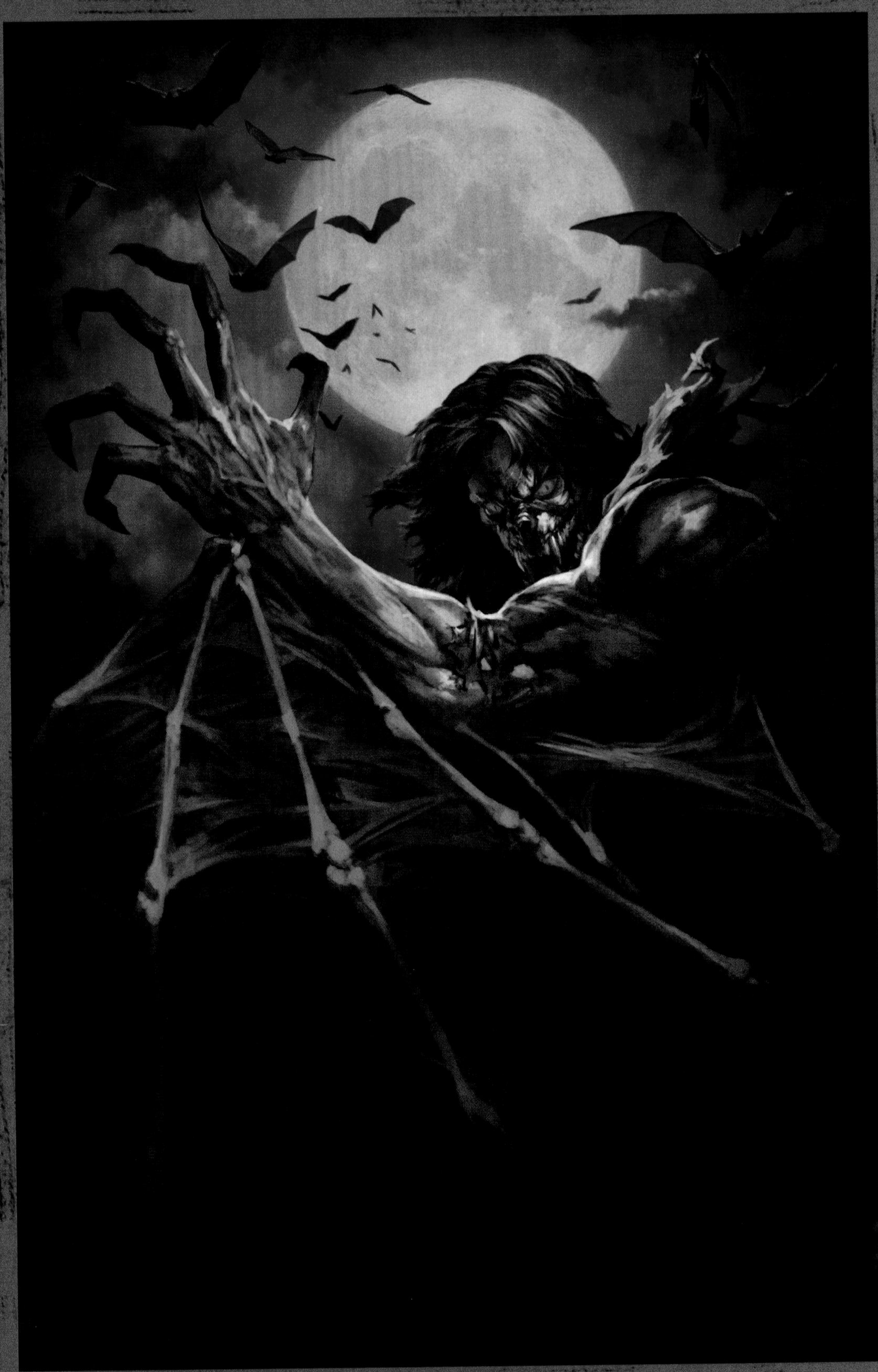

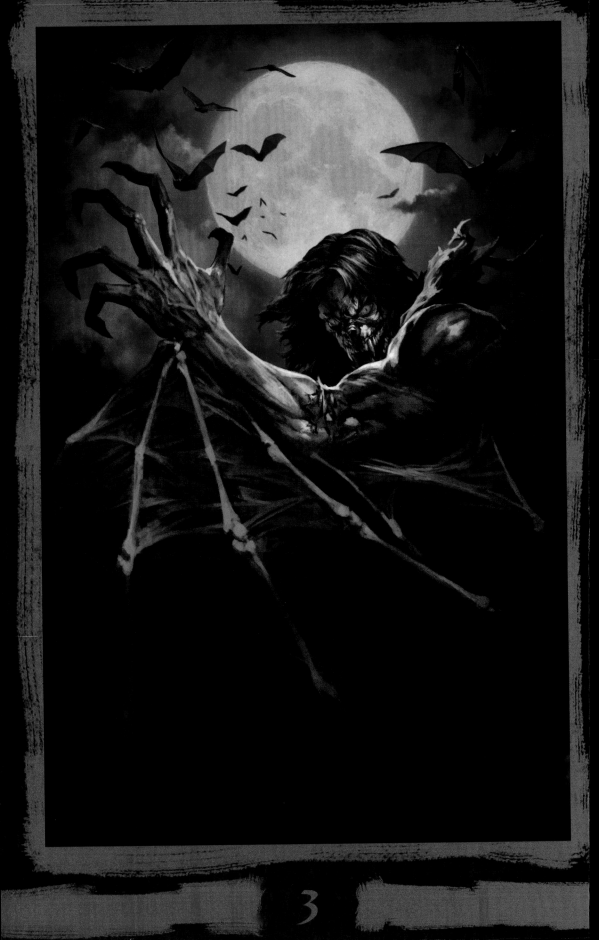

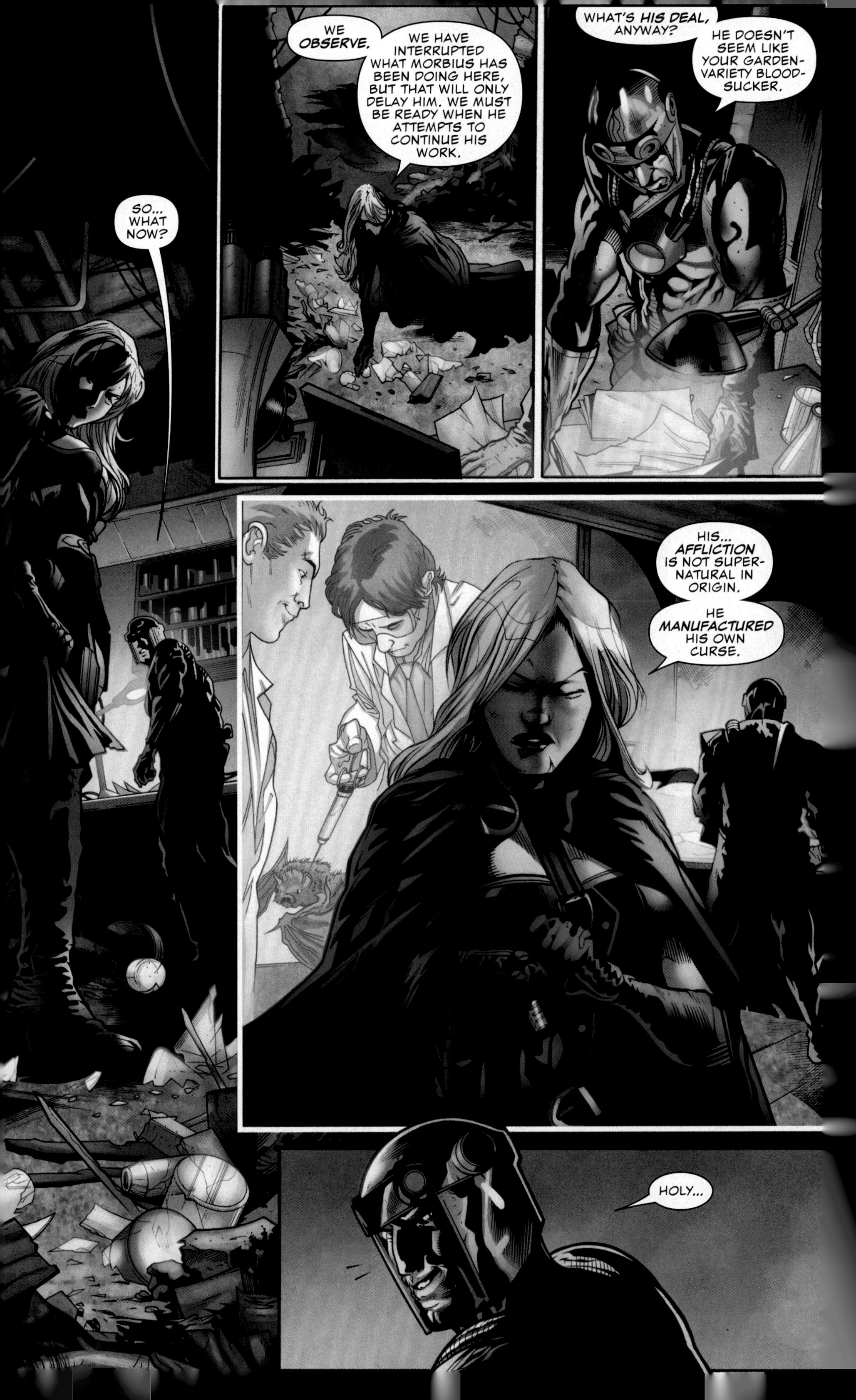
SO... WHAT NOW?
WE OBSERVE.
WE HAVE INTERRUPTED WHAT MORBIUS HAS BEEN DOING HERE, BUT THAT WILL ONLY DELAY HIM. WE MUST BE READY WHEN HE ATTEMPTS TO CONTINUE HIS WORK.
WHAT'S HIS DEAL, ANYWAY?
HE DOESN'T SEEM LIKE YOUR GARDEN-VARIETY BLOOD-SUCKER.
HIS... AFFLICTION IS NOT SUPER-NATURAL IN ORIGIN.
HE MANUFACTURED HIS OWN CURSE.
HOLY...

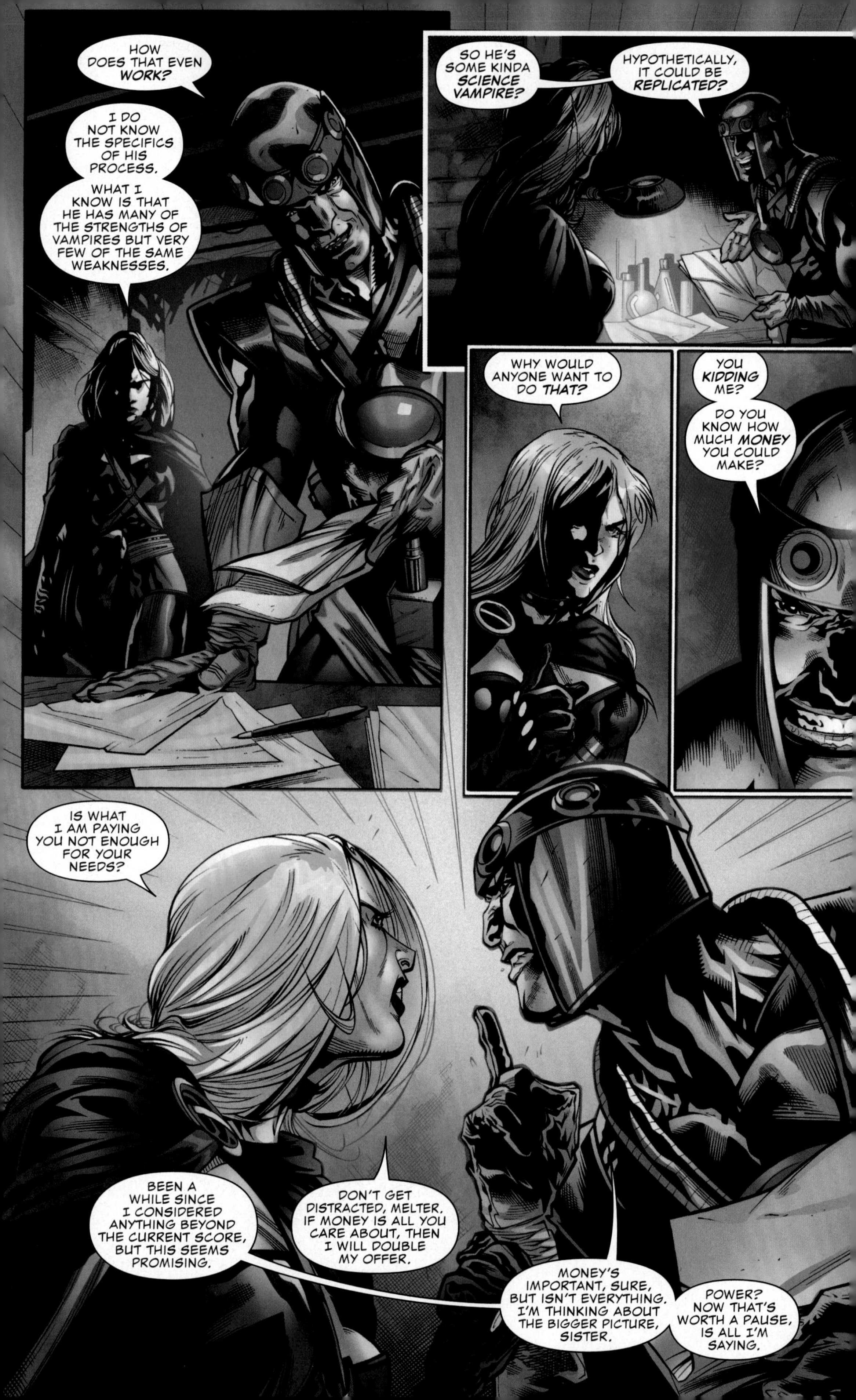
HOW DOES THAT EVEN WORK?
I DO NOT KNOW THE SPECIFICS OF HIS PROCESS.
WHAT I KNOW IS THAT HE HAS MANY OF THE STRENGTHS OF VAMPIRES BUT VERY FEW OF THE SAME WEAKNESSES.
SO HE'S SOME KINDA SCIENCE VAMPIRE?
HYPOTHETICALLY, IT COULD BE REPLICATED?
WHY WOULD ANYONE WANT TO DO THAT?
YOU KIDDING ME?
DO YOU KNOW HOW MUCH MONEY YOU COULD MAKE?
IS WHAT I AM PAYING YOU NOT ENOUGH FOR YOUR NEEDS?
BEEN A WHILE SINCE I CONSIDERED ANYTHING BEYOND THE CURRENT SCORE, BUT THIS SEEMS PROMISING.
DON'T GET DISTRACTED, MELTER. IF MONEY IS ALL YOU CARE ABOUT, THEN I WILL DOUBLE MY OFFER.
MONEY'S IMPORTANT, SURE, BUT ISN'T EVERYTHING. I'M THINKING ABOUT THE BIGGER PICTURE, SISTER.
POWER? NOW THAT'S WORTH A PAUSE, IS ALL I'M SAYING.

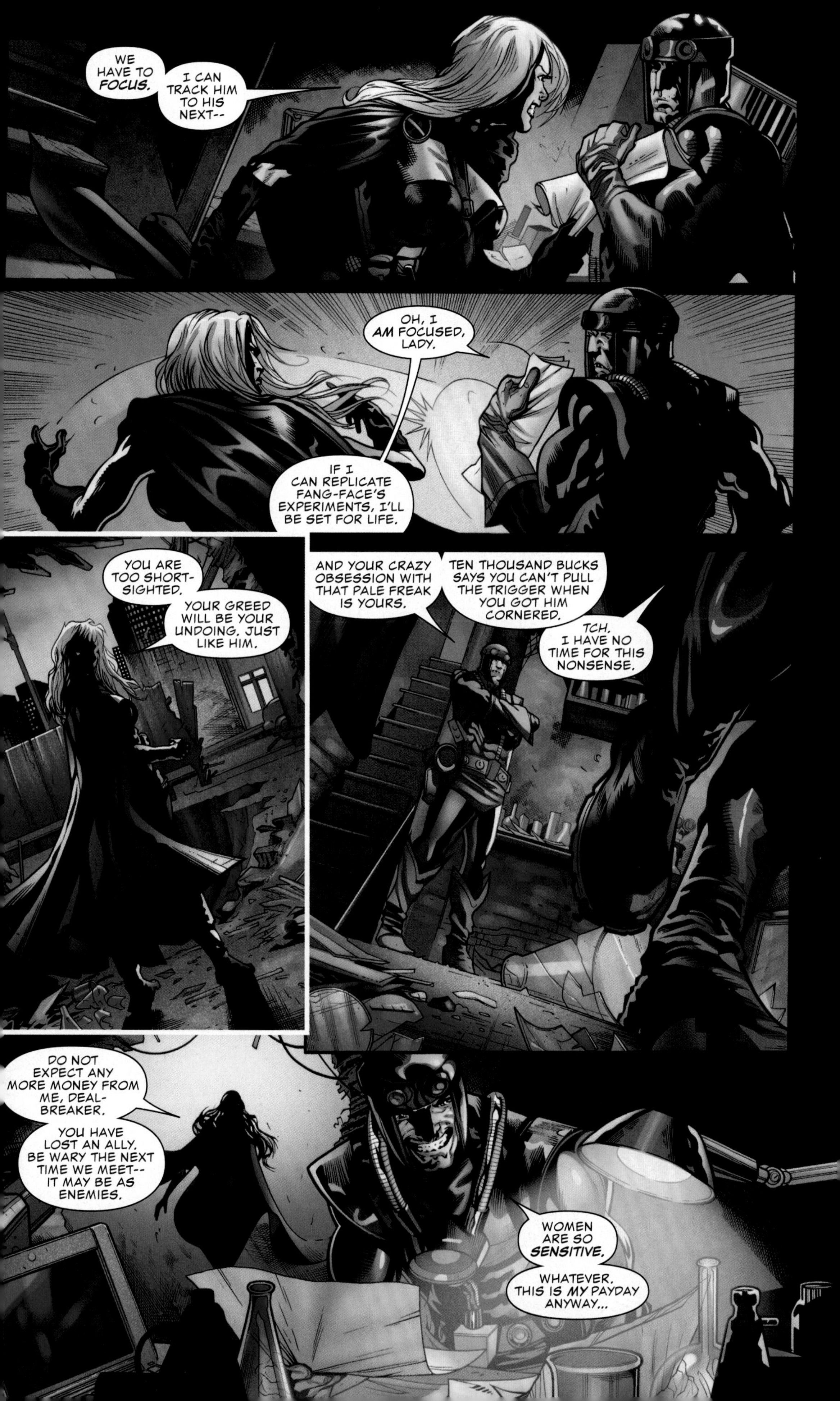

WE HAVE TO *FOCUS.*
I CAN TRACK HIM TO HIS NEXT--
OH, I *AM* FOCUSED, LADY.
IF I CAN REPLICATE FANG-FACE'S EXPERIMENTS, I'LL BE SET FOR LIFE.
YOU ARE TOO SHORT-SIGHTED.
YOUR GREED WILL BE YOUR UNDOING. JUST LIKE HIM.
AND YOUR CRAZY OBSESSION WITH THAT PALE FREAK IS YOURS.
TEN THOUSAND BUCKS SAYS YOU CAN'T PULL THE TRIGGER WHEN YOU GOT HIM CORNERED.
TCH. I HAVE NO TIME FOR THIS NONSENSE.
DO NOT EXPECT ANY MORE MONEY FROM ME, DEAL-BREAKER.
YOU HAVE LOST AN ALLY. BE WARY THE NEXT TIME WE MEET-- IT MAY BE AS ENEMIES.
WOMEN ARE SO *SENSITIVE.*
WHATEVER. THIS IS *MY* PAYDAY ANYWAY...

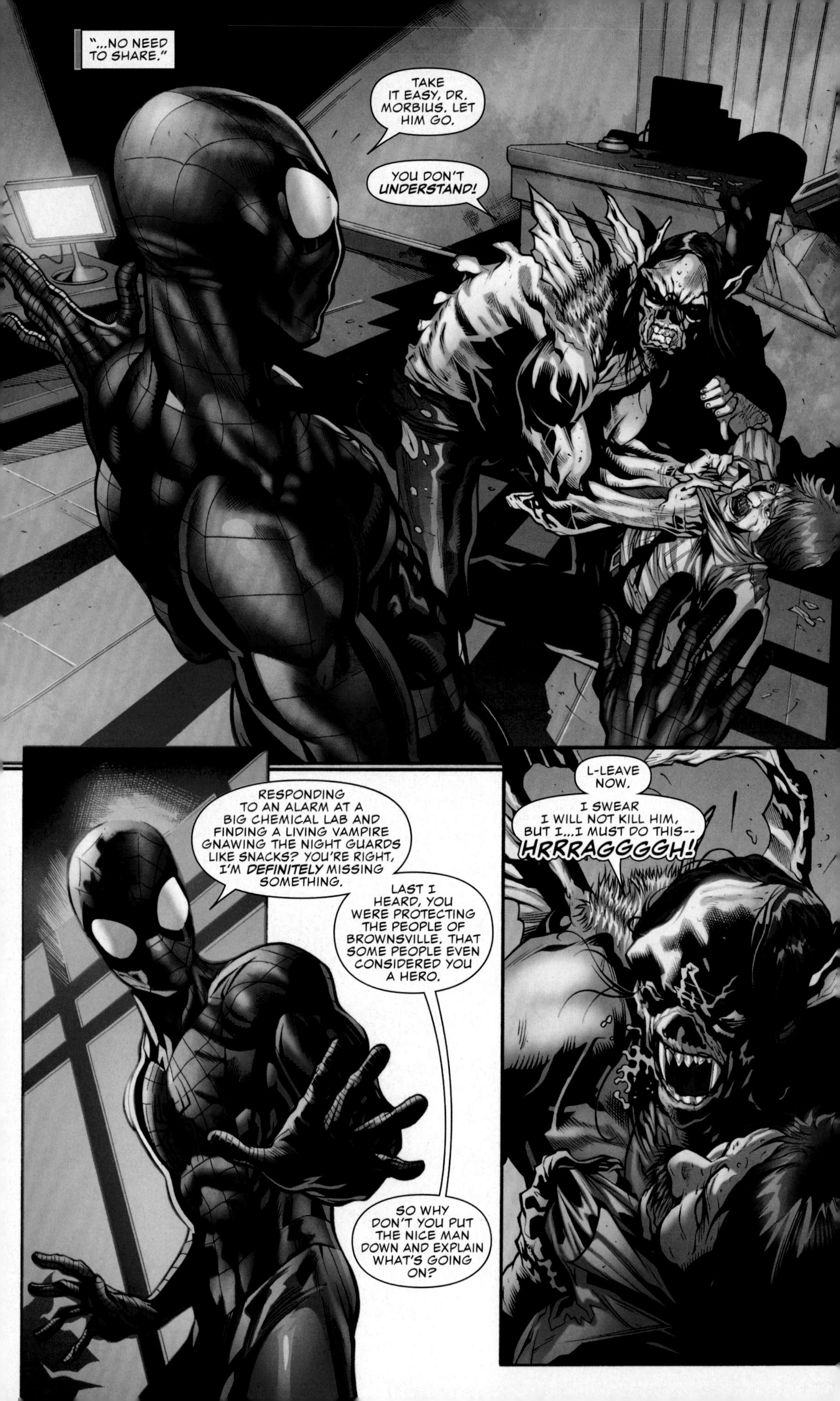
"...NO NEED TO SHARE."
TAKE IT EASY, DR. MORBIUS. LET HIM GO.
YOU DON'T *UNDERSTAND!*
RESPONDING TO AN ALARM AT A BIG CHEMICAL LAB AND FINDING A LIVING VAMPIRE GNAWING THE NIGHT GUARDS LIKE SNACKS? YOU'RE RIGHT, I'M *DEFINITELY* MISSING SOMETHING.
LAST I HEARD, YOU WERE PROTECTING THE PEOPLE OF BROWNSVILLE. THAT SOME PEOPLE EVEN CONSIDERED YOU A HERO.
SO WHY DON'T YOU PUT THE NICE MAN DOWN AND EXPLAIN WHAT'S GOING ON?
L-LEAVE NOW.
I SWEAR I WILL NOT KILL HIM, BUT I...I MUST DO THIS--
HRRRAGGGGH!

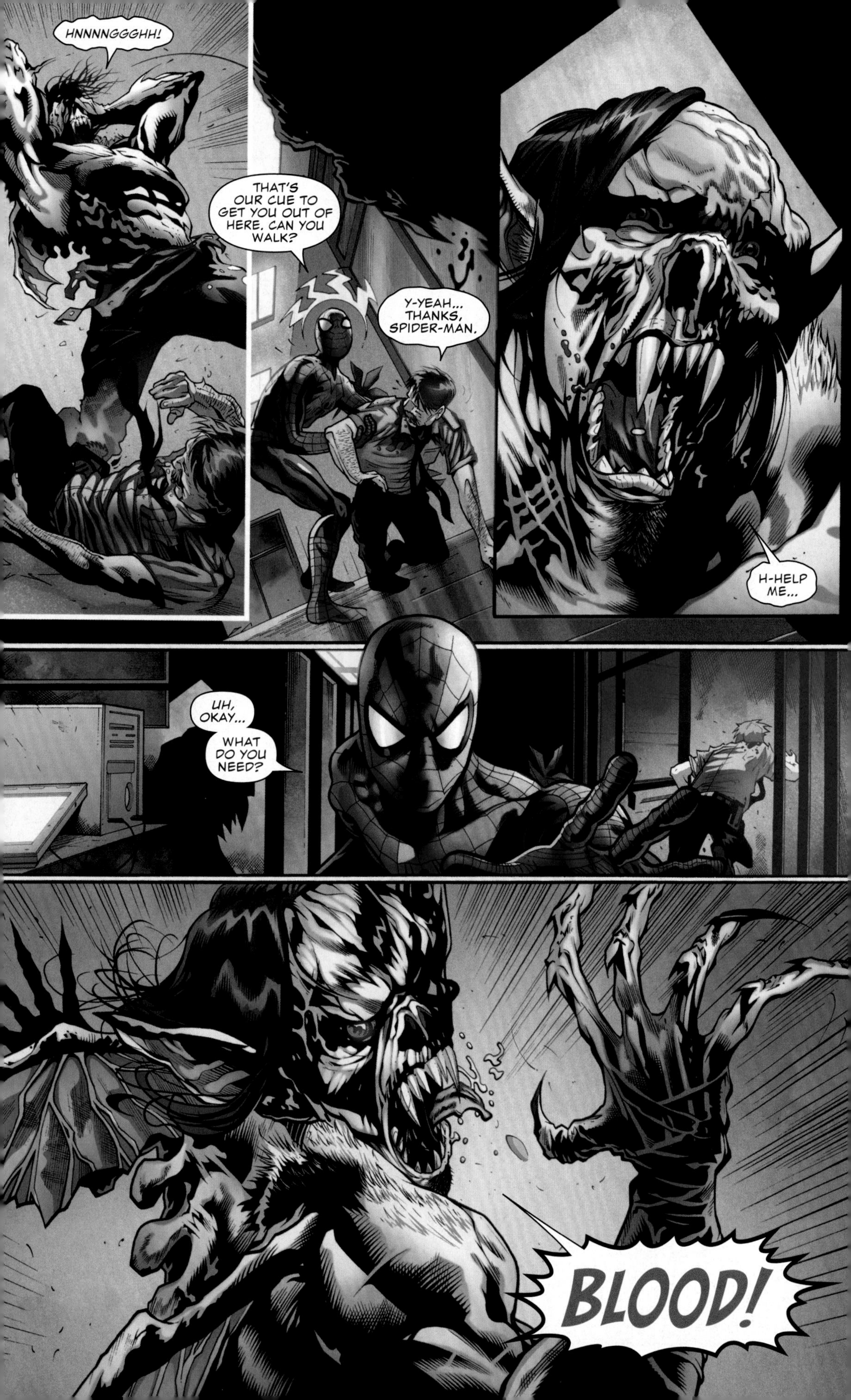
HNNNNGGGHH!
THAT'S OUR CUE TO GET YOU OUT OF HERE. CAN YOU WALK?
Y-YEAH... THANKS, SPIDER-MAN.
H-HELP ME...
UH, OKAY...
WHAT DO YOU NEED?
BLOOD!

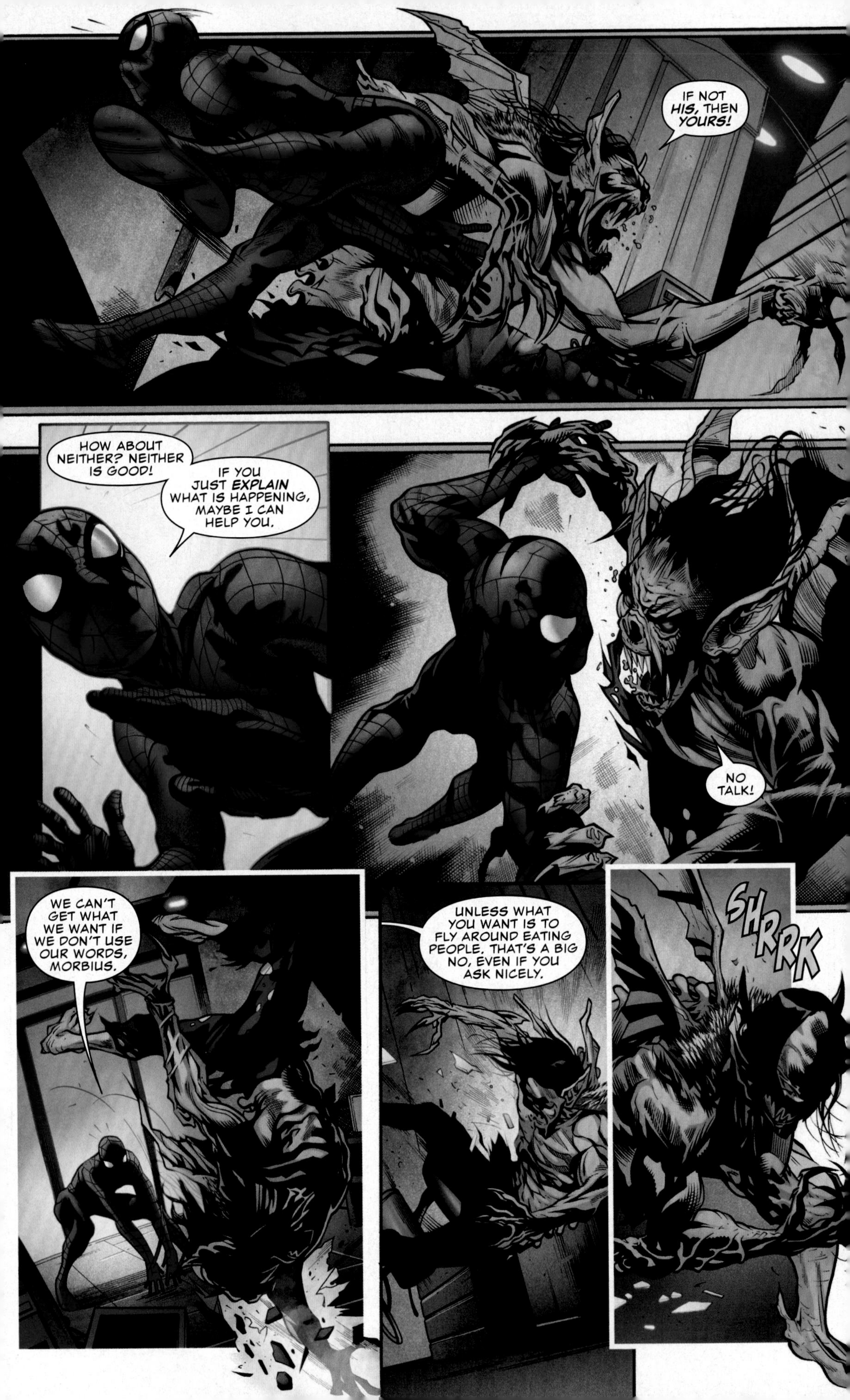
IF NOT HIS, THEN YOURS!
HOW ABOUT NEITHER? NEITHER IS GOOD!
IF YOU JUST EXPLAIN WHAT IS HAPPENING, MAYBE I CAN HELP YOU.
NO TALK!
WE CAN'T GET WHAT WE WANT IF WE DON'T USE OUR WORDS, MORBIUS.
UNLESS WHAT YOU WANT IS TO FLY AROUND EATING PEOPLE. THAT'S A BIG NO, EVEN IF YOU ASK NICELY.
SHRRK

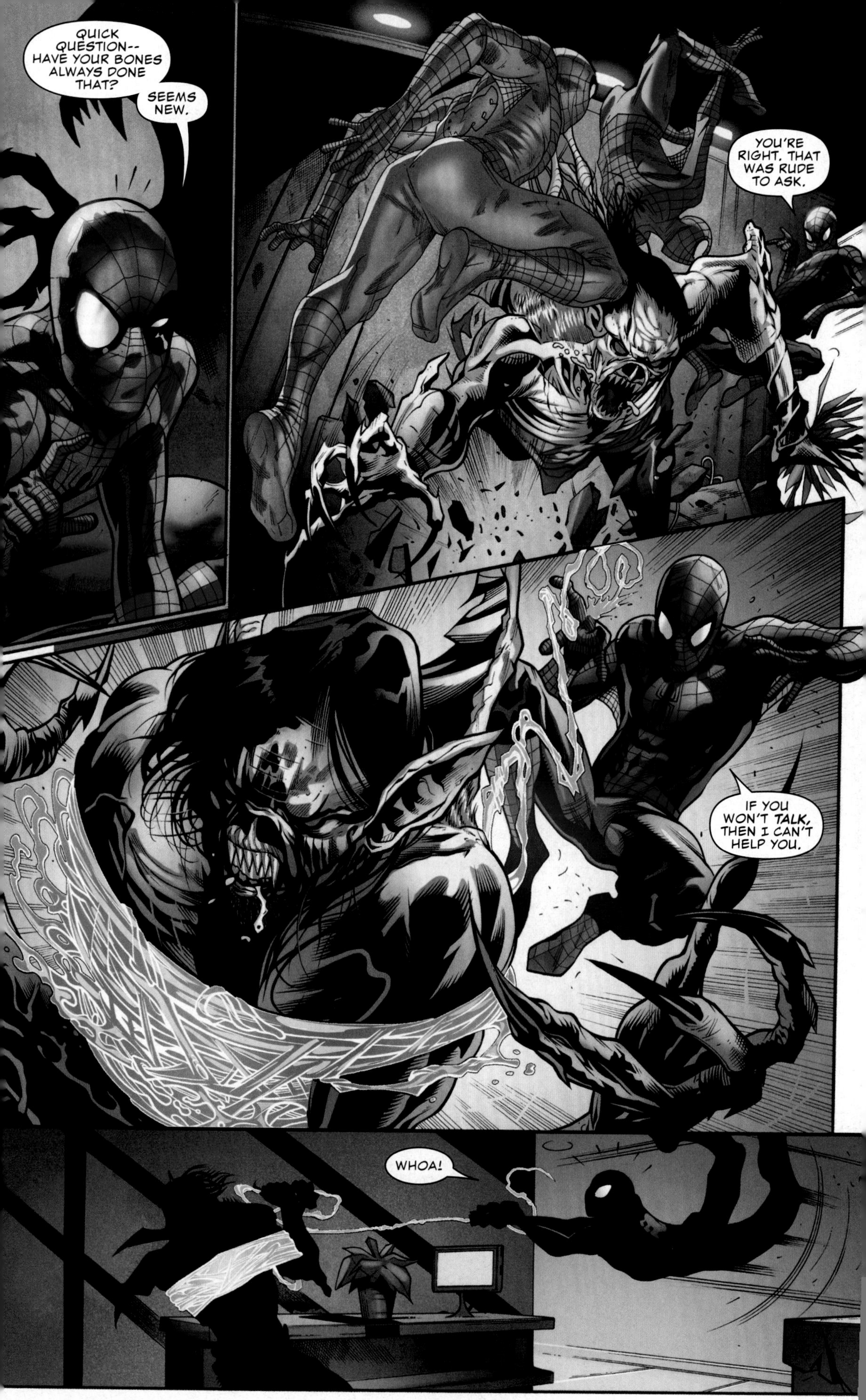
QUICK QUESTION-- HAVE YOUR BONES ALWAYS DONE THAT?
SEEMS NEW.
YOU'RE RIGHT. THAT WAS RUDE TO ASK.
IF YOU WON'T TALK, THEN I CAN'T HELP YOU.
WHOA!

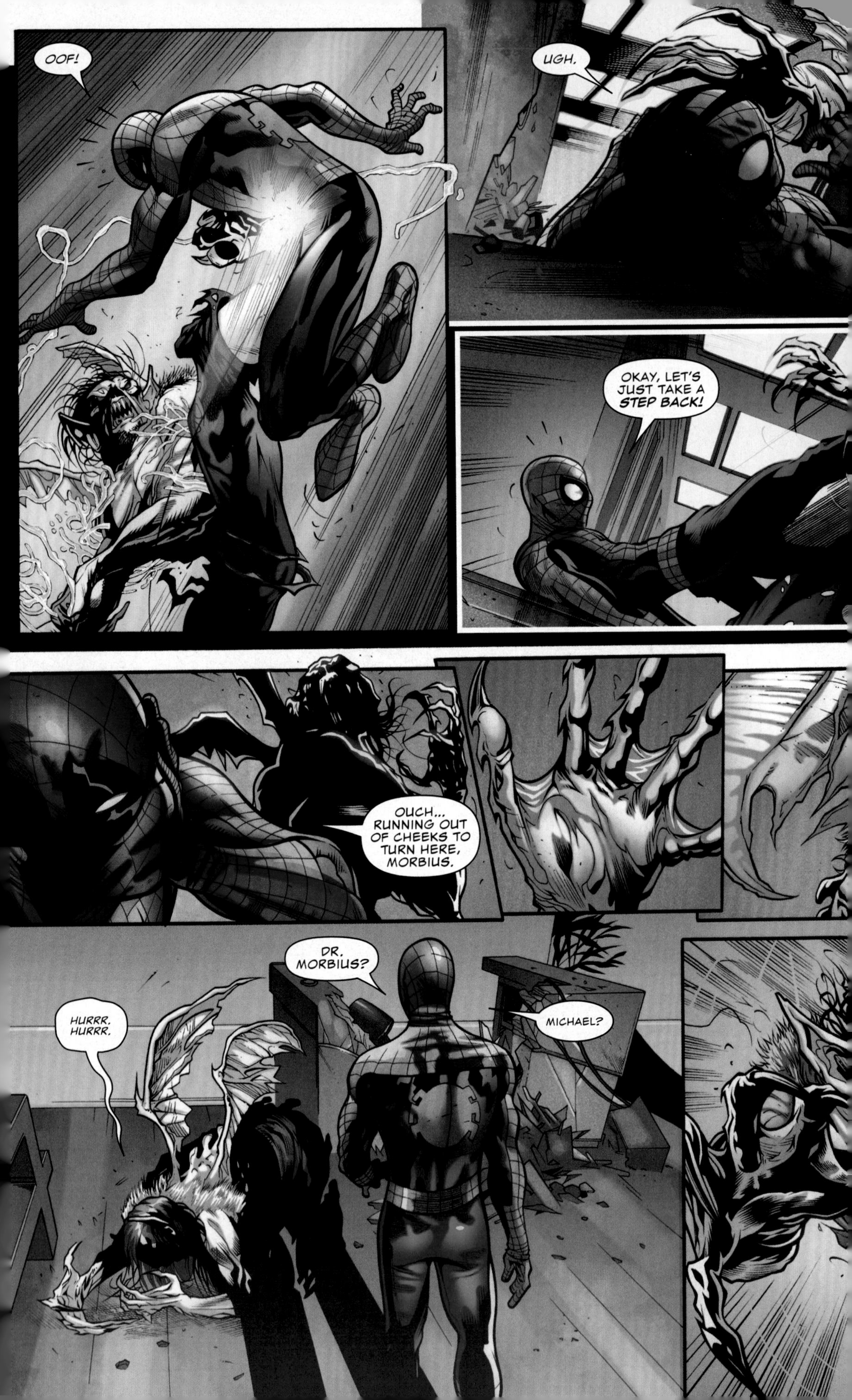
OOF!
UGH.
OKAY, LET'S JUST TAKE A STEP BACK!
OUCH... RUNNING OUT OF CHEEKS TO TURN HERE, MORBIUS.
HURRR. HURRR.
DR. MORBIUS?
MICHAEL?

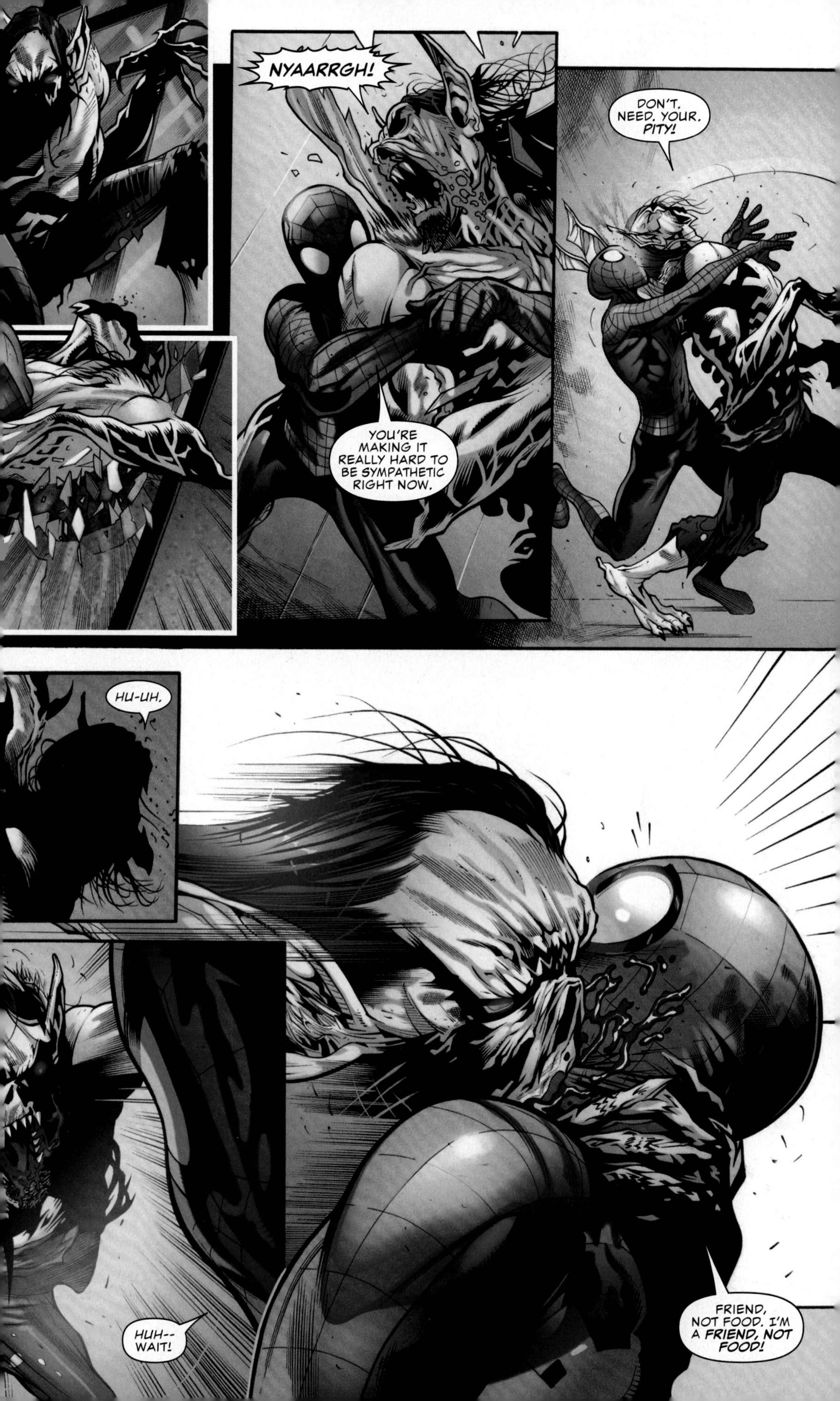
NYAARRGH!
YOU'RE MAKING IT REALLY HARD TO BE SYMPATHETIC RIGHT NOW.
DON'T. NEED. YOUR. PITY!
HU-UH.
HUH-- WAIT!
FRIEND, NOT FOOD. I'M A FRIEND, NOT FOOD!

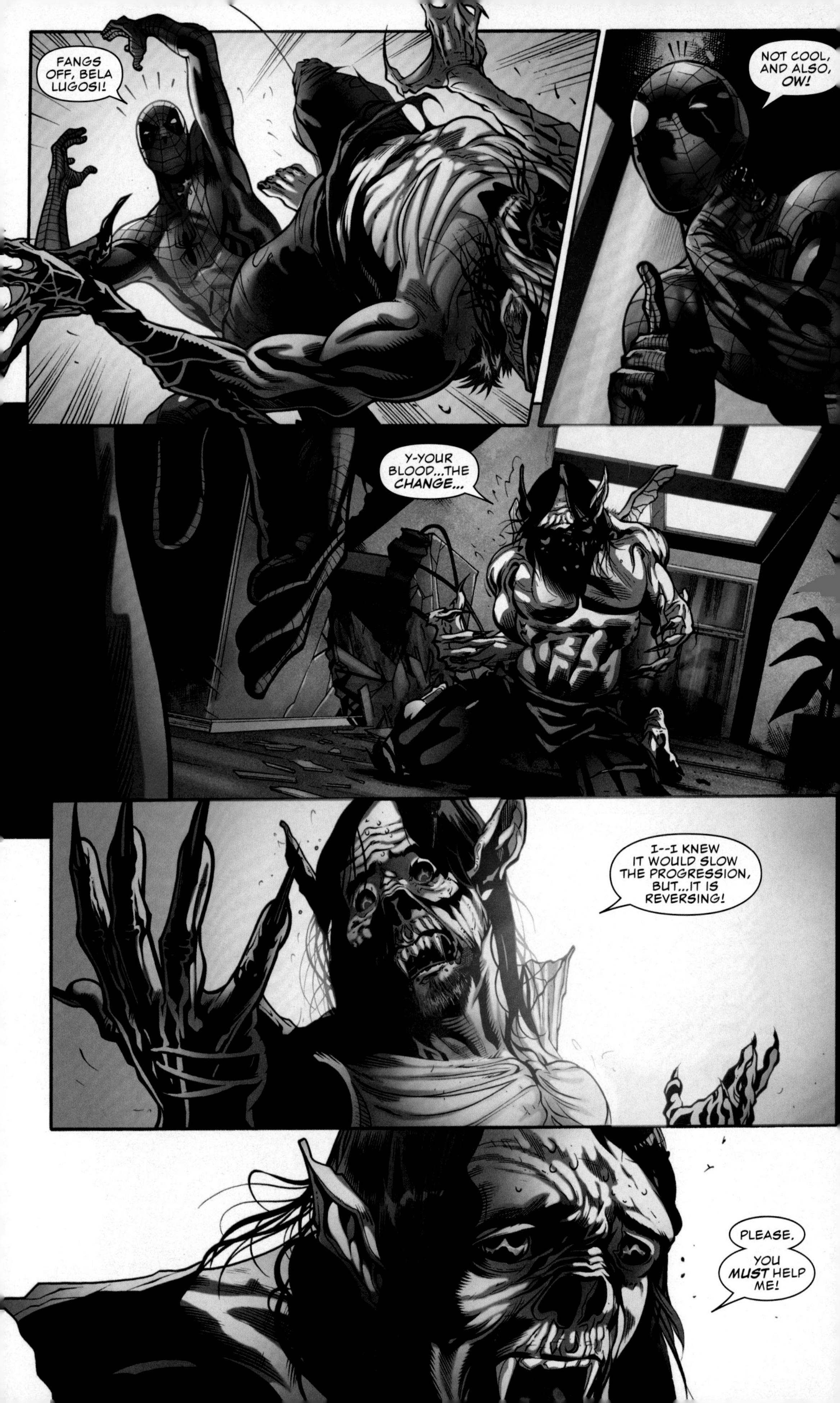
FANGS OFF, BELA LUGOSI!
NOT COOL, AND ALSO, OW!
Y-YOUR BLOOD...THE CHANGE...
I--I KNEW IT WOULD SLOW THE PROGRESSION, BUT...IT IS REVERSING!
PLEASE.
YOU MUST HELP ME!

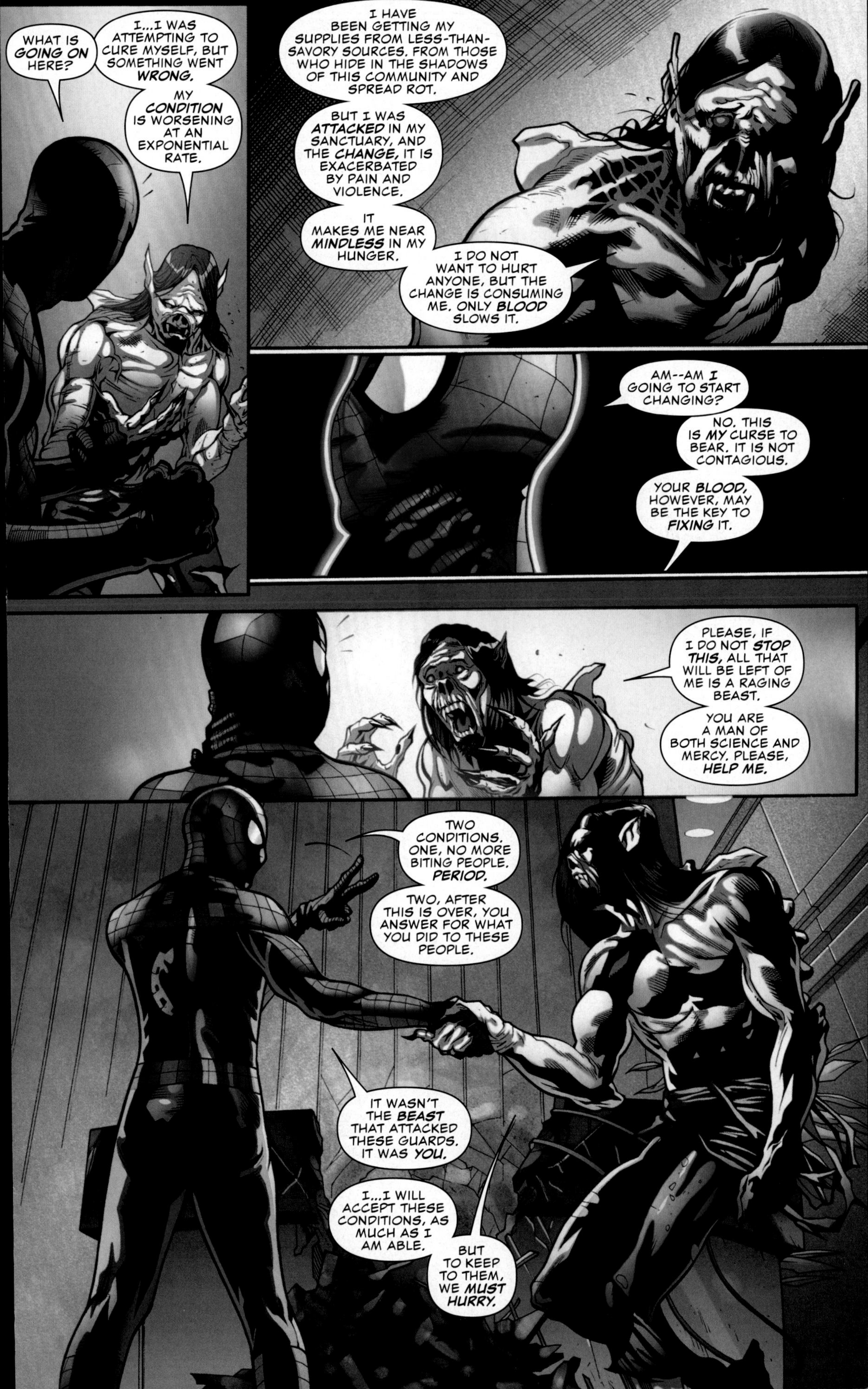
WHAT IS GOING ON HERE?
I...I WAS ATTEMPTING TO CURE MYSELF, BUT SOMETHING WENT WRONG.
MY CONDITION IS WORSENING AT AN EXPONENTIAL RATE.
I HAVE BEEN GETTING MY SUPPLIES FROM LESS-THAN-SAVORY SOURCES, FROM THOSE WHO HIDE IN THE SHADOWS OF THIS COMMUNITY AND SPREAD ROT.
BUT I WAS ATTACKED IN MY SANCTUARY, AND THE CHANGE, IT IS EXACERBATED BY PAIN AND VIOLENCE.
IT MAKES ME NEAR MINDLESS IN MY HUNGER.
I DO NOT WANT TO HURT ANYONE, BUT THE CHANGE IS CONSUMING ME. ONLY BLOOD SLOWS IT.
AM--AM I GOING TO START CHANGING?
NO. THIS IS MY CURSE TO BEAR. IT IS NOT CONTAGIOUS.
YOUR BLOOD, HOWEVER, MAY BE THE KEY TO FIXING IT.
PLEASE, IF I DO NOT STOP THIS, ALL THAT WILL BE LEFT OF ME IS A RAGING BEAST.
YOU ARE A MAN OF BOTH SCIENCE AND MERCY. PLEASE, HELP ME.
TWO CONDITIONS. ONE, NO MORE BITING PEOPLE. PERIOD.
TWO, AFTER THIS IS OVER, YOU ANSWER FOR WHAT YOU DID TO THESE PEOPLE.
IT WASN'T THE BEAST THAT ATTACKED THESE GUARDS. IT WAS YOU.
I...I WILL ACCEPT THESE CONDITIONS, AS MUCH AS I AM ABLE.
BUT TO KEEP TO THEM, WE MUST HURRY.

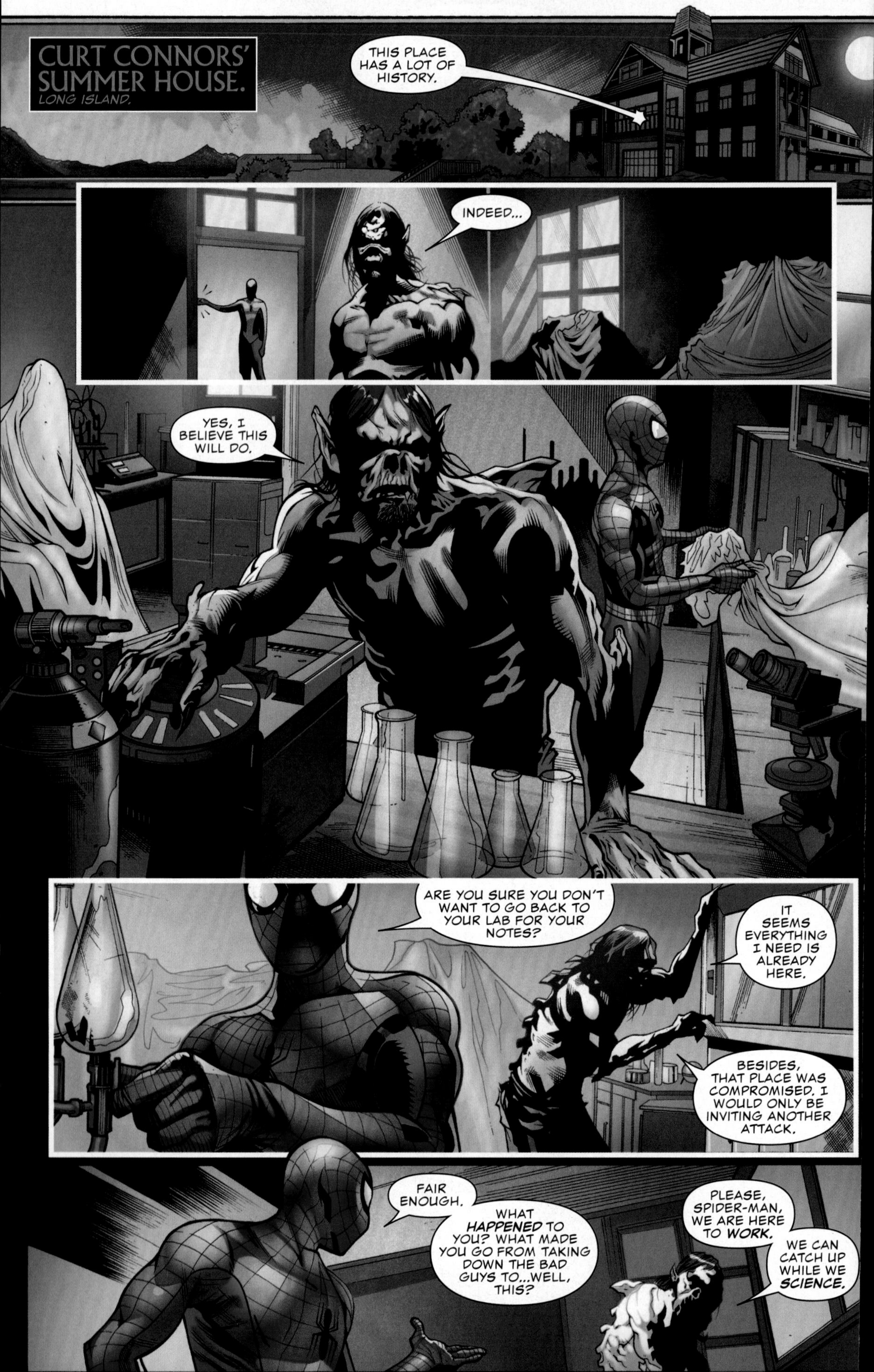
CURT CONNORS' SUMMER HOUSE.
LONG ISLAND.
THIS PLACE HAS A LOT OF HISTORY.
INDEED...
YES, I BELIEVE THIS WILL DO.
ARE YOU SURE YOU DON'T WANT TO GO BACK TO YOUR LAB FOR YOUR NOTES?
IT SEEMS EVERYTHING I NEED IS ALREADY HERE.
BESIDES, THAT PLACE WAS COMPROMISED. I WOULD ONLY BE INVITING ANOTHER ATTACK.
FAIR ENOUGH.
WHAT HAPPENED TO YOU? WHAT MADE YOU GO FROM TAKING DOWN THE BAD GUYS TO...WELL, THIS?
PLEASE, SPIDER-MAN, WE ARE HERE TO WORK.
WE CAN CATCH UP WHILE WE SCIENCE.

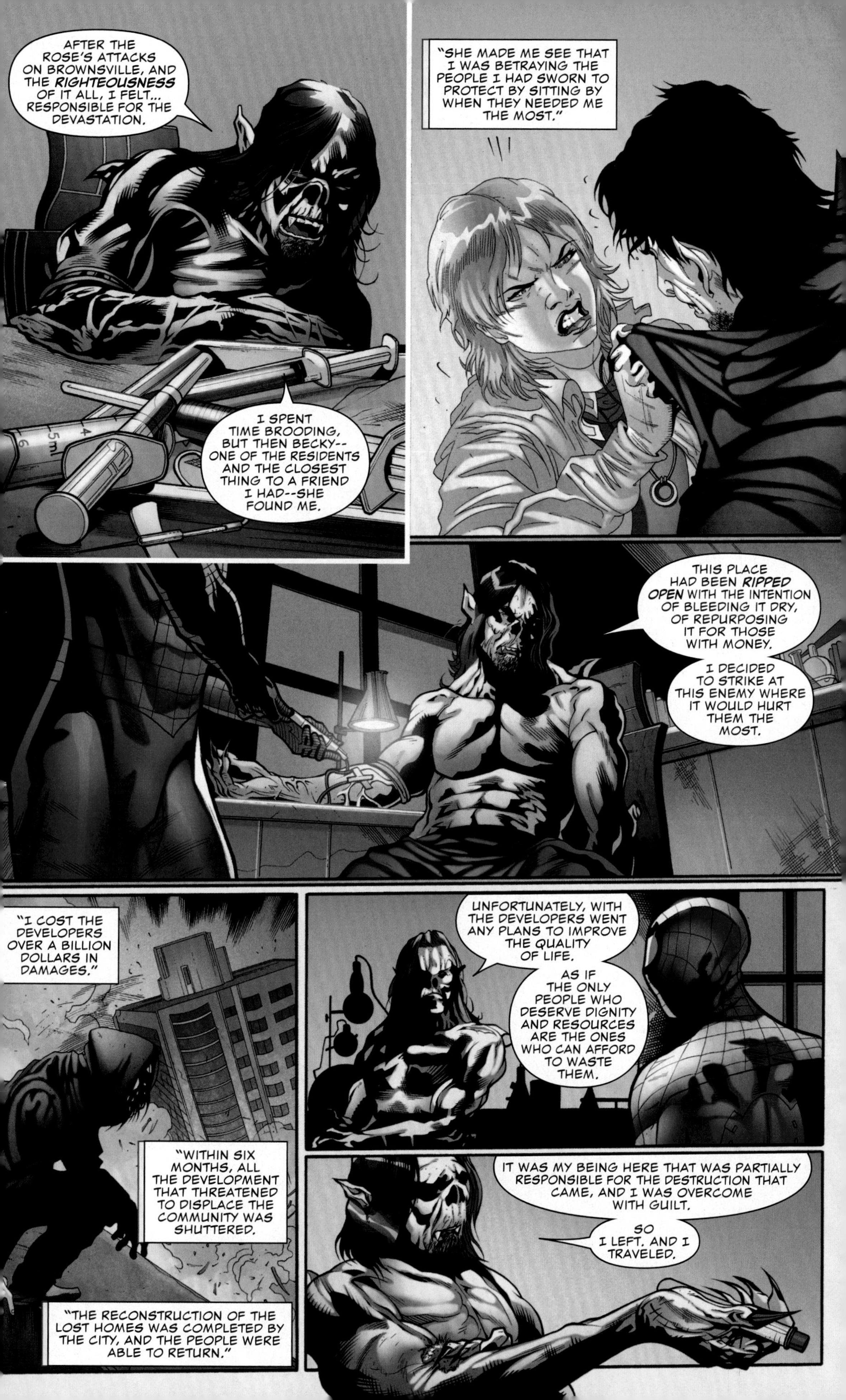
AFTER THE ROSE'S ATTACKS ON BROWNSVILLE, AND THE *RIGHTEOUSNESS* OF IT ALL, I FELT... RESPONSIBLE FOR THE DEVASTATION.
I SPENT TIME BROODING, BUT THEN BECKY-- ONE OF THE RESIDENTS AND THE CLOSEST THING TO A FRIEND I HAD--SHE FOUND ME.
"SHE MADE ME SEE THAT I WAS BETRAYING THE PEOPLE I HAD SWORN TO PROTECT BY SITTING BY WHEN THEY NEEDED ME THE MOST."
THIS PLACE HAD BEEN *RIPPED OPEN* WITH THE INTENTION OF BLEEDING IT DRY, OF REPURPOSING IT FOR THOSE WITH MONEY.
I DECIDED TO STRIKE AT THIS ENEMY WHERE IT WOULD HURT THEM THE MOST.
"I COST THE DEVELOPERS OVER A BILLION DOLLARS IN DAMAGES."
"WITHIN SIX MONTHS, ALL THE DEVELOPMENT THAT THREATENED TO DISPLACE THE COMMUNITY WAS SHUTTERED.
"THE RECONSTRUCTION OF THE LOST HOMES WAS COMPLETED BY THE CITY, AND THE PEOPLE WERE ABLE TO RETURN."
UNFORTUNATELY, WITH THE DEVELOPERS WENT ANY PLANS TO IMPROVE THE QUALITY OF LIFE.
AS IF THE ONLY PEOPLE WHO DESERVE DIGNITY AND RESOURCES ARE THE ONES WHO CAN AFFORD TO WASTE THEM.
IT WAS MY BEING HERE THAT WAS PARTIALLY RESPONSIBLE FOR THE DESTRUCTION THAT CAME, AND I WAS OVERCOME WITH GUILT.
SO I LEFT. AND I TRAVELED.

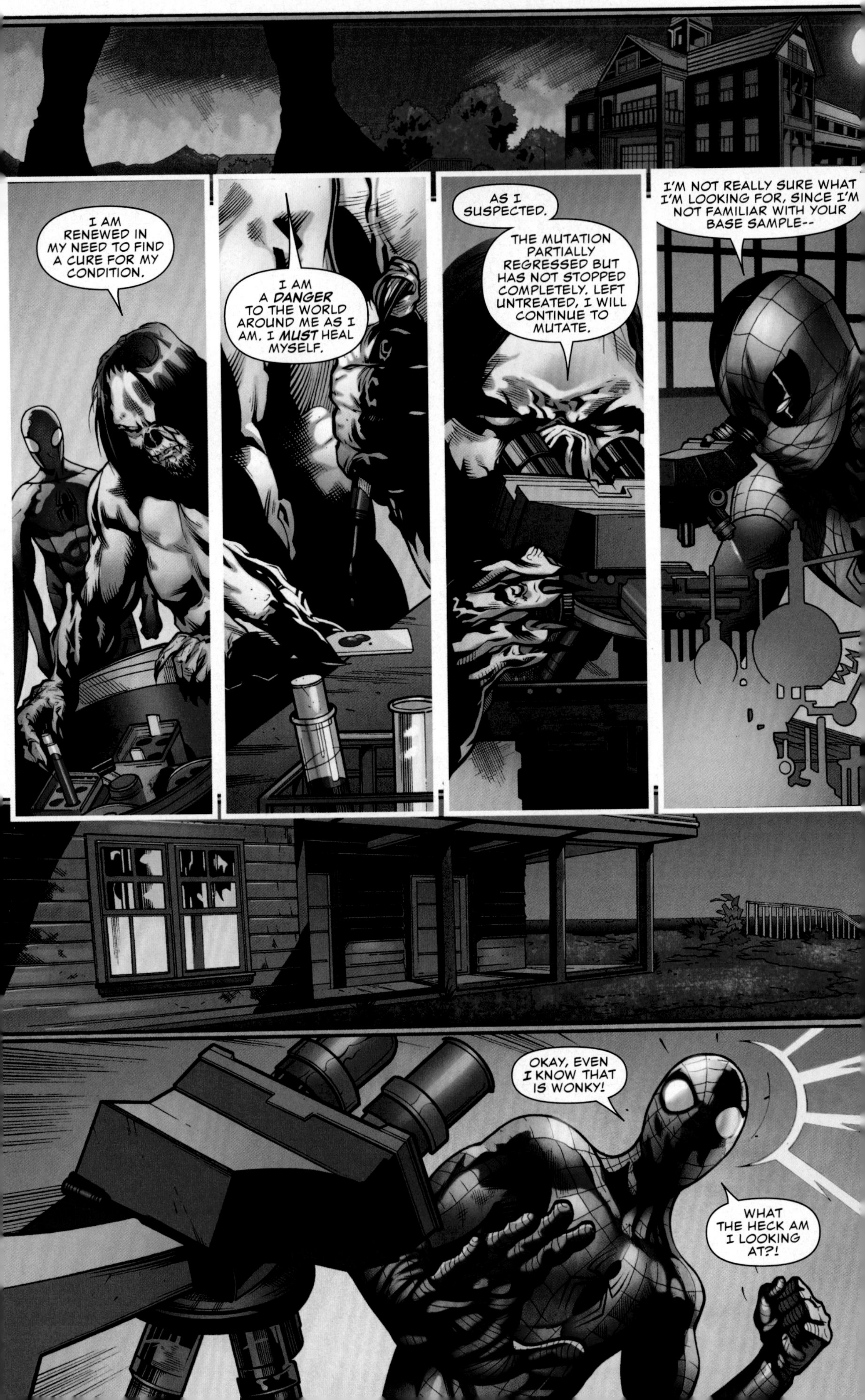
I AM RENEWED IN MY NEED TO FIND A CURE FOR MY CONDITION.
I AM A *DANGER* TO THE WORLD AROUND ME AS I AM. I *MUST* HEAL MYSELF.
AS I SUSPECTED.
THE MUTATION PARTIALLY REGRESSED BUT HAS NOT STOPPED COMPLETELY. LEFT UNTREATED, I WILL CONTINUE TO MUTATE.
I'M NOT REALLY SURE WHAT I'M LOOKING FOR, SINCE I'M NOT FAMILIAR WITH YOUR BASE SAMPLE--
OKAY, EVEN *I* KNOW THAT IS WONKY!
WHAT THE HECK AM I LOOKING AT?!

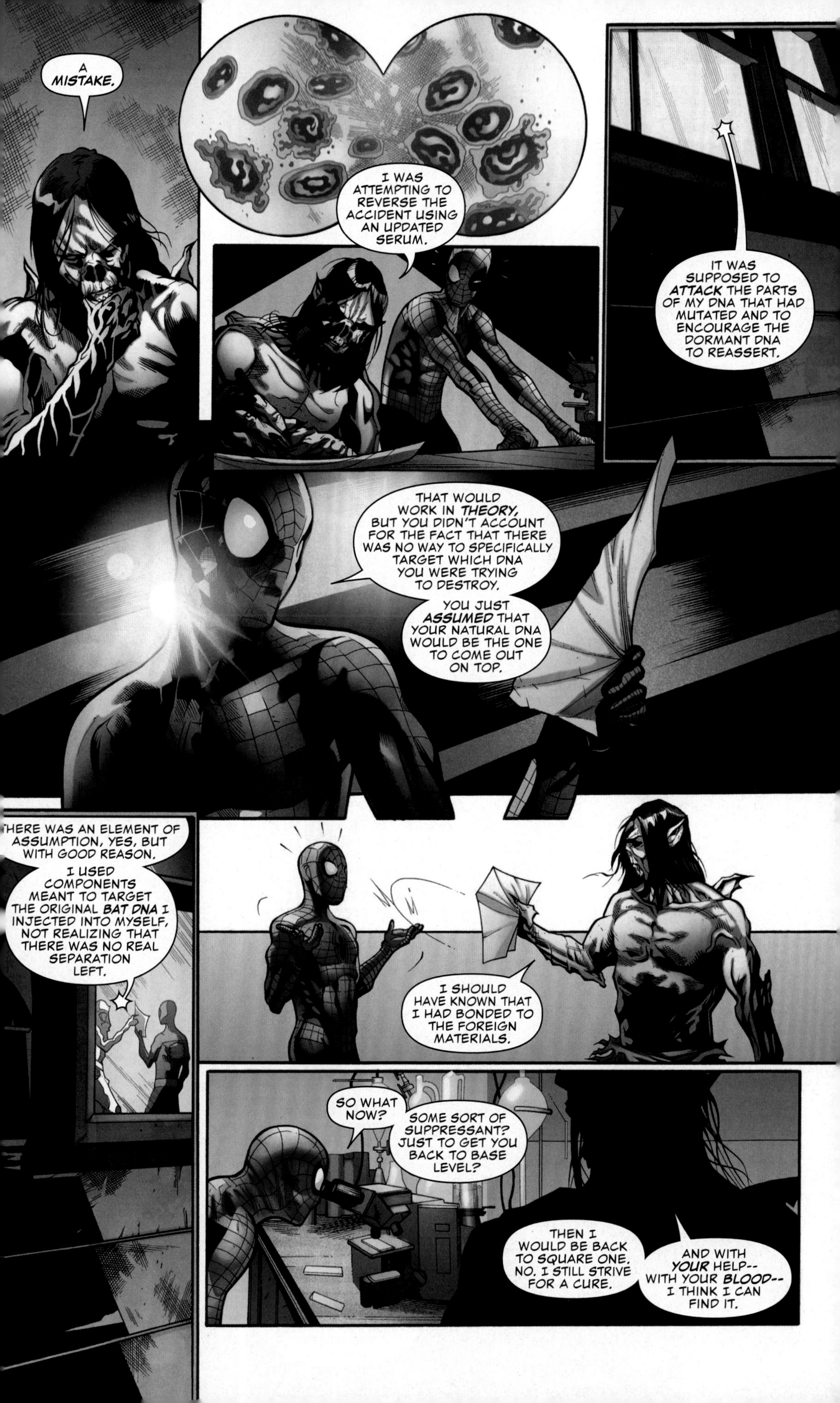

A MISTAKE.
I WAS ATTEMPTING TO REVERSE THE ACCIDENT USING AN UPDATED SERUM.
IT WAS SUPPOSED TO ATTACK THE PARTS OF MY DNA THAT HAD MUTATED AND TO ENCOURAGE THE DORMANT DNA TO REASSERT.
THAT WOULD WORK IN THEORY, BUT YOU DIDN'T ACCOUNT FOR THE FACT THAT THERE WAS NO WAY TO SPECIFICALLY TARGET WHICH DNA YOU WERE TRYING TO DESTROY.
YOU JUST ASSUMED THAT YOUR NATURAL DNA WOULD BE THE ONE TO COME OUT ON TOP.
THERE WAS AN ELEMENT OF ASSUMPTION, YES, BUT WITH GOOD REASON.
I USED COMPONENTS MEANT TO TARGET THE ORIGINAL BAT DNA I INJECTED INTO MYSELF, NOT REALIZING THAT THERE WAS NO REAL SEPARATION LEFT.
I SHOULD HAVE KNOWN THAT I HAD BONDED TO THE FOREIGN MATERIALS.
SO WHAT NOW?
SOME SORT OF SUPPRESSANT? JUST TO GET YOU BACK TO BASE LEVEL?
THEN I WOULD BE BACK TO SQUARE ONE. NO. I STILL STRIVE FOR A CURE.
AND WITH YOUR HELP-- WITH YOUR BLOOD-- I THINK I CAN FIND IT.

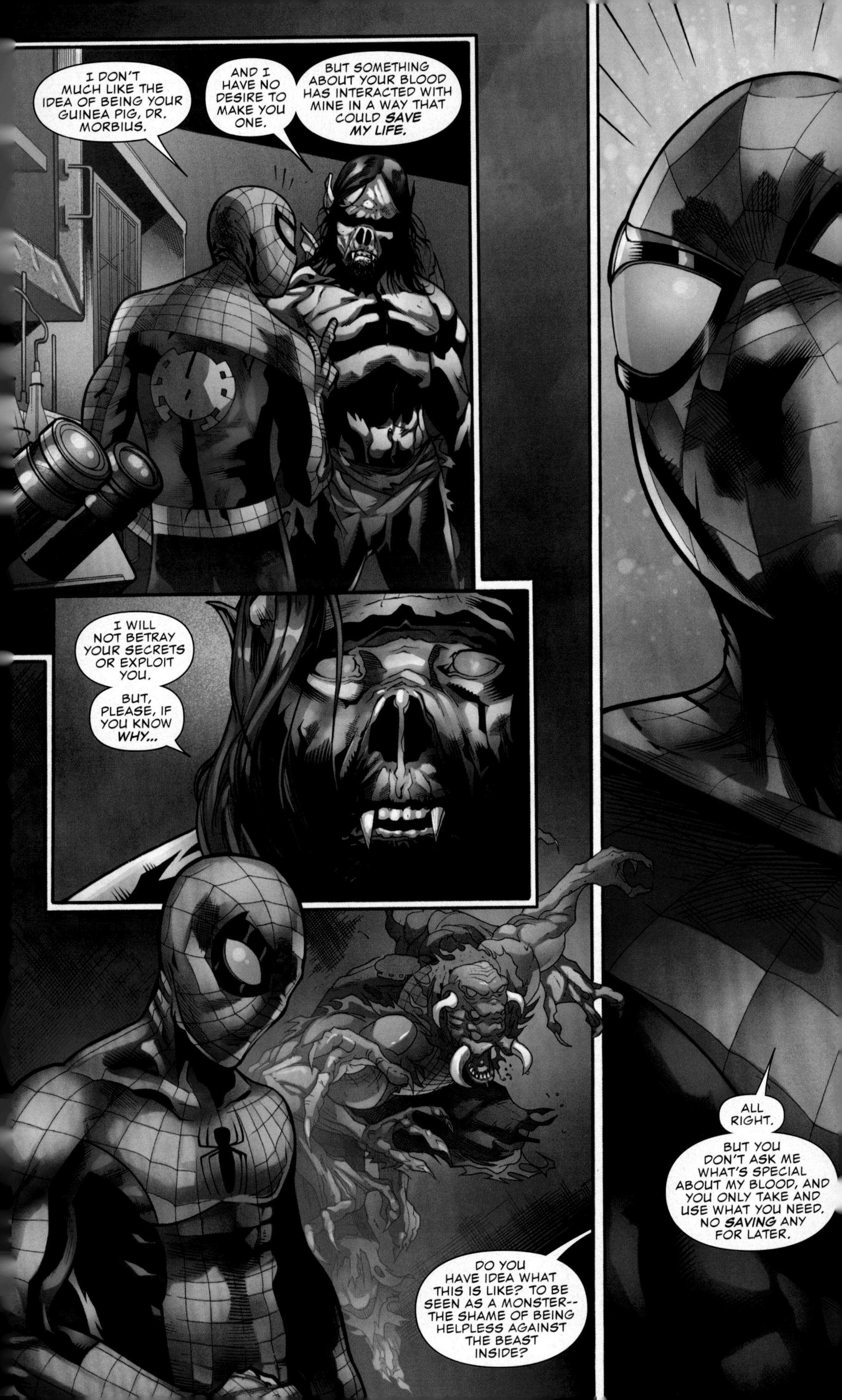
I DON'T MUCH LIKE THE IDEA OF BEING YOUR GUINEA PIG, DR. MORBIUS.
AND I HAVE NO DESIRE TO MAKE YOU ONE.
BUT SOMETHING ABOUT YOUR BLOOD HAS INTERACTED WITH MINE IN A WAY THAT COULD SAVE MY LIFE.
I WILL NOT BETRAY YOUR SECRETS OR EXPLOIT YOU.
BUT, PLEASE, IF YOU KNOW WHY...
DO YOU HAVE IDEA WHAT THIS IS LIKE? TO BE SEEN AS A MONSTER-- THE SHAME OF BEING HELPLESS AGAINST THE BEAST INSIDE?
ALL RIGHT.
BUT YOU DON'T ASK ME WHAT'S SPECIAL ABOUT MY BLOOD, AND YOU ONLY TAKE AND USE WHAT YOU NEED. NO SAVING ANY FOR LATER.

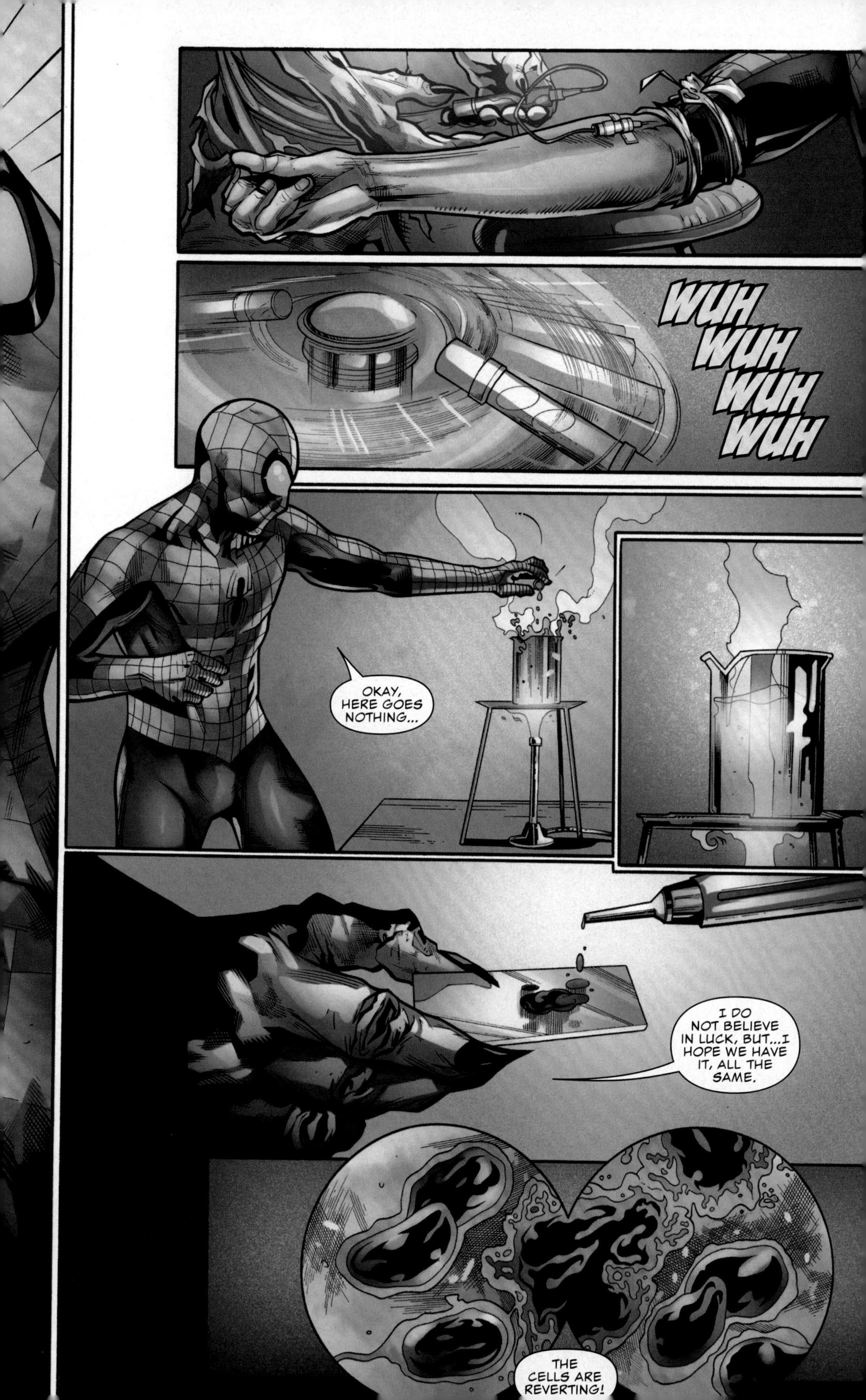
WUH WUH WUH WUH
OKAY, HERE GOES NOTHING...
I DO NOT BELIEVE IN LUCK, BUT...I HOPE WE HAVE IT, ALL THE SAME.
THE CELLS ARE REVERTING!

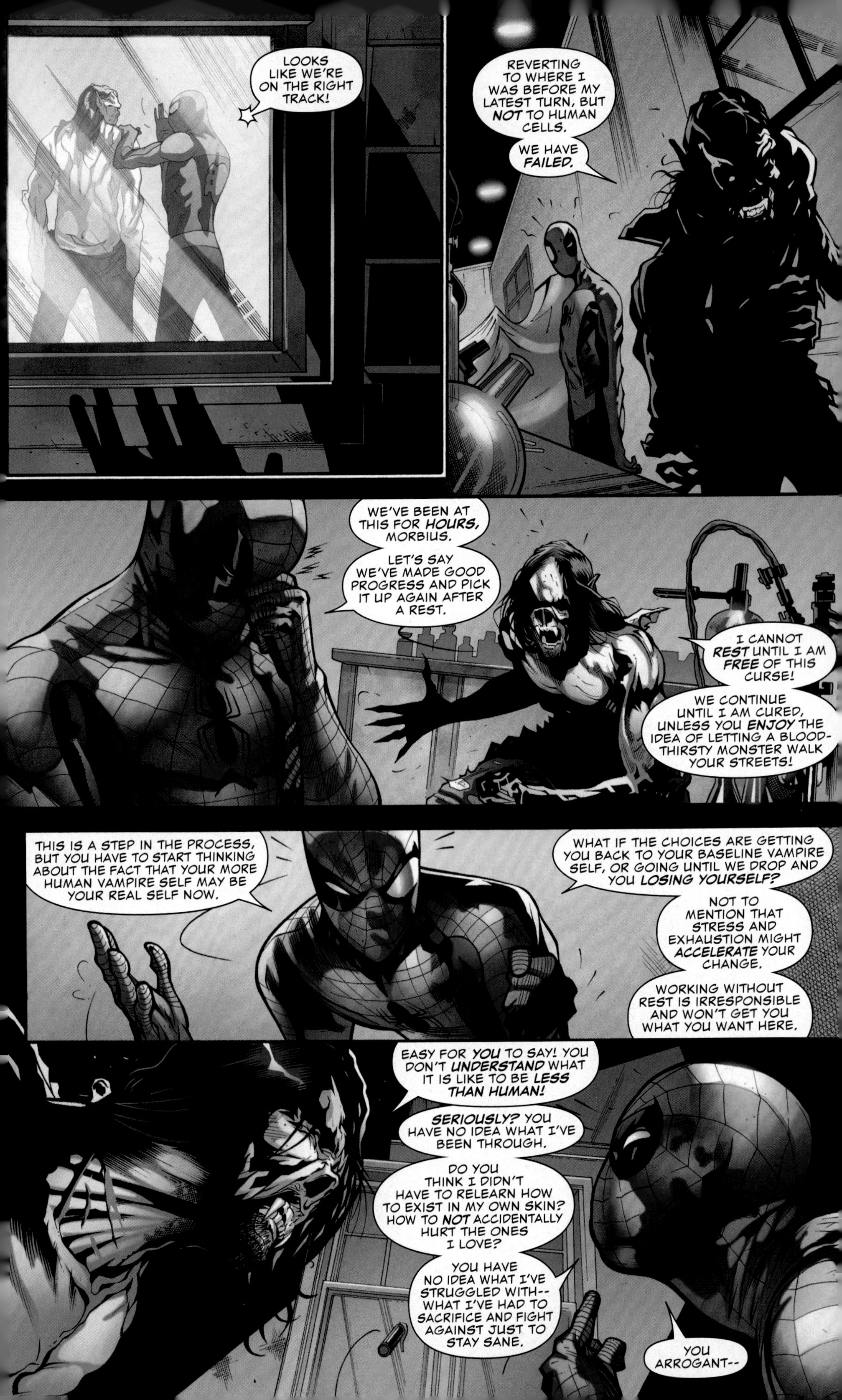
LOOKS LIKE WE'RE ON THE RIGHT TRACK!
REVERTING TO WHERE I WAS BEFORE MY LATEST TURN, BUT NOT TO HUMAN CELLS.
WE HAVE FAILED.
WE'VE BEEN AT THIS FOR HOURS, MORBIUS.
LET'S SAY WE'VE MADE GOOD PROGRESS AND PICK IT UP AGAIN AFTER A REST.
I CANNOT REST UNTIL I AM FREE OF THIS CURSE!
WE CONTINUE UNTIL I AM CURED, UNLESS YOU ENJOY THE IDEA OF LETTING A BLOOD-THIRSTY MONSTER WALK YOUR STREETS!
THIS IS A STEP IN THE PROCESS, BUT YOU HAVE TO START THINKING ABOUT THE FACT THAT YOUR MORE HUMAN VAMPIRE SELF MAY BE YOUR REAL SELF NOW.
WHAT IF THE CHOICES ARE GETTING YOU BACK TO YOUR BASELINE VAMPIRE SELF, OR GOING UNTIL WE DROP AND YOU LOSING YOURSELF?
NOT TO MENTION THAT STRESS AND EXHAUSTION MIGHT ACCELERATE YOUR CHANGE.
WORKING WITHOUT REST IS IRRESPONSIBLE AND WON'T GET YOU WHAT YOU WANT HERE.
EASY FOR YOU TO SAY! YOU DON'T UNDERSTAND WHAT IT IS LIKE TO BE LESS THAN HUMAN!
SERIOUSLY? YOU HAVE NO IDEA WHAT I'VE BEEN THROUGH.
DO YOU THINK I DIDN'T HAVE TO RELEARN HOW TO EXIST IN MY OWN SKIN? HOW TO NOT ACCIDENTALLY HURT THE ONES I LOVE?
YOU HAVE NO IDEA WHAT I'VE STRUGGLED WITH-- WHAT I'VE HAD TO SACRIFICE AND FIGHT AGAINST JUST TO STAY SANE.
YOU ARROGANT--

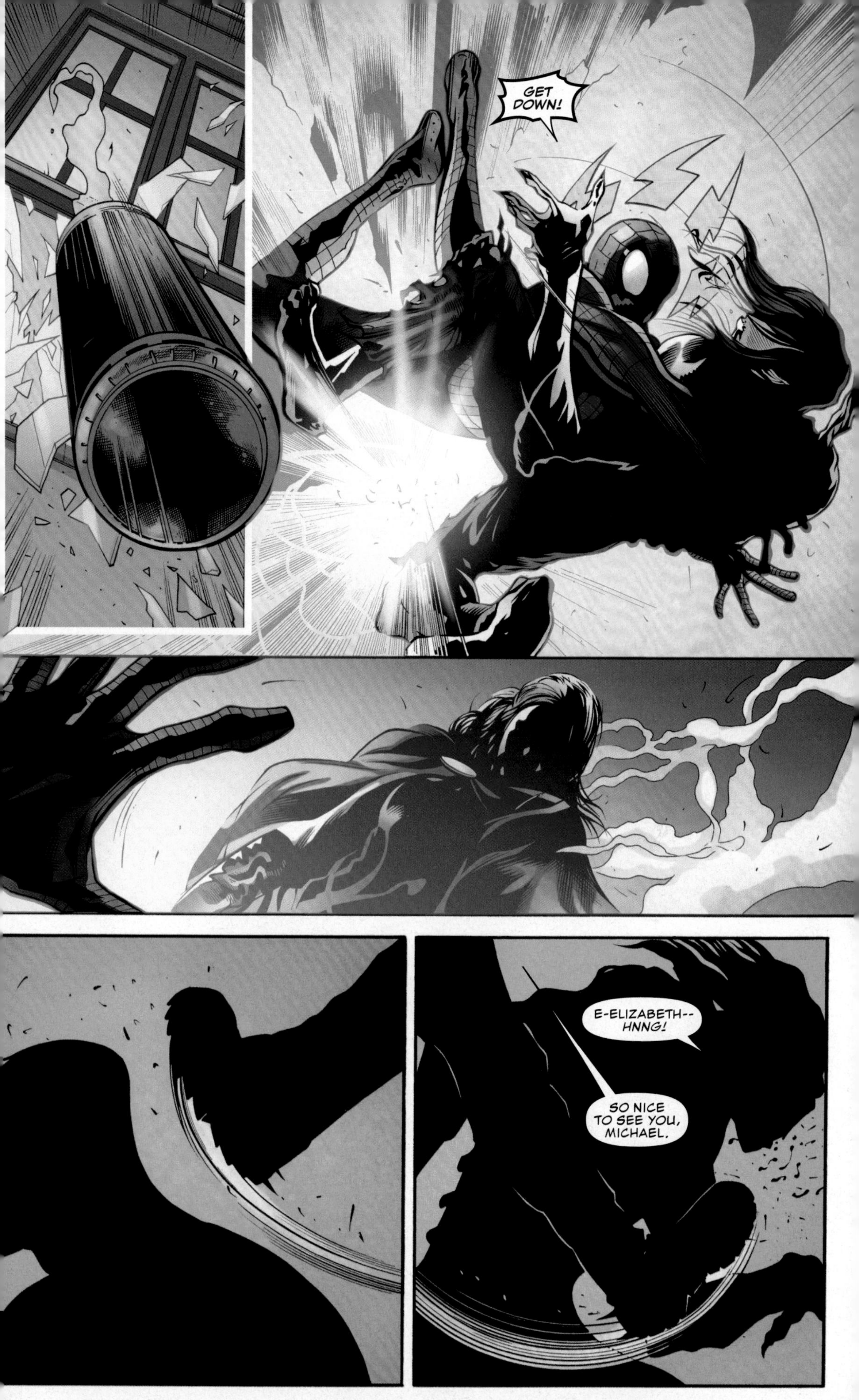
GET DOWN!
E-ELIZABETH--HNNG!
SO NICE TO SEE YOU, MICHAEL.

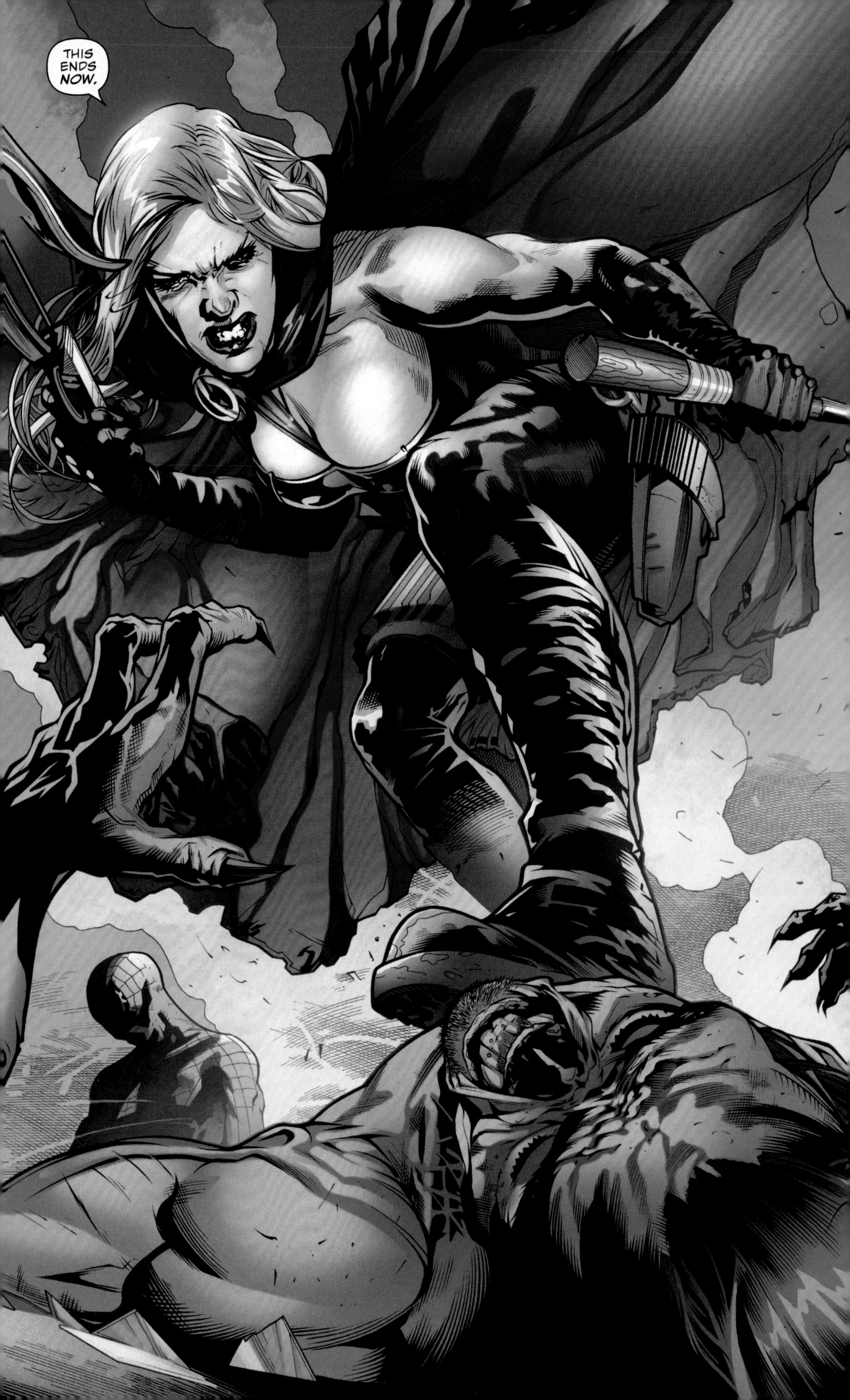
THIS ENDS NOW.

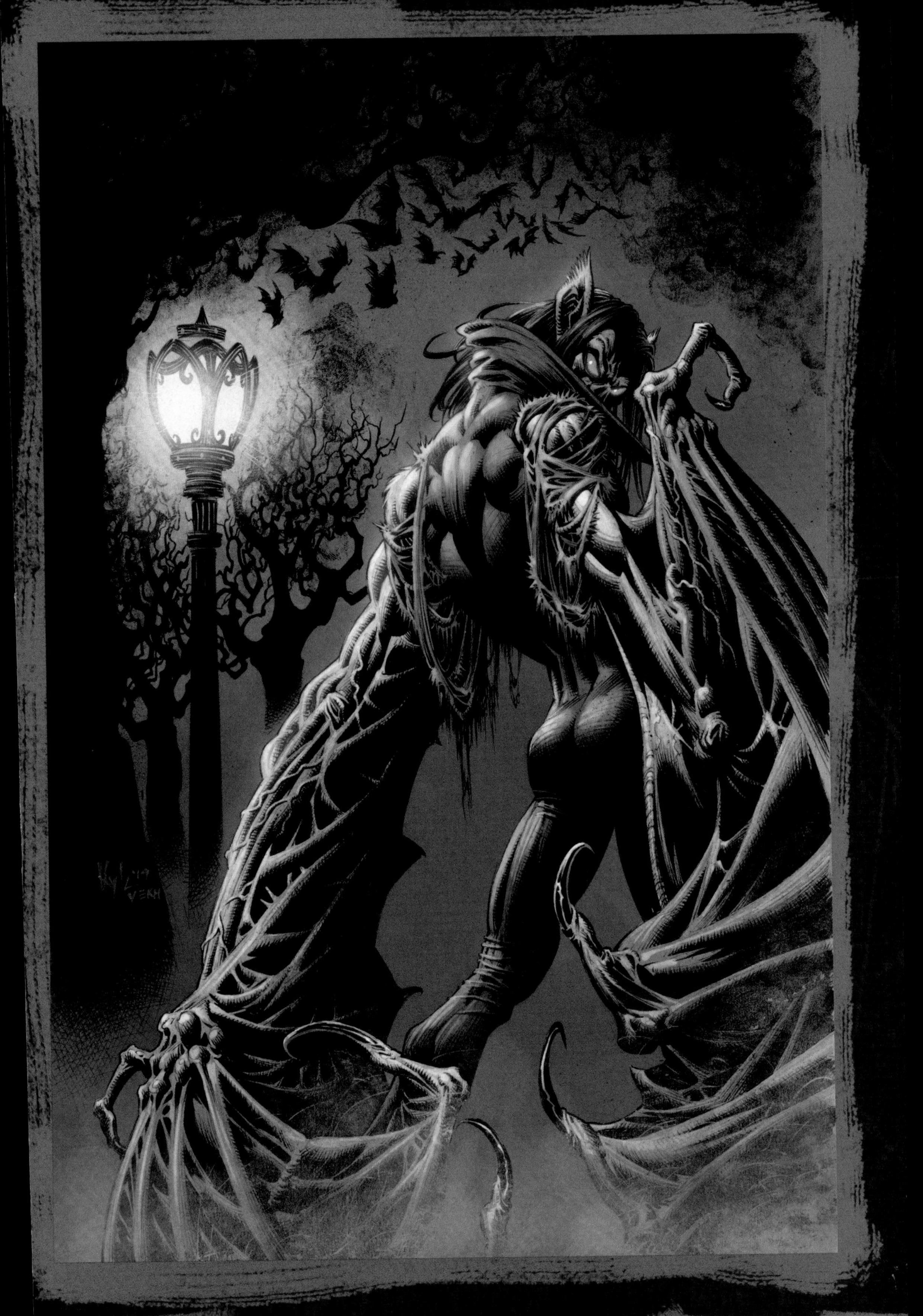

#1 variant by **KYLE HOTZ** *&* **DAN BROWN**

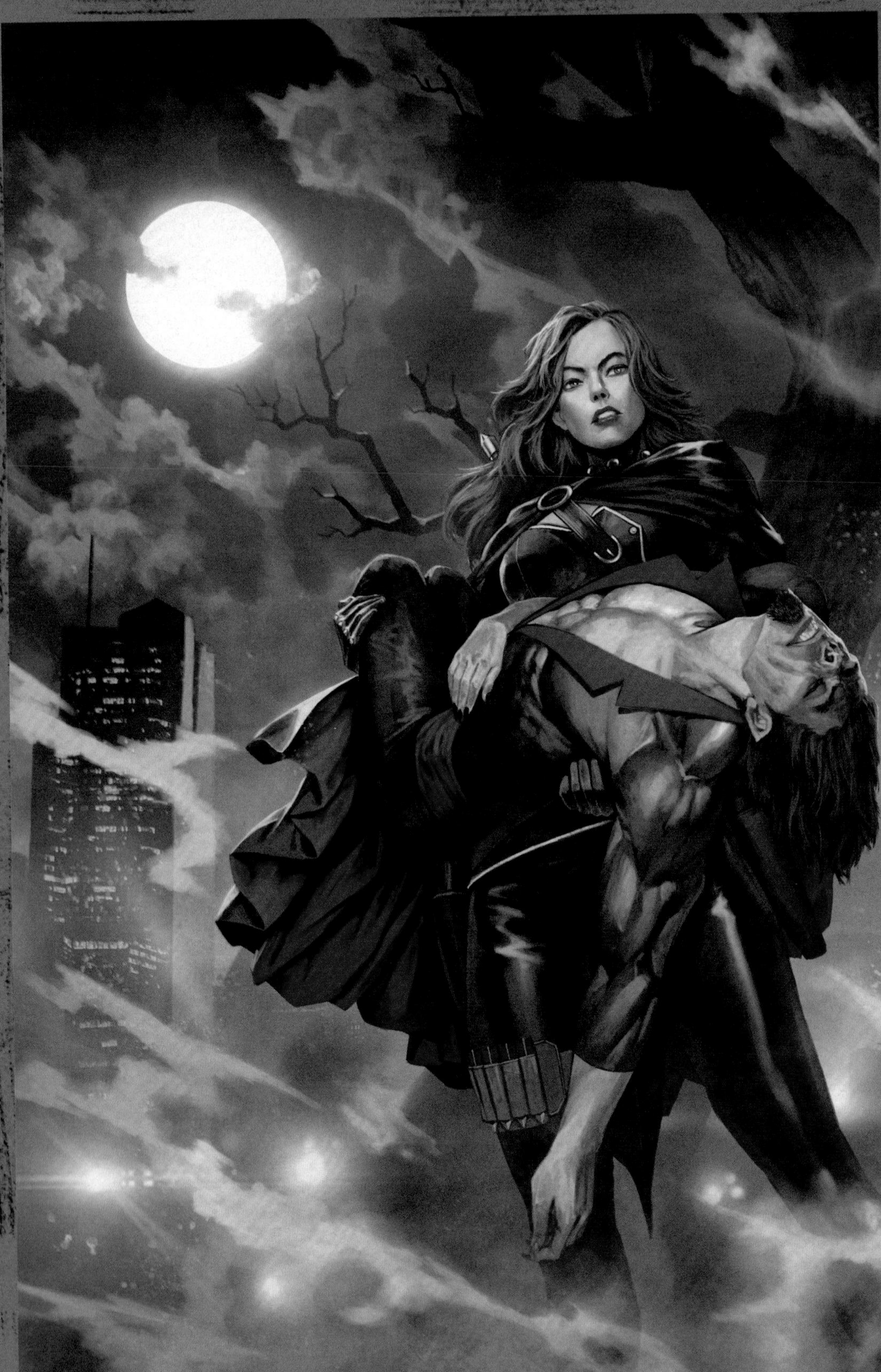

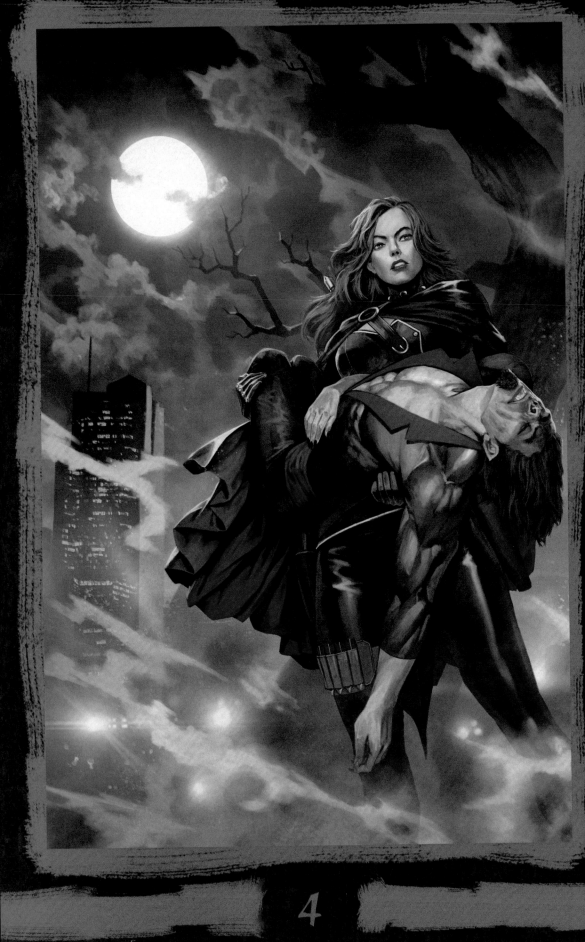

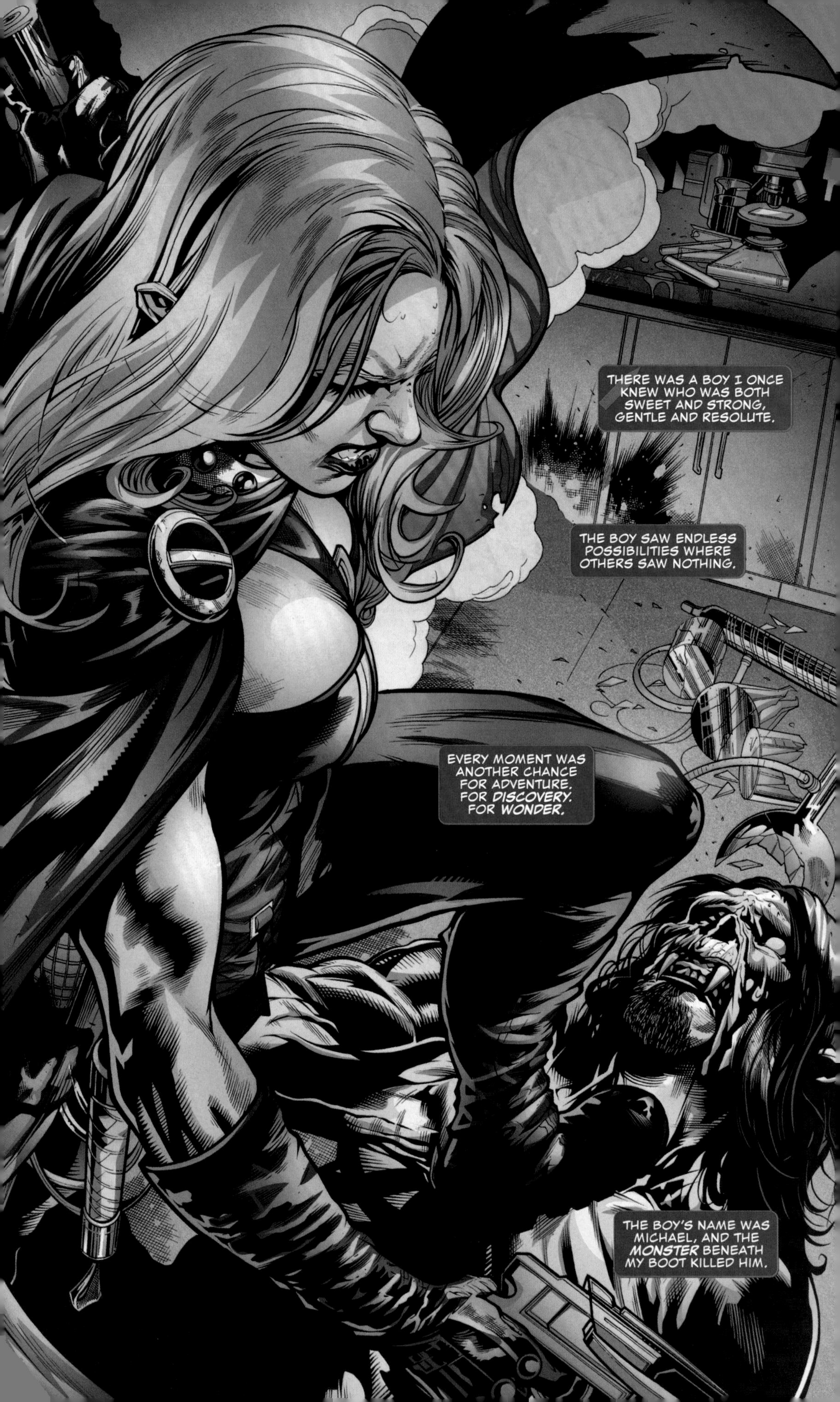
THERE WAS A BOY I ONCE KNEW WHO WAS BOTH SWEET AND STRONG, GENTLE AND RESOLUTE.
THE BOY SAW ENDLESS POSSIBILITIES WHERE OTHERS SAW NOTHING.
EVERY MOMENT WAS ANOTHER CHANCE FOR ADVENTURE. FOR *DISCOVERY*. FOR *WONDER*.
THE BOY'S NAME WAS MICHAEL, AND THE *MONSTER* BENEATH MY BOOT KILLED HIM.

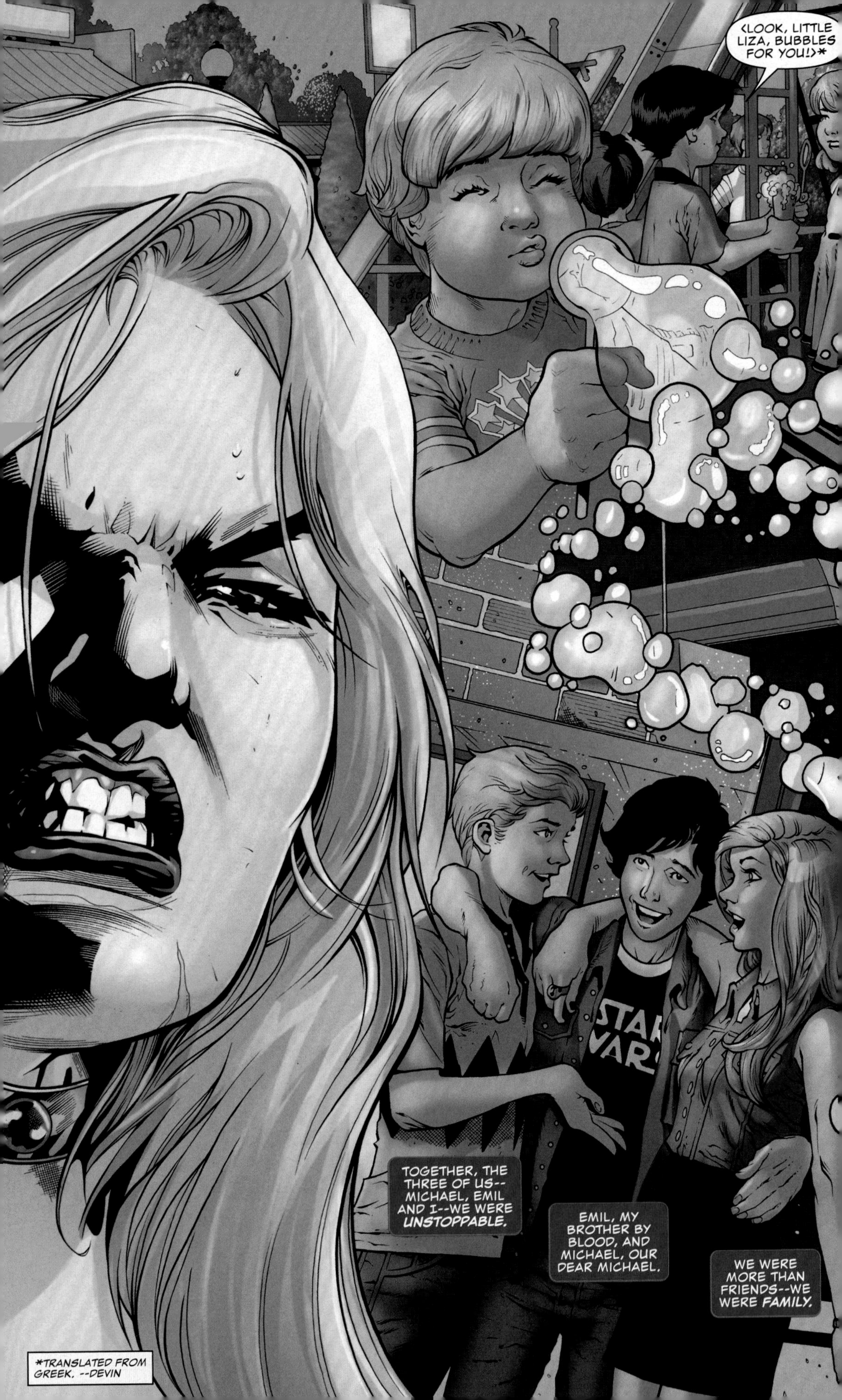

<LOOK, LITTLE LIZA, BUBBLES FOR YOU!>*
TOGETHER, THE THREE OF US--MICHAEL, EMIL AND I--WE WERE UNSTOPPABLE.
EMIL, MY BROTHER BY BLOOD, AND MICHAEL, OUR DEAR MICHAEL.
WE WERE MORE THAN FRIENDS--WE WERE FAMILY.
STAR WARS
*TRANSLATED FROM GREEK. --DEVIN

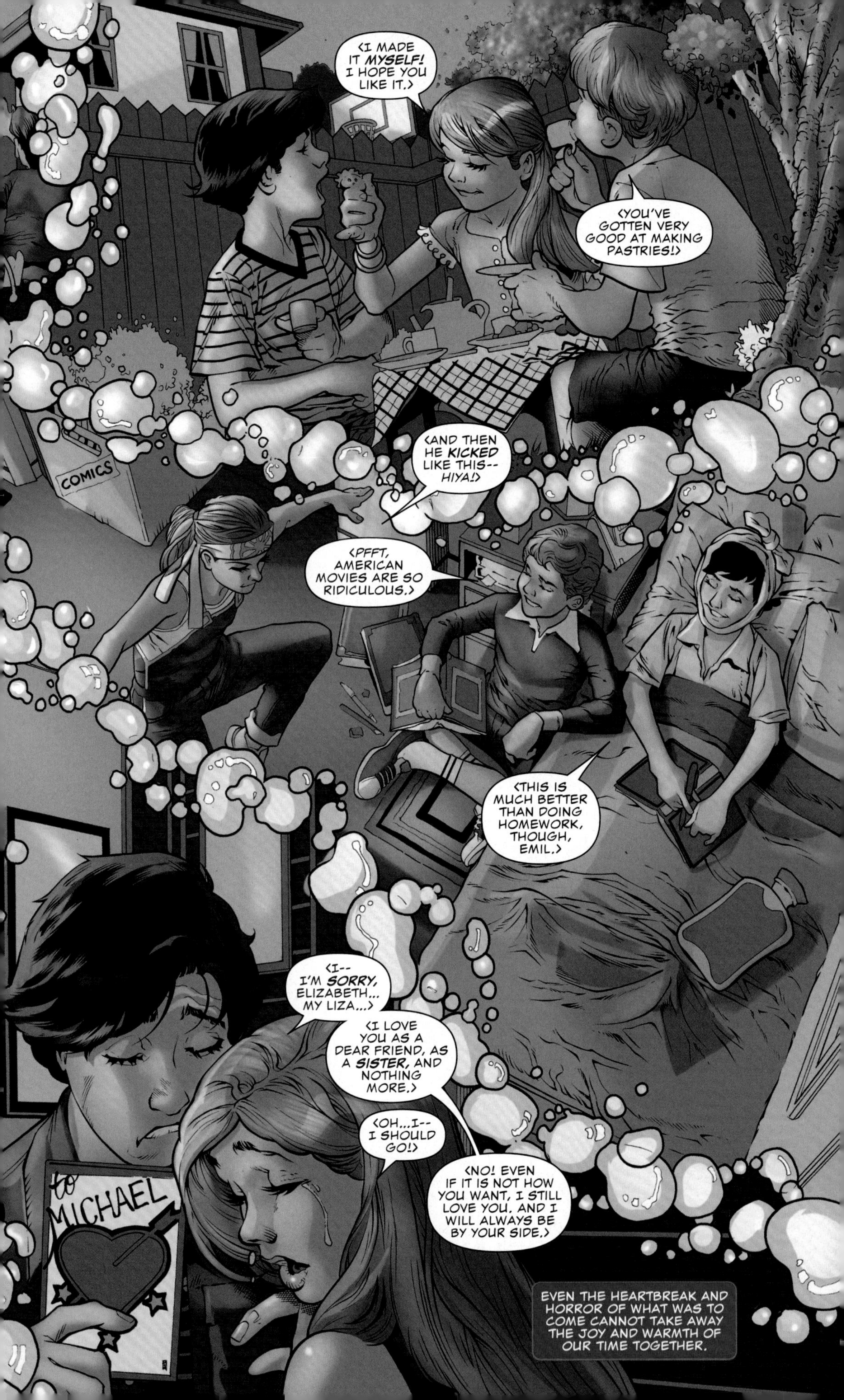

‹I MADE IT MYSELF! I HOPE YOU LIKE IT.›
‹YOU'VE GOTTEN VERY GOOD AT MAKING PASTRIES!›
COMICS
‹AND THEN HE KICKED LIKE THIS-- HIYA!›
‹PFFT, AMERICAN MOVIES ARE SO RIDICULOUS.›
‹THIS IS MUCH BETTER THAN DOING HOMEWORK, THOUGH, EMIL.›
‹I-- I'M SORRY, ELIZABETH... MY LIZA...›
‹I LOVE YOU AS A DEAR FRIEND, AS A SISTER, AND NOTHING MORE.›
‹OH...I-- I SHOULD GO!›
‹NO! EVEN IF IT IS NOT HOW YOU WANT, I STILL LOVE YOU. AND I WILL ALWAYS BE BY YOUR SIDE.›
to MICHAEL
EVEN THE HEARTBREAK AND HORROR OF WHAT WAS TO COME CANNOT TAKE AWAY THE JOY AND WARMTH OF OUR TIME TOGETHER.

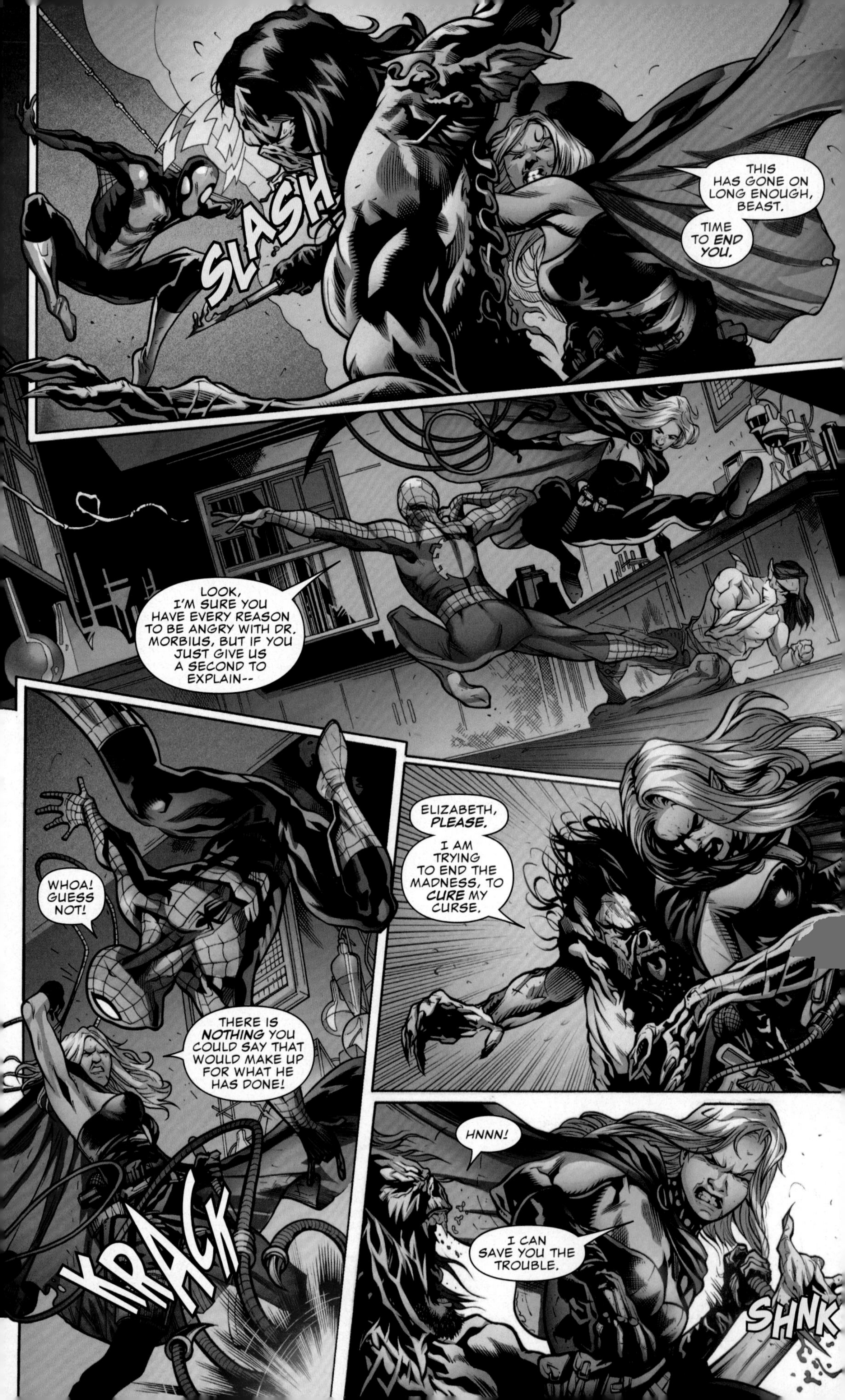
SLASH
THIS HAS GONE ON LONG ENOUGH, BEAST.
TIME TO END YOU.
LOOK, I'M SURE YOU HAVE EVERY REASON TO BE ANGRY WITH DR. MORBIUS, BUT IF YOU JUST GIVE US A SECOND TO EXPLAIN--
WHOA! GUESS NOT!
THERE IS NOTHING YOU COULD SAY THAT WOULD MAKE UP FOR WHAT HE HAS DONE!
KRACK
ELIZABETH, PLEASE.
I AM TRYING TO END THE MADNESS, TO CURE MY CURSE.
HNNN!
I CAN SAVE YOU THE TROUBLE.
SHNK

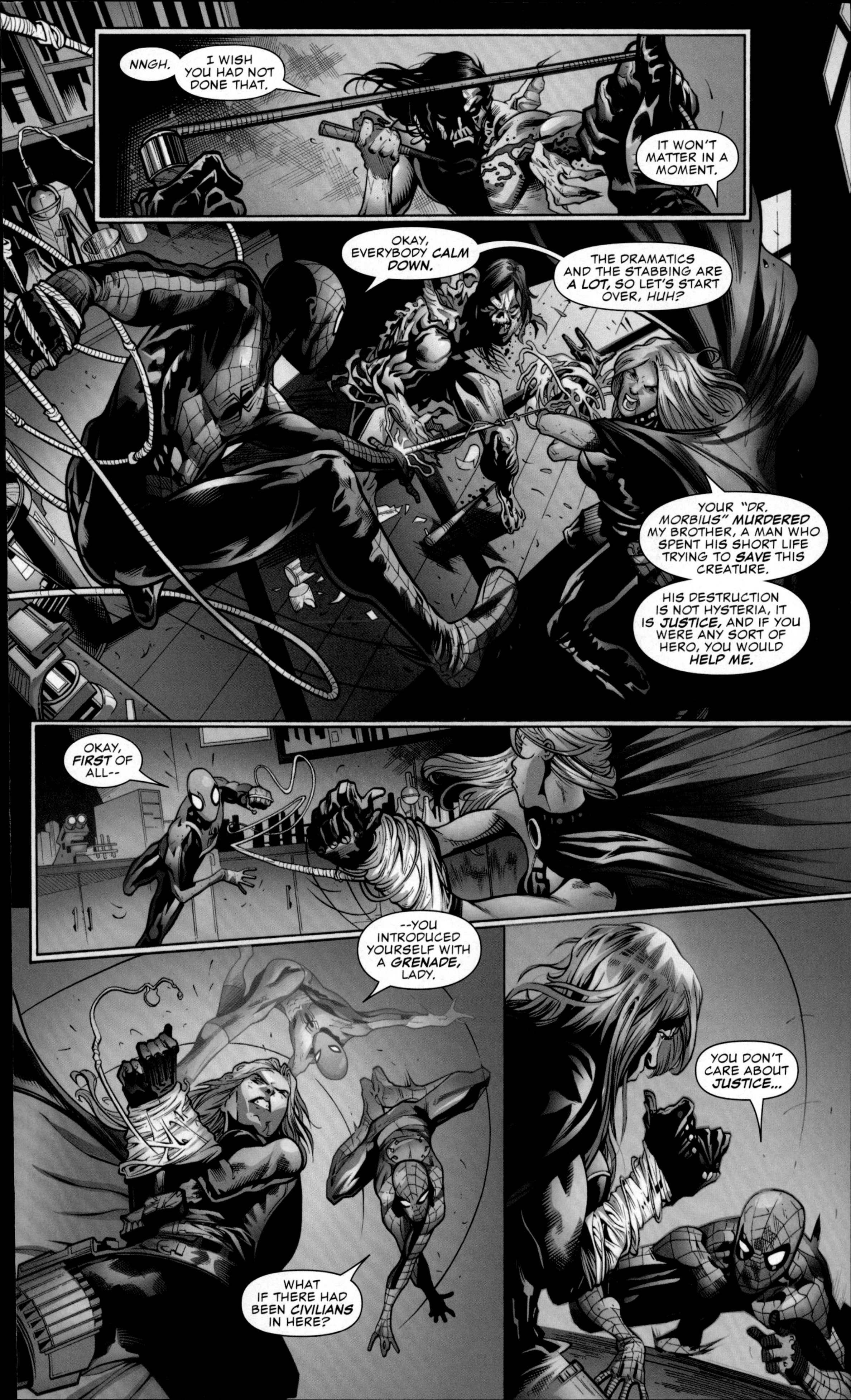
NNGH.
I WISH YOU HAD NOT DONE THAT.
IT WON'T MATTER IN A MOMENT.
OKAY, EVERYBODY CALM DOWN.
THE DRAMATICS AND THE STABBING ARE A LOT, SO LET'S START OVER, HUH?
YOUR "DR. MORBIUS" MURDERED MY BROTHER, A MAN WHO SPENT HIS SHORT LIFE TRYING TO SAVE THIS CREATURE.
HIS DESTRUCTION IS NOT HYSTERIA, IT IS JUSTICE, AND IF YOU WERE ANY SORT OF HERO, YOU WOULD HELP ME.
OKAY, FIRST OF ALL--
--YOU INTRODUCED YOURSELF WITH A GRENADE, LADY.
WHAT IF THERE HAD BEEN CIVILIANS IN HERE?
YOU DON'T CARE ABOUT JUSTICE...

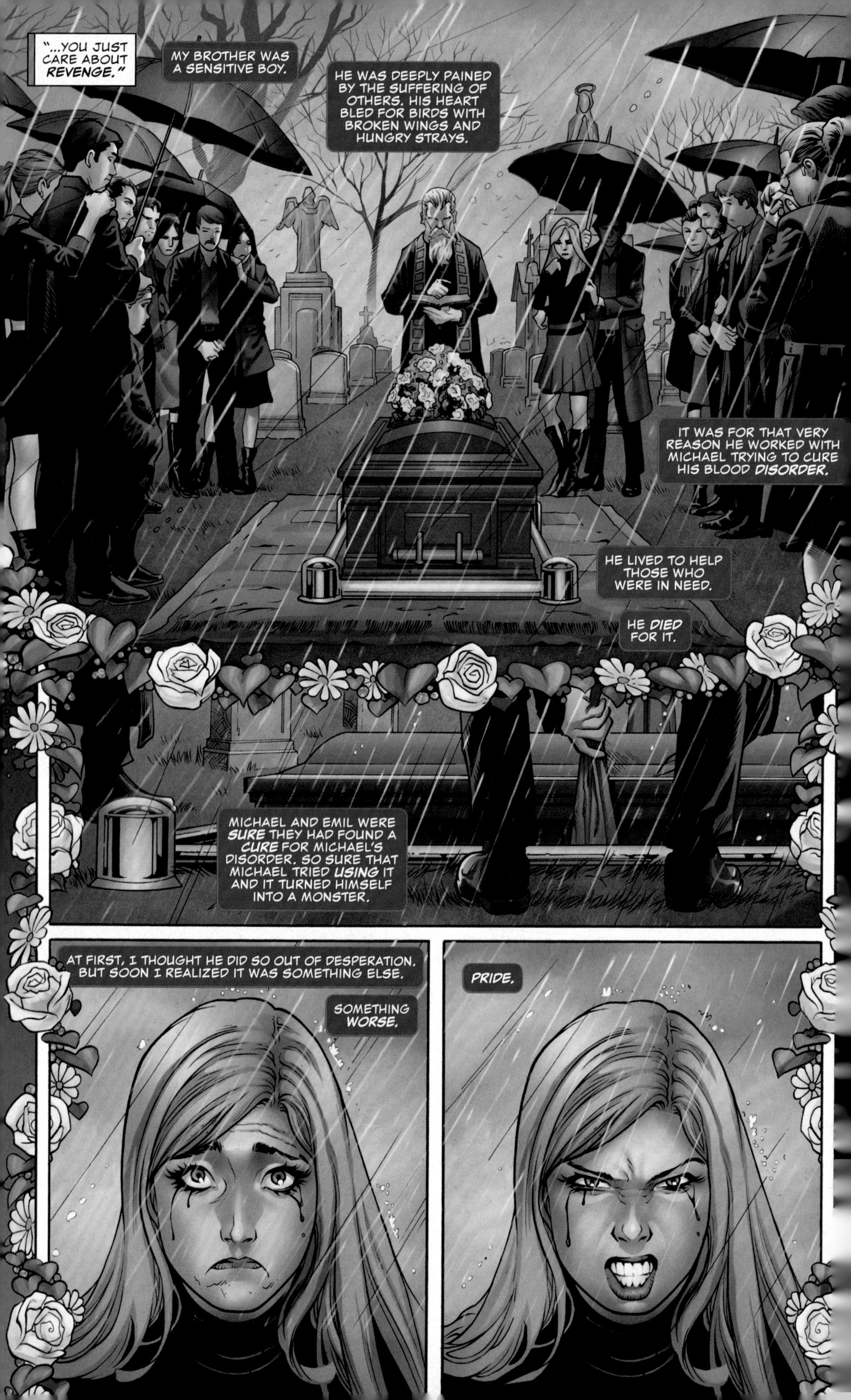
"...YOU JUST CARE ABOUT REVENGE."
MY BROTHER WAS A SENSITIVE BOY.
HE WAS DEEPLY PAINED BY THE SUFFERING OF OTHERS. HIS HEART BLED FOR BIRDS WITH BROKEN WINGS AND HUNGRY STRAYS.
IT WAS FOR THAT VERY REASON HE WORKED WITH MICHAEL TRYING TO CURE HIS BLOOD DISORDER.
HE LIVED TO HELP THOSE WHO WERE IN NEED.
HE DIED FOR IT.
MICHAEL AND EMIL WERE SURE THEY HAD FOUND A CURE FOR MICHAEL'S DISORDER. SO SURE THAT MICHAEL TRIED USING IT AND IT TURNED HIMSELF INTO A MONSTER.
AT FIRST, I THOUGHT HE DID SO OUT OF DESPERATION. BUT SOON I REALIZED IT WAS SOMETHING ELSE.
SOMETHING WORSE.
PRIDE.

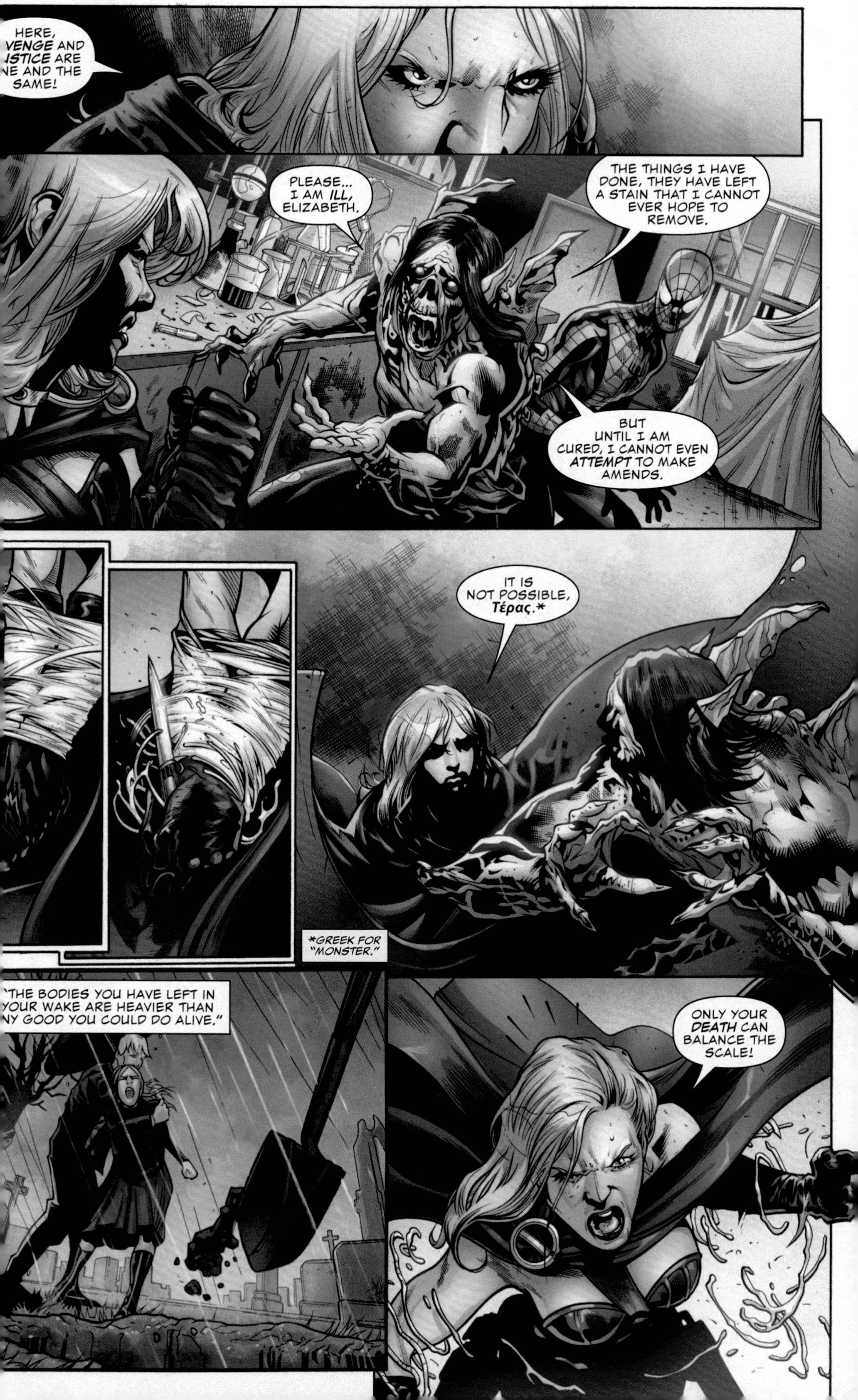
HERE, VENGE AND ISTICE ARE NE AND THE SAME!
PLEASE... I AM ILL, ELIZABETH.
THE THINGS I HAVE DONE, THEY HAVE LEFT A STAIN THAT I CANNOT EVER HOPE TO REMOVE.
BUT UNTIL I AM CURED, I CANNOT EVEN ATTEMPT TO MAKE AMENDS.
IT IS NOT POSSIBLE, Τέρας.*
*GREEK FOR "MONSTER."
"THE BODIES YOU HAVE LEFT IN YOUR WAKE ARE HEAVIER THAN NY GOOD YOU COULD DO ALIVE."
ONLY YOUR DEATH CAN BALANCE THE SCALE!

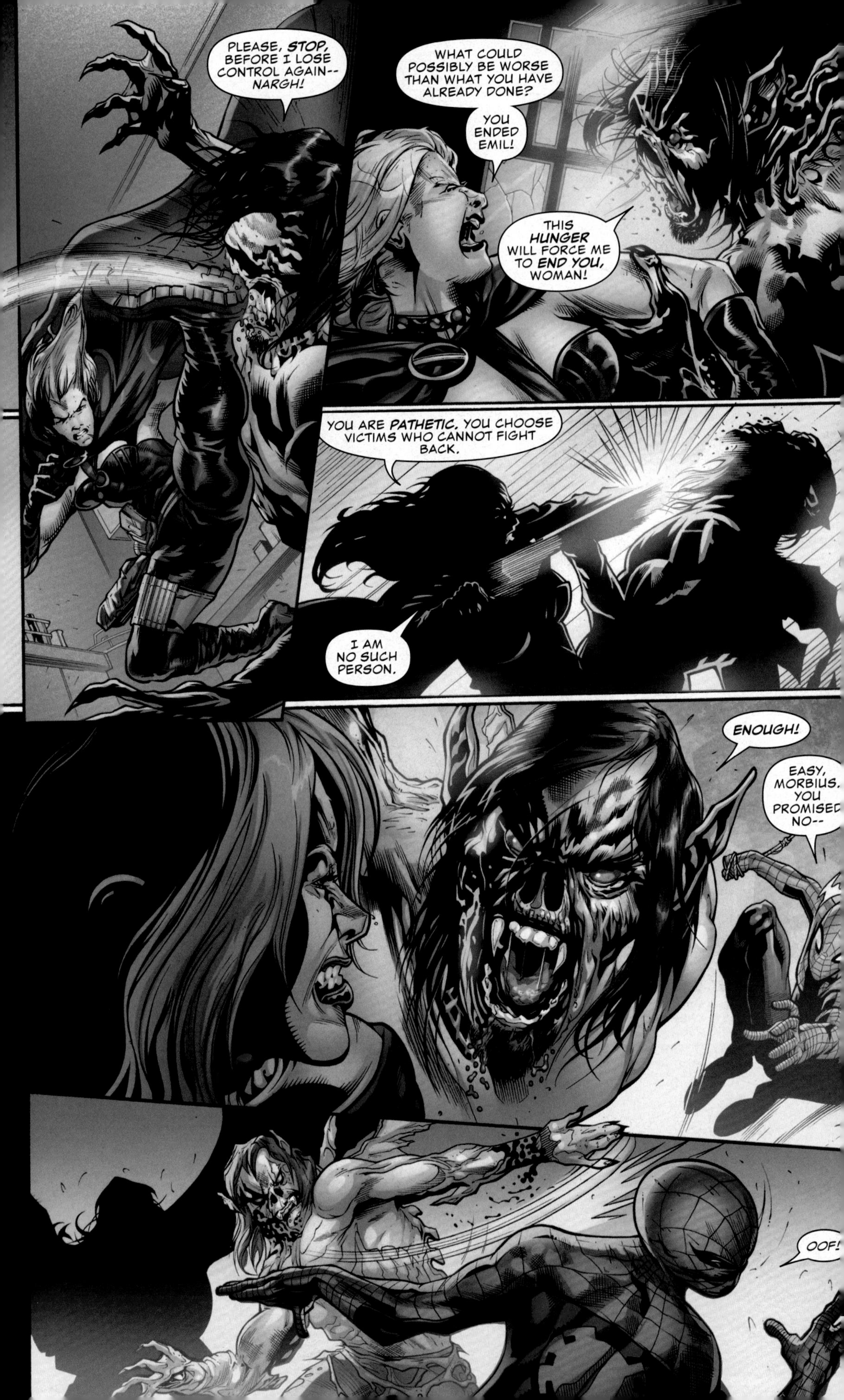

PLEASE, STOP, BEFORE I LOSE CONTROL AGAIN-- NARGH!
WHAT COULD POSSIBLY BE WORSE THAN WHAT YOU HAVE ALREADY DONE?
YOU ENDED EMIL!
THIS HUNGER WILL FORCE ME TO END YOU, WOMAN!
YOU ARE PATHETIC. YOU CHOOSE VICTIMS WHO CANNOT FIGHT BACK.
I AM NO SUCH PERSON.
ENOUGH!
EASY, MORBIUS. YOU PROMISED NO--
OOF!

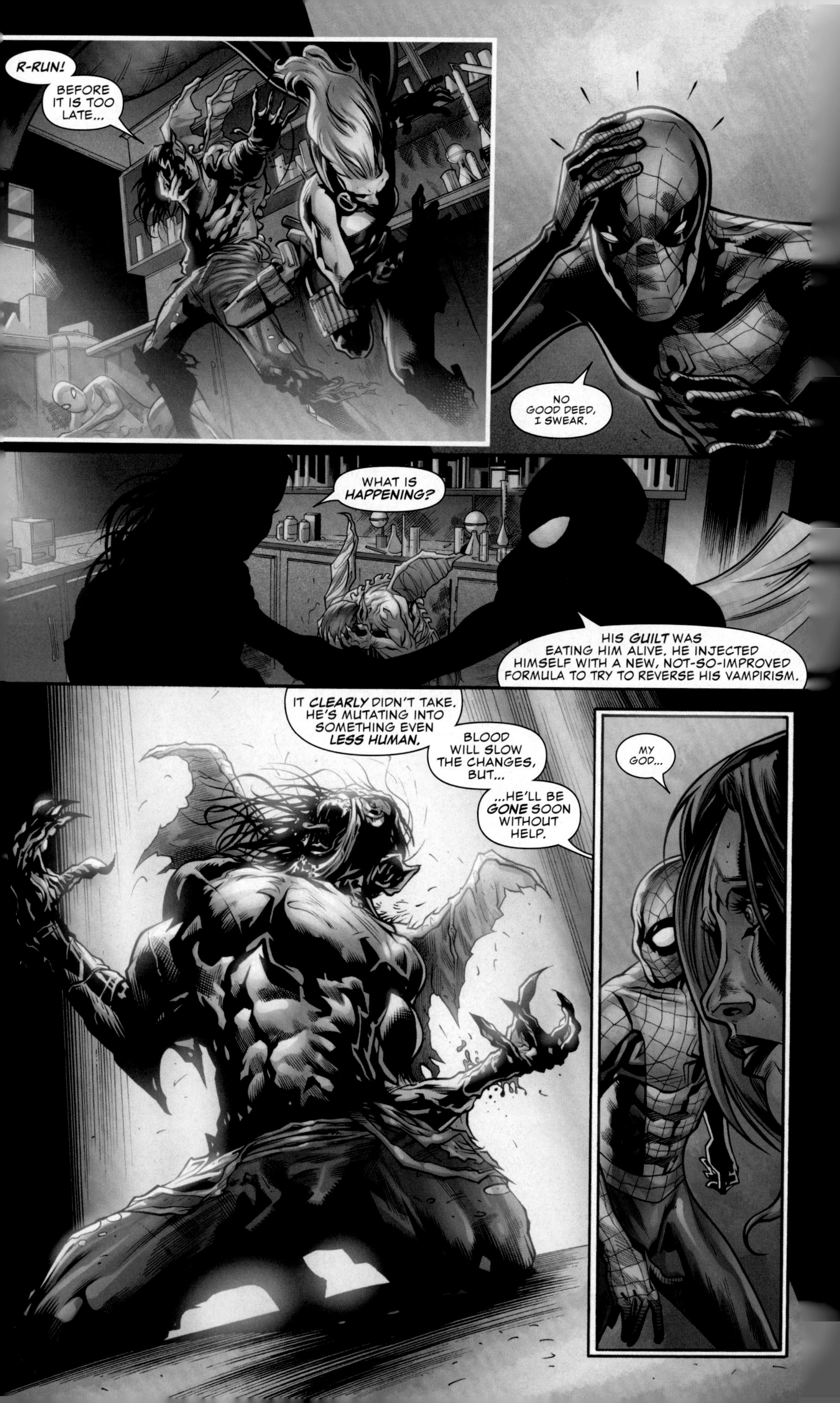
R-RUN!
BEFORE IT IS TOO LATE...
NO GOOD DEED, I SWEAR.
WHAT IS HAPPENING?
HIS GUILT WAS EATING HIM ALIVE. HE INJECTED HIMSELF WITH A NEW, NOT-SO-IMPROVED FORMULA TO TRY TO REVERSE HIS VAMPIRISM.
IT CLEARLY DIDN'T TAKE. HE'S MUTATING INTO SOMETHING EVEN LESS HUMAN.
BLOOD WILL SLOW THE CHANGES, BUT...
...HE'LL BE GONE SOON WITHOUT HELP.
MY GOD...

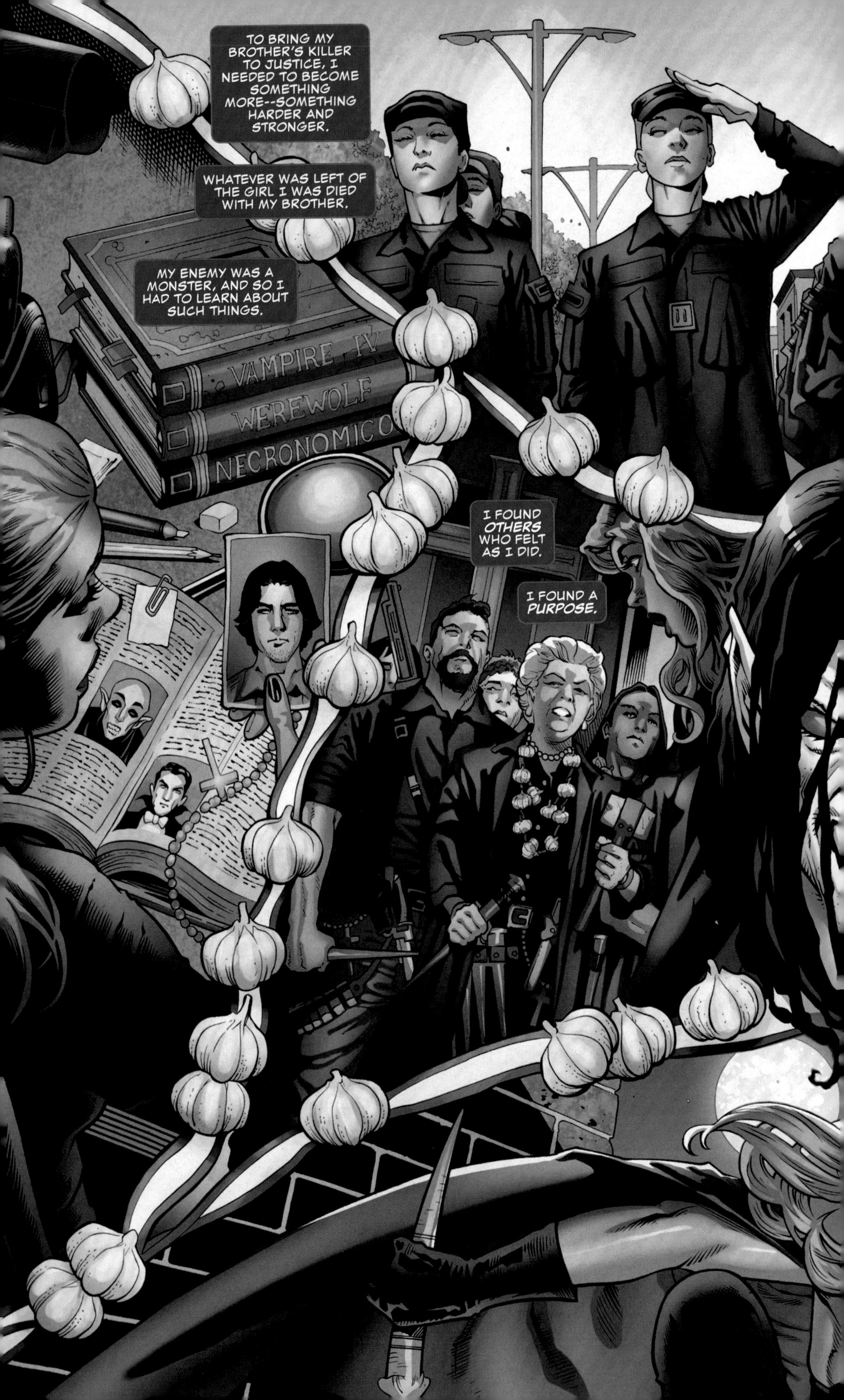
TO BRING MY BROTHER'S KILLER TO JUSTICE, I NEEDED TO BECOME SOMETHING MORE--SOMETHING HARDER AND STRONGER.
WHATEVER WAS LEFT OF THE GIRL I WAS DIED WITH MY BROTHER.
MY ENEMY WAS A MONSTER, AND SO I HAD TO LEARN ABOUT SUCH THINGS.
VAMPIRE IV
WEREWOLF
NECRONOMICO
I FOUND OTHERS WHO FELT AS I DID.
I FOUND A PURPOSE.

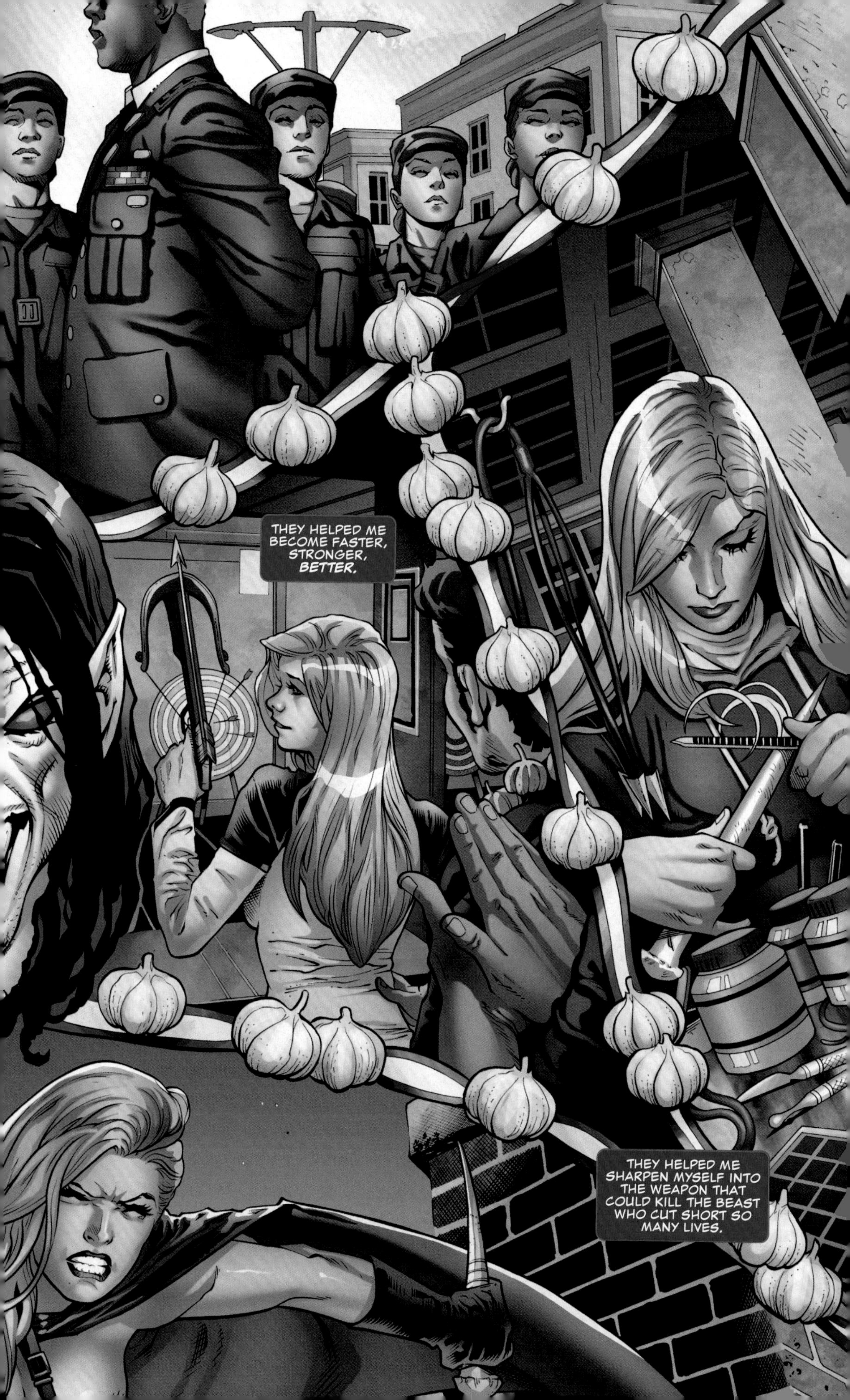
THEY HELPED ME BECOME FASTER, STRONGER, BETTER.
THEY HELPED ME SHARPEN MYSELF INTO THE WEAPON THAT COULD KILL THE BEAST WHO CUT SHORT SO MANY LIVES.

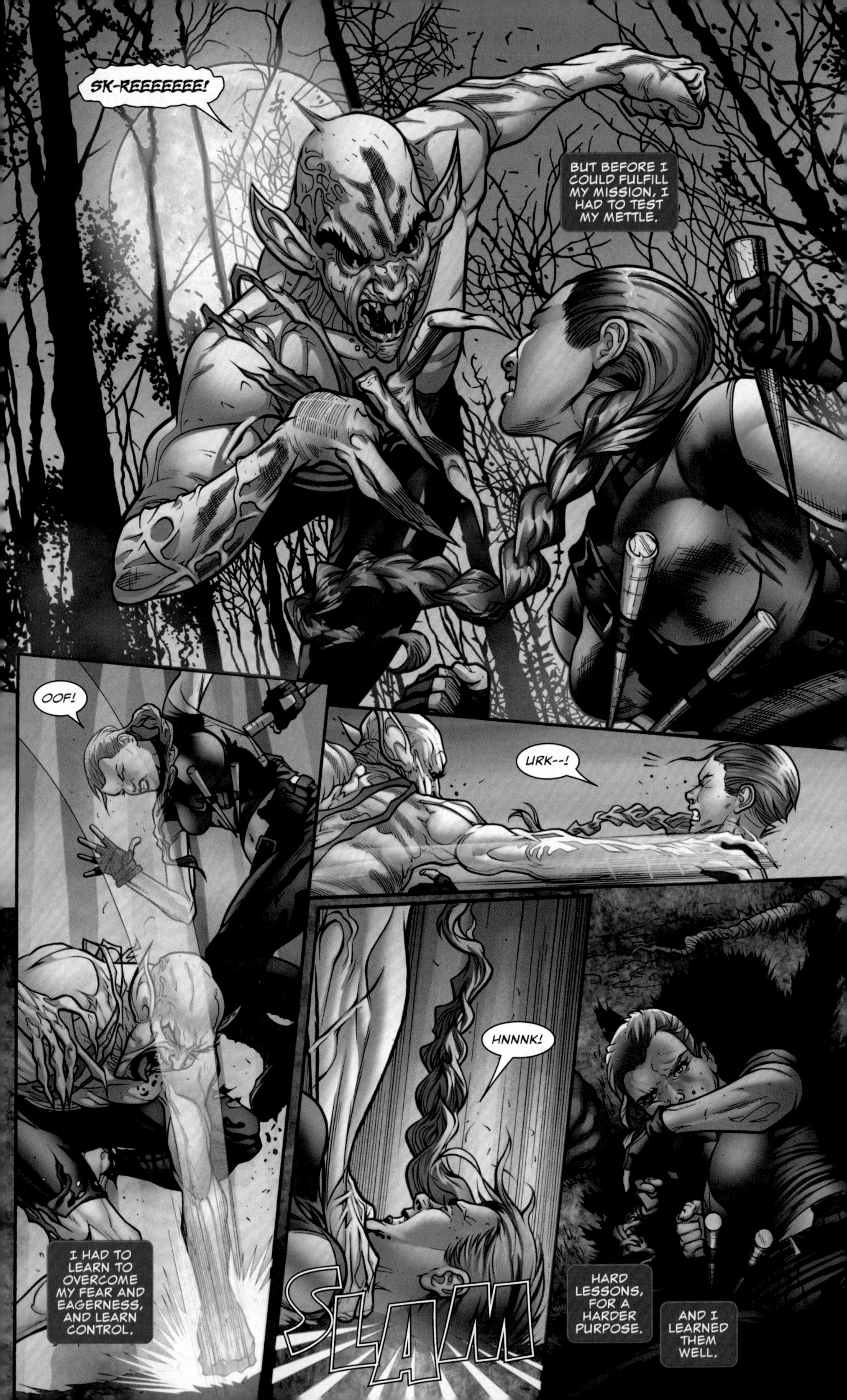
SK-REEEEEEEE!
BUT BEFORE I COULD FULFILL MY MISSION, I HAD TO TEST MY METTLE.
OOF!
URK--!
I HAD TO LEARN TO OVERCOME MY FEAR AND EAGERNESS, AND LEARN CONTROL.
HNNNK!
SLAM
HARD LESSONS, FOR A HARDER PURPOSE.
AND I LEARNED THEM WELL.

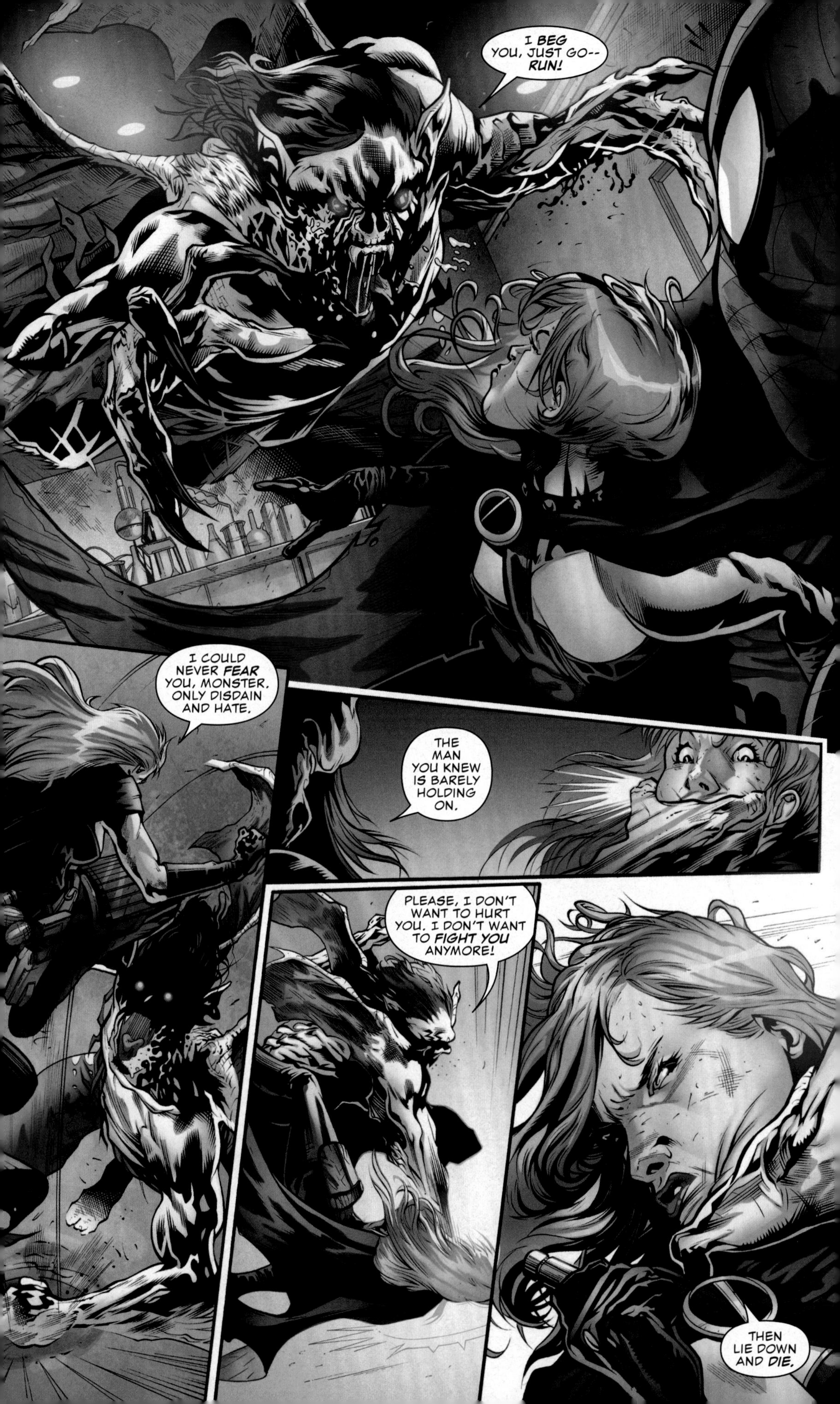

I BEG YOU, JUST GO-- RUN!
I COULD NEVER FEAR YOU, MONSTER. ONLY DISDAIN AND HATE.
THE MAN YOU KNEW IS BARELY HOLDING ON.
PLEASE, I DON'T WANT TO HURT YOU. I DON'T WANT TO FIGHT YOU ANYMORE!
THEN LIE DOWN AND DIE.

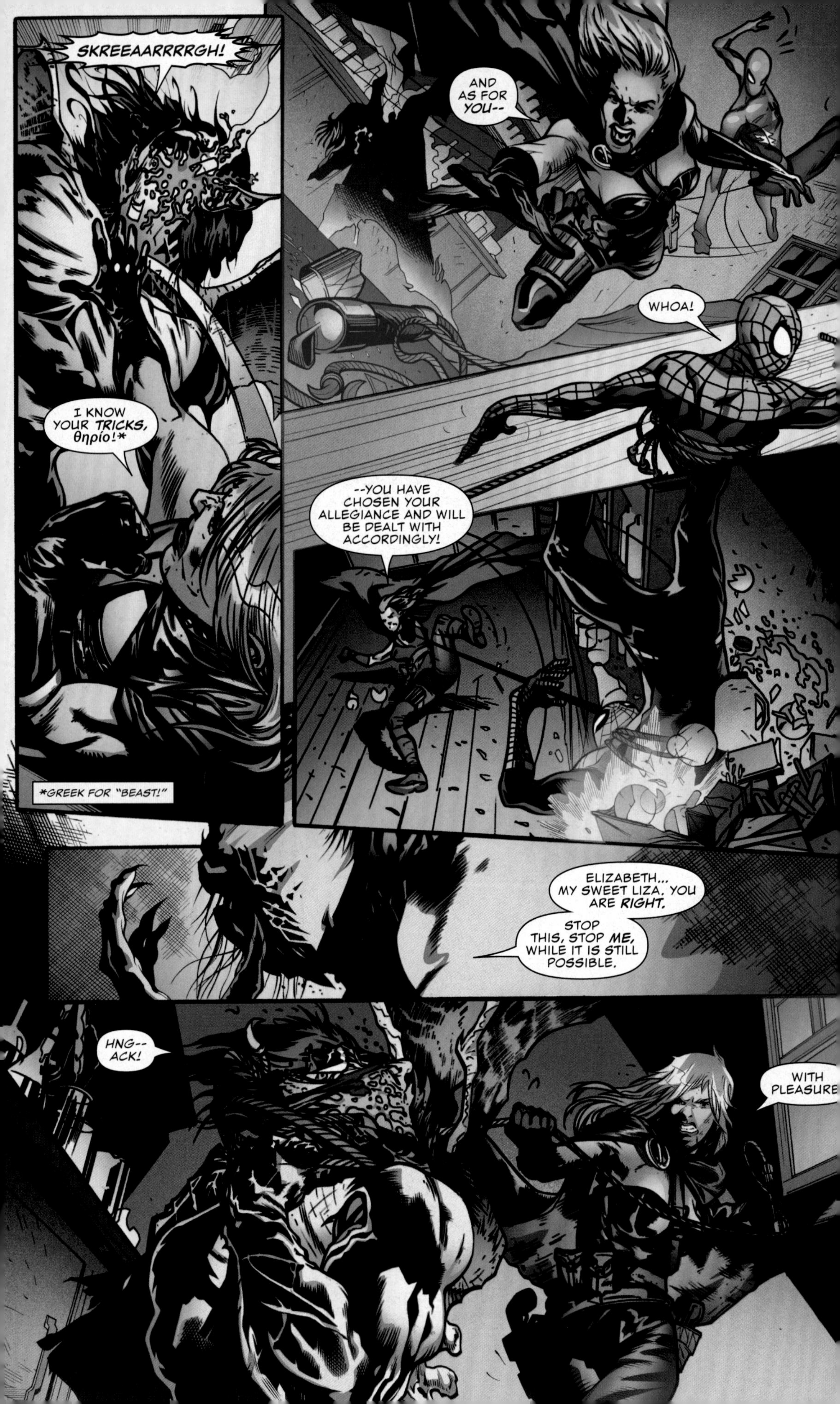
SKREEAARRRRGH!
AND AS FOR YOU--
WHOA!
--YOU HAVE CHOSEN YOUR ALLEGIANCE AND WILL BE DEALT WITH ACCORDINGLY!
I KNOW YOUR TRICKS, θηρίο!*
*GREEK FOR "BEAST!"
ELIZABETH... MY SWEET LIZA. YOU ARE RIGHT.
STOP THIS, STOP ME, WHILE IT IS STILL POSSIBLE.
HNG-- ACK!
WITH PLEASURE

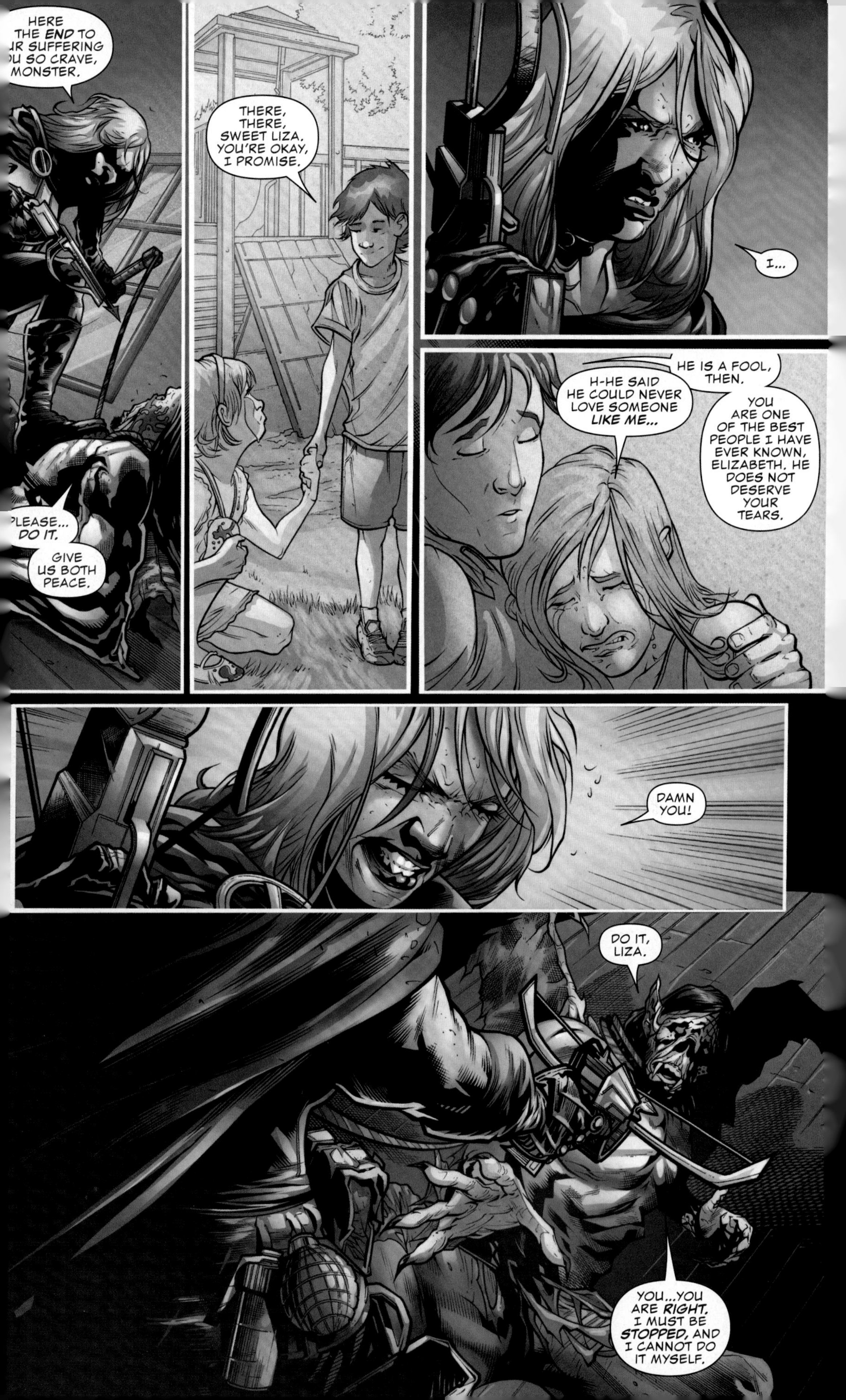

HERE THE END TO UR SUFFERING OU SO CRAVE, MONSTER.
PLEASE... DO IT.
GIVE US BOTH PEACE.
THERE, THERE, SWEET LIZA. YOU'RE OKAY, I PROMISE.
I...
H-HE SAID HE COULD NEVER LOVE SOMEONE LIKE ME...
HE IS A FOOL, THEN.
YOU ARE ONE OF THE BEST PEOPLE I HAVE EVER KNOWN, ELIZABETH. HE DOES NOT DESERVE YOUR TEARS.
DAMN YOU!
DO IT, LIZA.
YOU...YOU ARE RIGHT. I MUST BE STOPPED, AND I CANNOT DO IT MYSELF.

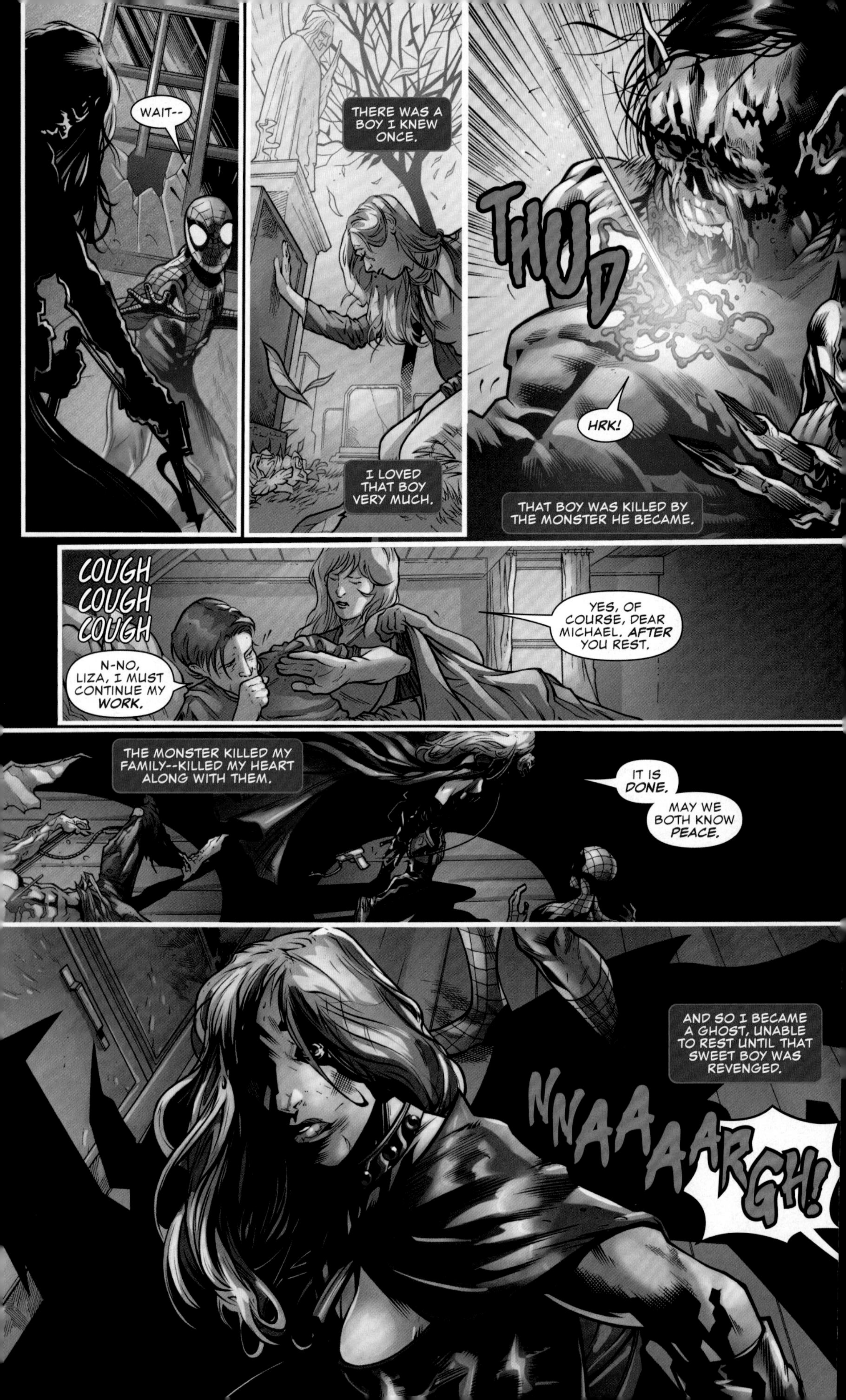

WAIT--
THERE WAS A BOY I KNEW ONCE.
I LOVED THAT BOY VERY MUCH.
THUD
HRK!
THAT BOY WAS KILLED BY THE MONSTER HE BECAME.
COUGH COUGH COUGH
N-NO, LIZA, I MUST CONTINUE MY WORK.
YES, OF COURSE, DEAR MICHAEL. AFTER YOU REST.
THE MONSTER KILLED MY FAMILY--KILLED MY HEART ALONG WITH THEM.
IT IS DONE.
MAY WE BOTH KNOW PEACE.
AND SO I BECAME A GHOST, UNABLE TO REST UNTIL THAT SWEET BOY WAS REVENGED.
NNAAAAARGH!

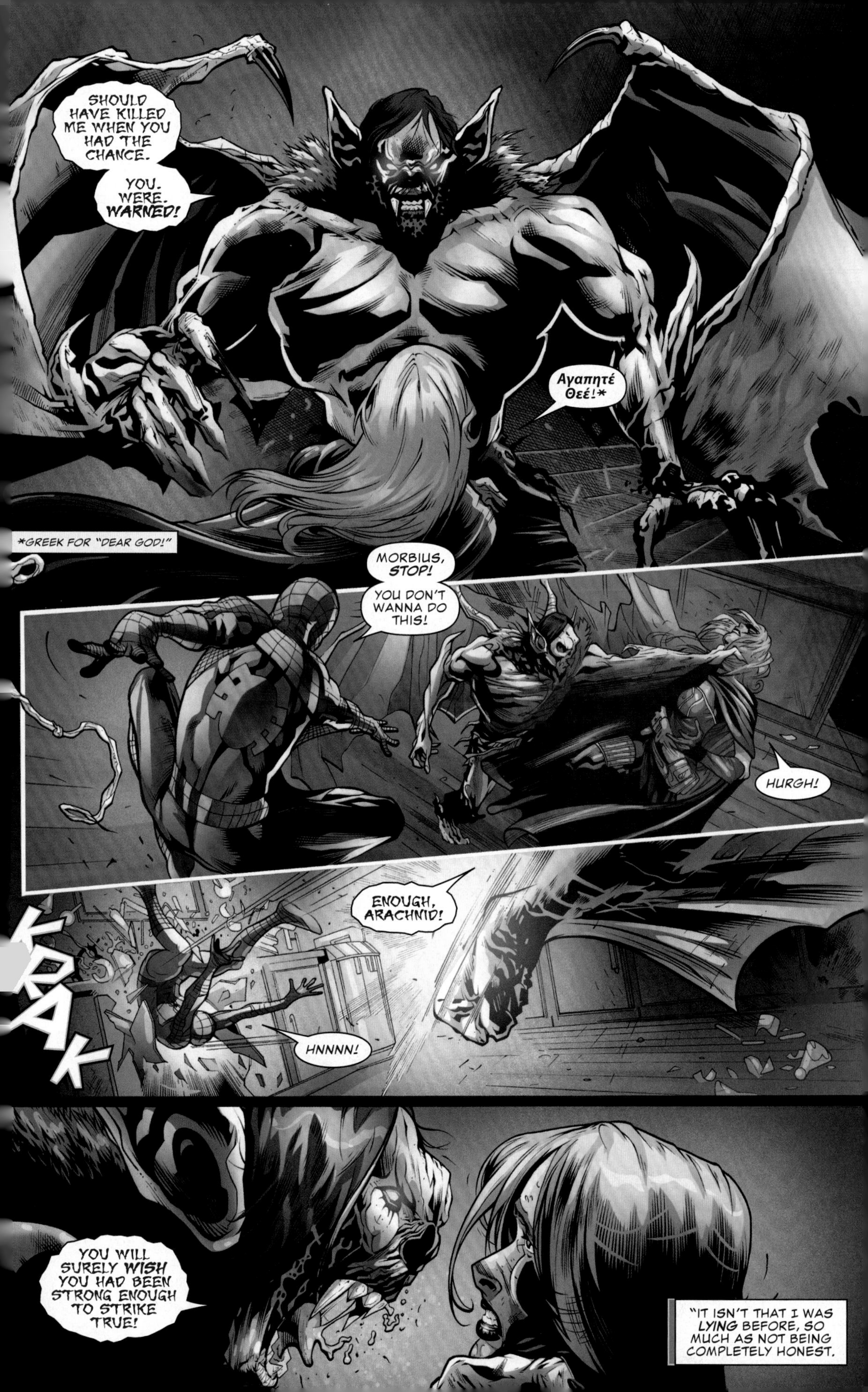
SHOULD HAVE KILLED ME WHEN YOU HAD THE CHANCE.
YOU. WERE. WARNED!
Αγαπητέ Θεέ!*
*GREEK FOR "DEAR GOD!"
MORBIUS, STOP!
YOU DON'T WANNA DO THIS!
HURGH!
ENOUGH, ARACHNID!
KRAK
HNNNN!
YOU WILL SURELY WISH YOU HAD BEEN STRONG ENOUGH TO STRIKE TRUE!
"IT ISN'T THAT I WAS LYING BEFORE, SO MUCH AS NOT BEING COMPLETELY HONEST.

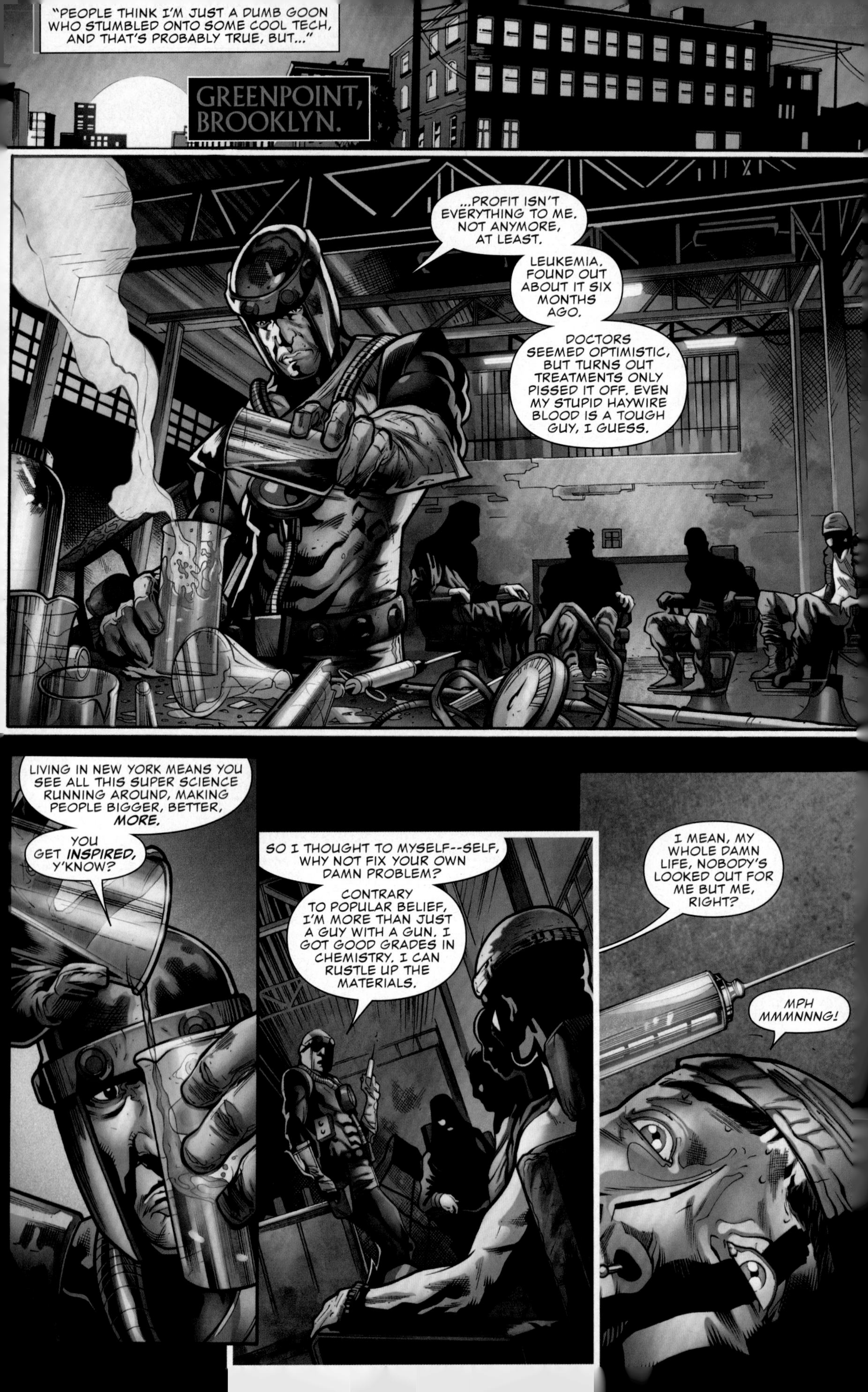
"PEOPLE THINK I'M JUST A DUMB GOON WHO STUMBLED ONTO SOME COOL TECH, AND THAT'S PROBABLY TRUE, BUT..."
GREENPOINT, BROOKLYN.
...PROFIT ISN'T EVERYTHING TO ME. NOT ANYMORE, AT LEAST.
LEUKEMIA. FOUND OUT ABOUT IT SIX MONTHS AGO.
DOCTORS SEEMED OPTIMISTIC, BUT TURNS OUT TREATMENTS ONLY PISSED IT OFF. EVEN MY STUPID HAYWIRE BLOOD IS A TOUGH GUY, I GUESS.
LIVING IN NEW YORK MEANS YOU SEE ALL THIS SUPER SCIENCE RUNNING AROUND, MAKING PEOPLE BIGGER, BETTER, *MORE.*
YOU GET *INSPIRED,* Y'KNOW?
SO I THOUGHT TO MYSELF--SELF, WHY NOT FIX YOUR OWN DAMN PROBLEM?
CONTRARY TO POPULAR BELIEF, I'M MORE THAN JUST A GUY WITH A GUN. I GOT GOOD GRADES IN CHEMISTRY. I CAN RUSTLE UP THE MATERIALS.
I MEAN, MY WHOLE DAMN LIFE, NOBODY'S LOOKED OUT FOR ME BUT ME, RIGHT?
MPH MMMNNNG!

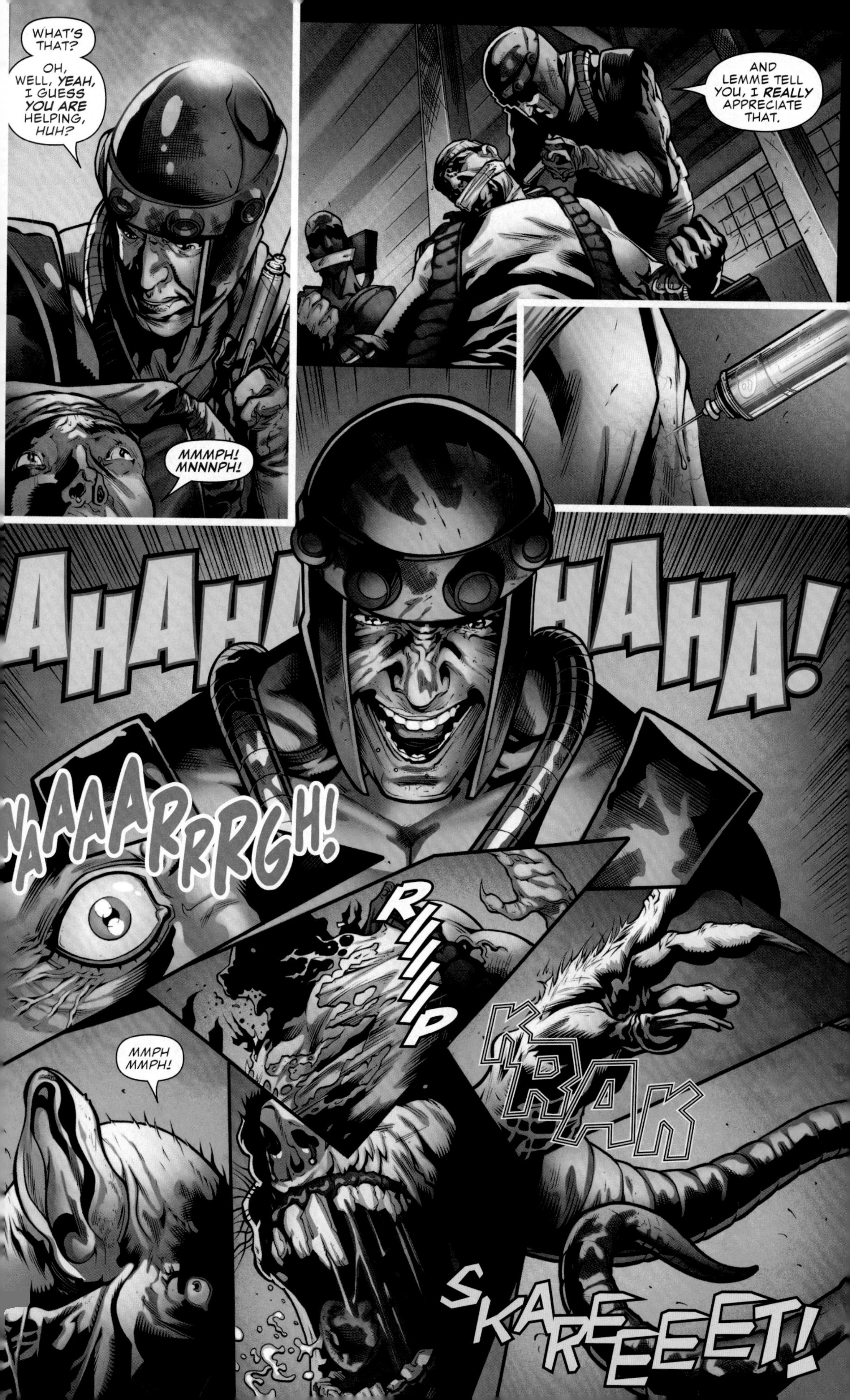
WHAT'S THAT? OH, WELL, YEAH, I GUESS YOU ARE HELPING, HUH?
AND LEMME TELL YOU, I REALLY APPRECIATE THAT.
MMMPH! MNNNPH!
AHAHAHAHAHAHA!
NAAAARRRGH!
RIIIIP
KRAK
MMPH MMPH!
SKAREEEEET!

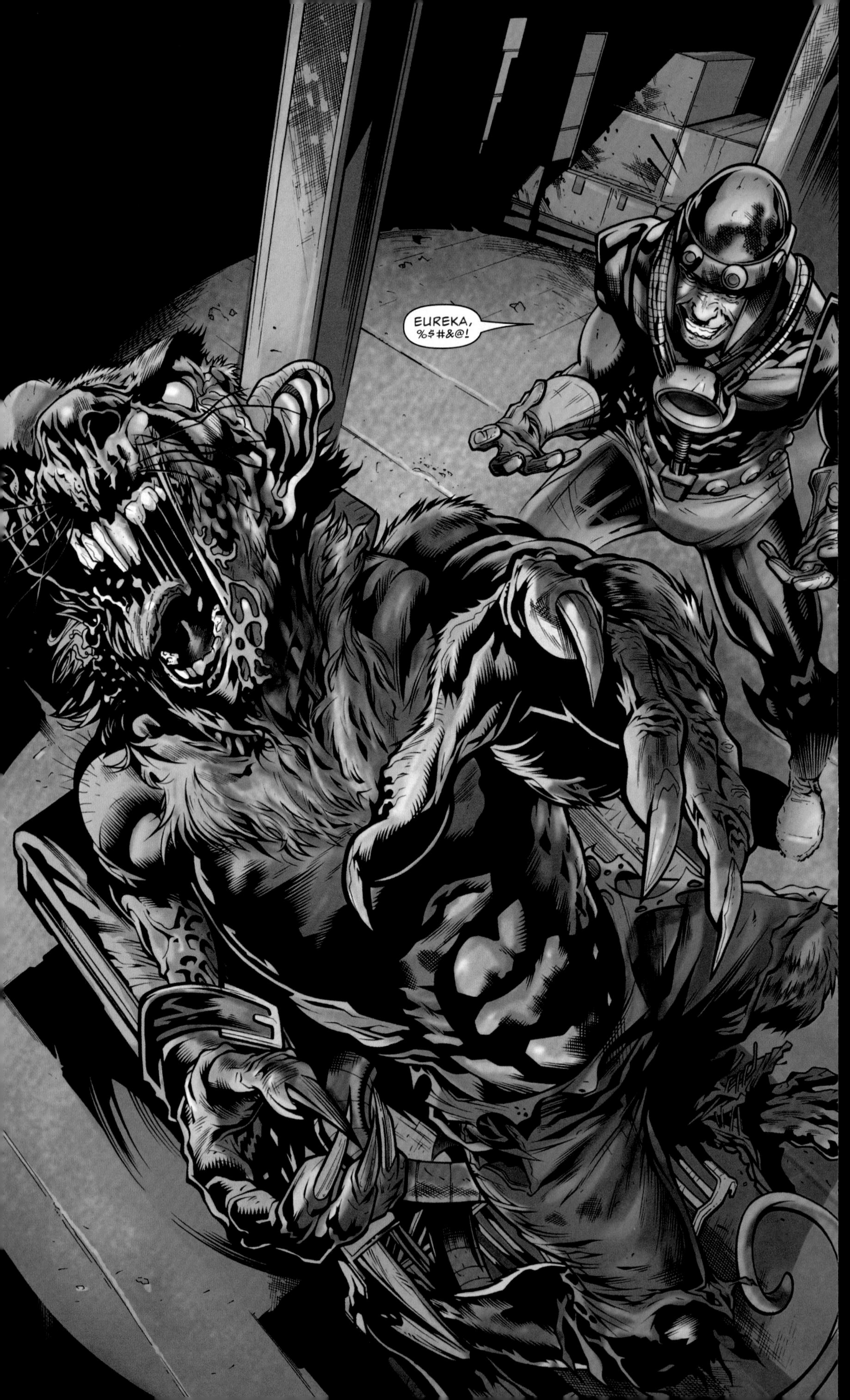
EUREKA, %$#&@!

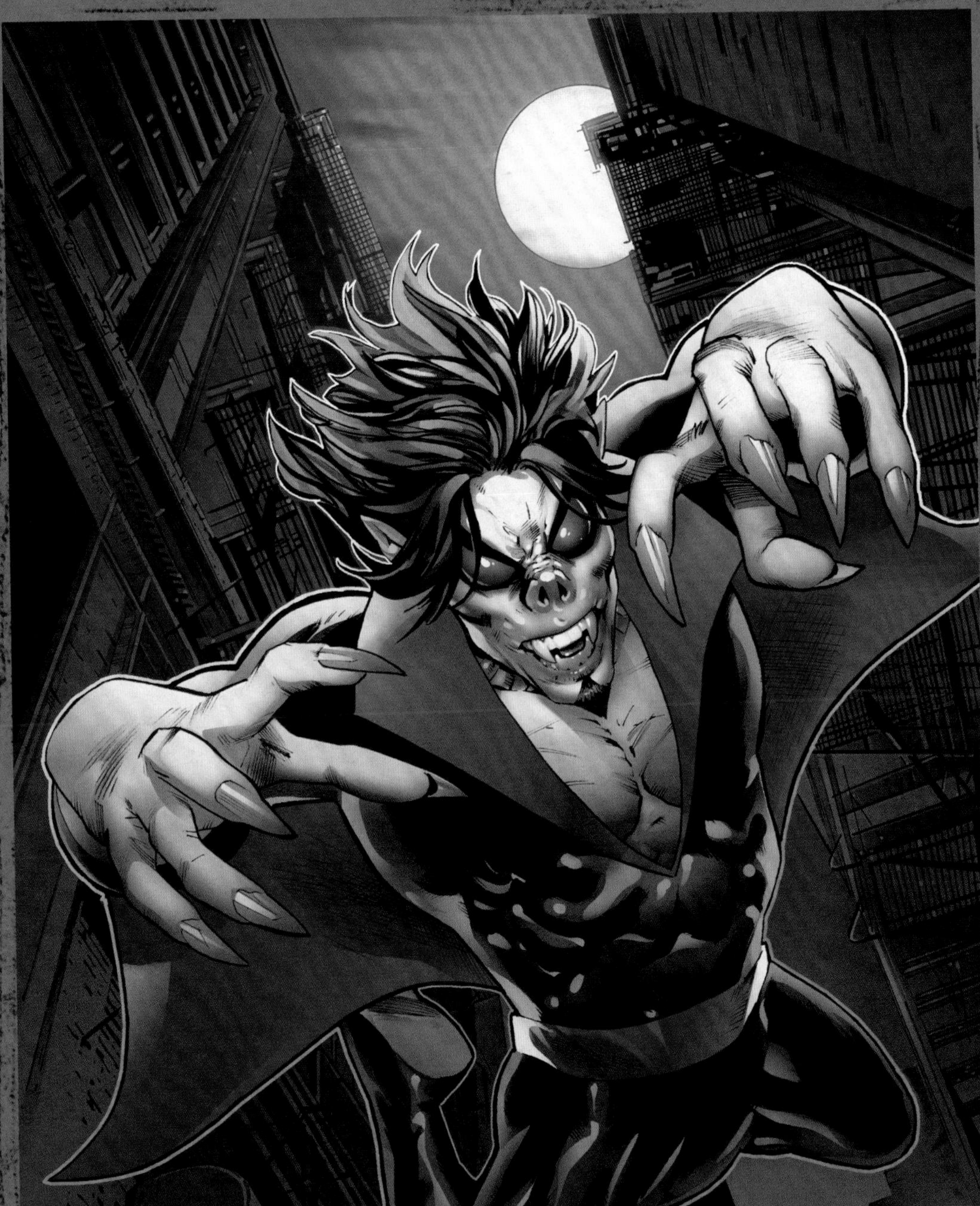
LAND

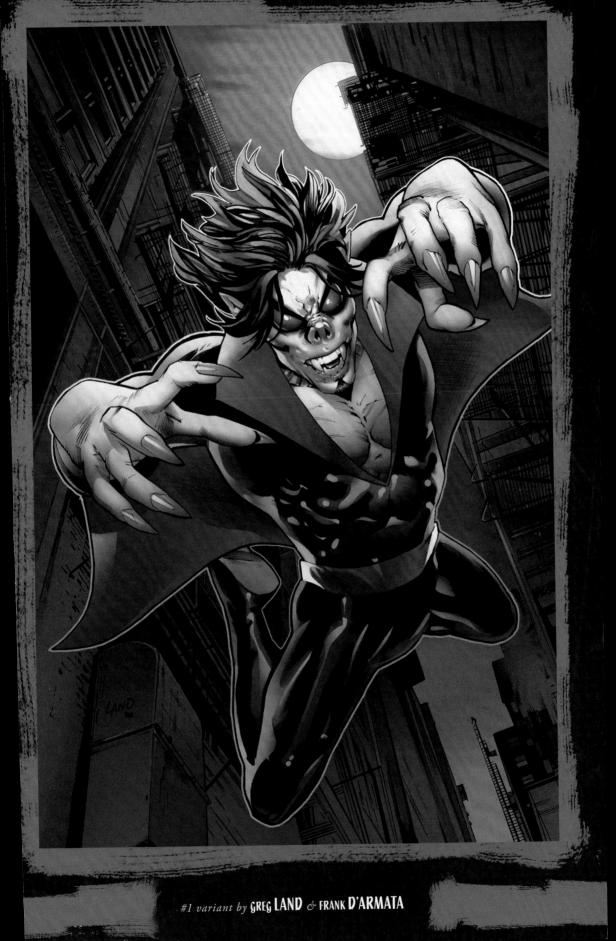

#1 variant by GREG LAND *&* FRANK D'ARMATA

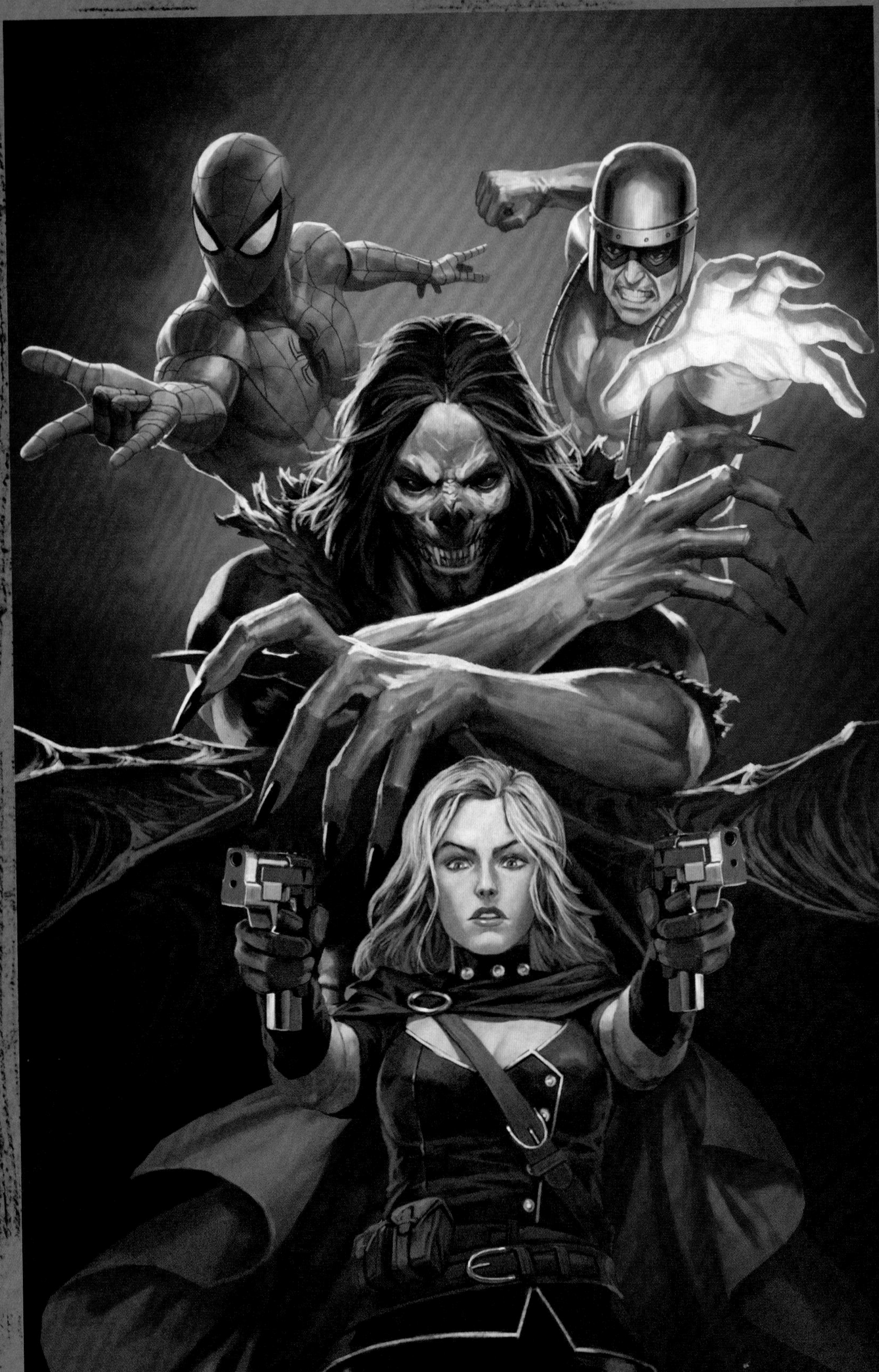

5

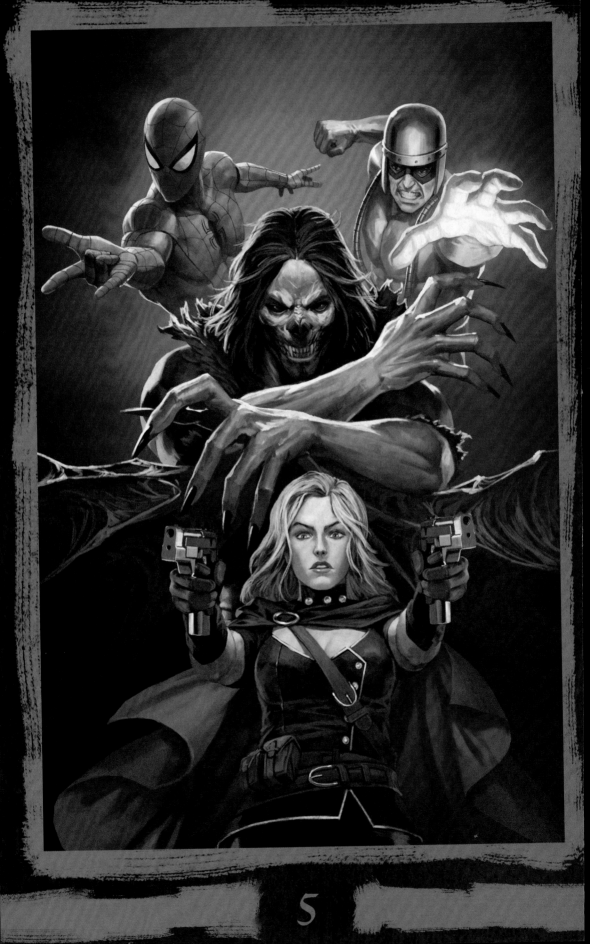

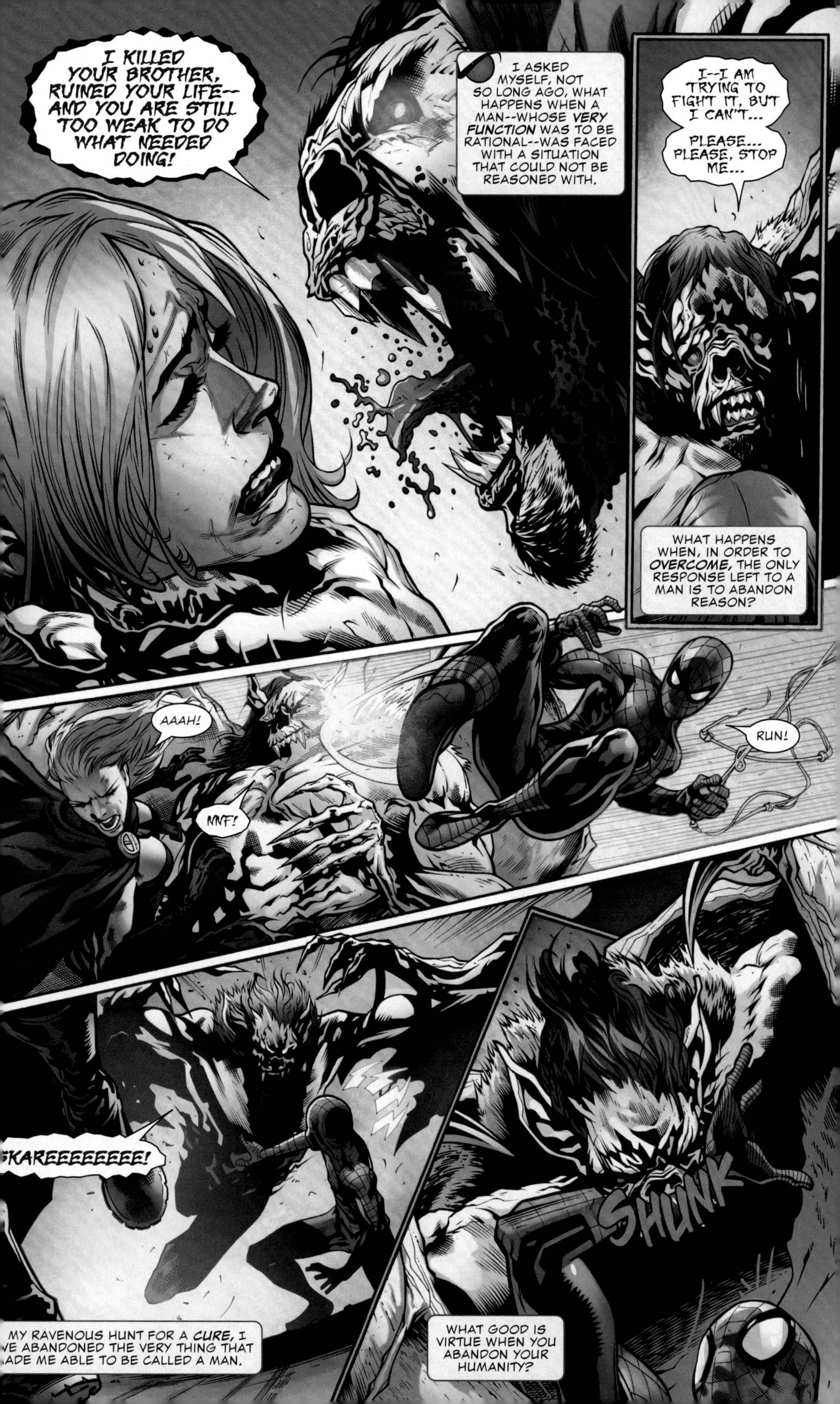

I KILLED YOUR BROTHER, RUINED YOUR LIFE-- AND YOU ARE STILL TOO WEAK TO DO WHAT NEEDED DOING!
I ASKED MYSELF, NOT SO LONG AGO, WHAT HAPPENS WHEN A MAN--WHOSE *VERY FUNCTION* WAS TO BE RATIONAL--WAS FACED WITH A SITUATION THAT COULD NOT BE REASONED WITH.
I--I AM TRYING TO FIGHT IT, BUT I CAN'T...
PLEASE... PLEASE, STOP ME...
WHAT HAPPENS WHEN, IN ORDER TO *OVERCOME,* THE ONLY RESPONSE LEFT TO A MAN IS TO ABANDON REASON?
AAAH!
RUN!
NNF!
SKAREEEEEEEEE!
SHUNK
MY RAVENOUS HUNT FOR A *CURE,* I
VE ABANDONED THE VERY THING THAT
ADE ME ABLE TO BE CALLED A MAN.
WHAT GOOD IS VIRTUE WHEN YOU ABANDON YOUR HUMANITY?

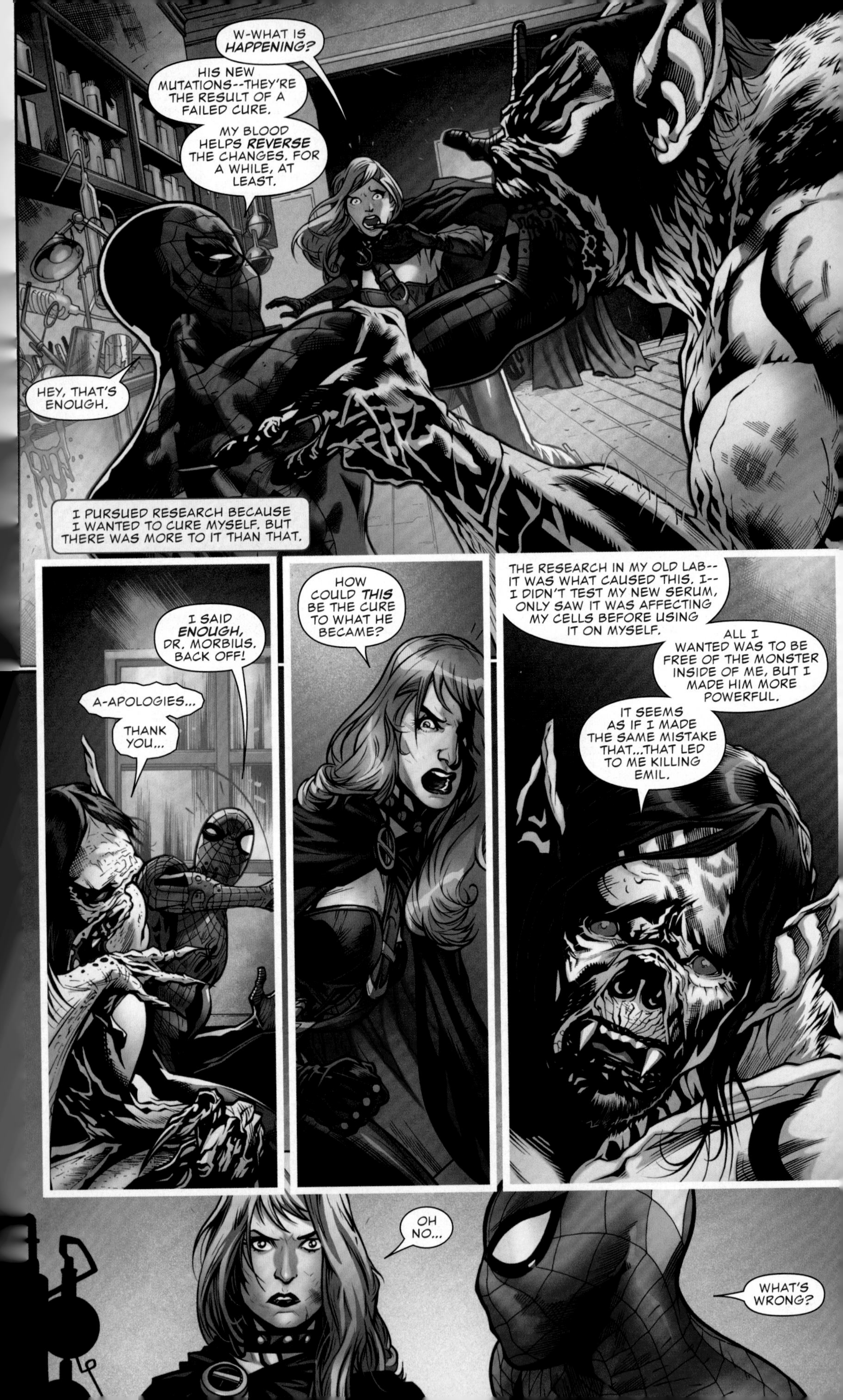
W-WHAT IS HAPPENING?
HIS NEW MUTATIONS--THEY'RE THE RESULT OF A FAILED CURE.
MY BLOOD HELPS REVERSE THE CHANGES. FOR A WHILE, AT LEAST.
HEY, THAT'S ENOUGH.
I PURSUED RESEARCH BECAUSE I WANTED TO CURE MYSELF. BUT THERE WAS MORE TO IT THAN THAT.
I SAID ENOUGH, DR. MORBIUS. BACK OFF!
A-APOLOGIES...
THANK YOU...
HOW COULD THIS BE THE CURE TO WHAT HE BECAME?
THE RESEARCH IN MY OLD LAB--IT WAS WHAT CAUSED THIS. I--I DIDN'T TEST MY NEW SERUM, ONLY SAW IT WAS AFFECTING MY CELLS BEFORE USING IT ON MYSELF.
ALL I WANTED WAS TO BE FREE OF THE MONSTER INSIDE OF ME, BUT I MADE HIM MORE POWERFUL.
IT SEEMS AS IF I MADE THE SAME MISTAKE THAT...THAT LED TO ME KILLING EMIL.
OH NO...
WHAT'S WRONG?

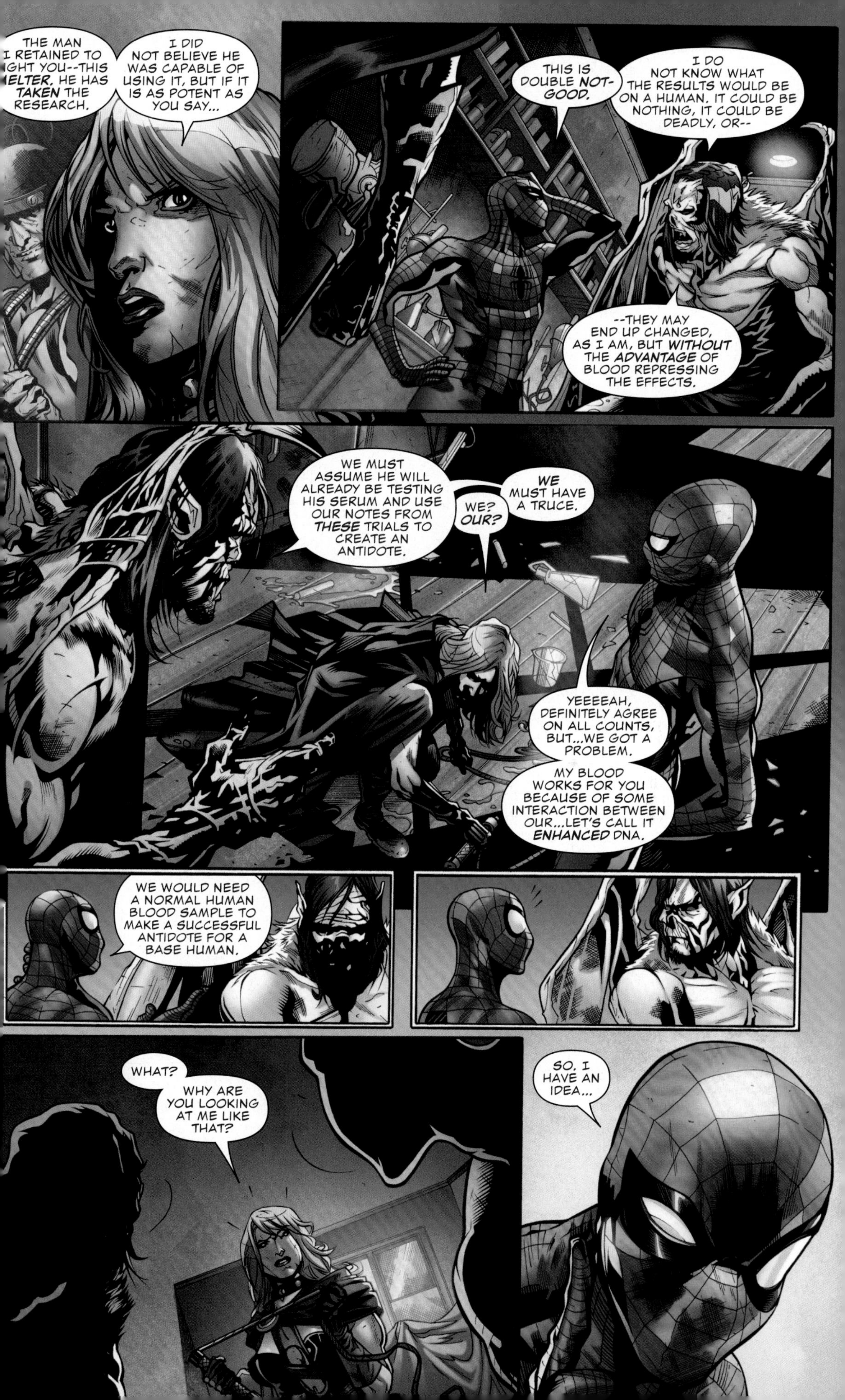

THE MAN I RETAINED TO ...IGHT YOU--THIS ...ELTER. HE HAS TAKEN THE RESEARCH.
I DID NOT BELIEVE HE WAS CAPABLE OF USING IT, BUT IF IT IS AS POTENT AS YOU SAY...
THIS IS DOUBLE NOT-GOOD.
I DO NOT KNOW WHAT THE RESULTS WOULD BE ON A HUMAN. IT COULD BE NOTHING, IT COULD BE DEADLY, OR--
--THEY MAY END UP CHANGED, AS I AM, BUT WITHOUT THE ADVANTAGE OF BLOOD REPRESSING THE EFFECTS.
WE MUST ASSUME HE WILL ALREADY BE TESTING HIS SERUM AND USE OUR NOTES FROM THESE TRIALS TO CREATE AN ANTIDOTE.
WE? OUR?
WE MUST HAVE A TRUCE.
YEEEEAH, DEFINITELY AGREE ON ALL COUNTS, BUT...WE GOT A PROBLEM.
MY BLOOD WORKS FOR YOU BECAUSE OF SOME INTERACTION BETWEEN OUR...LET'S CALL IT ENHANCED DNA.
WE WOULD NEED A NORMAL HUMAN BLOOD SAMPLE TO MAKE A SUCCESSFUL ANTIDOTE FOR A BASE HUMAN.
SO, I HAVE AN IDEA...
WHAT?
WHY ARE YOU LOOKING AT ME LIKE THAT?

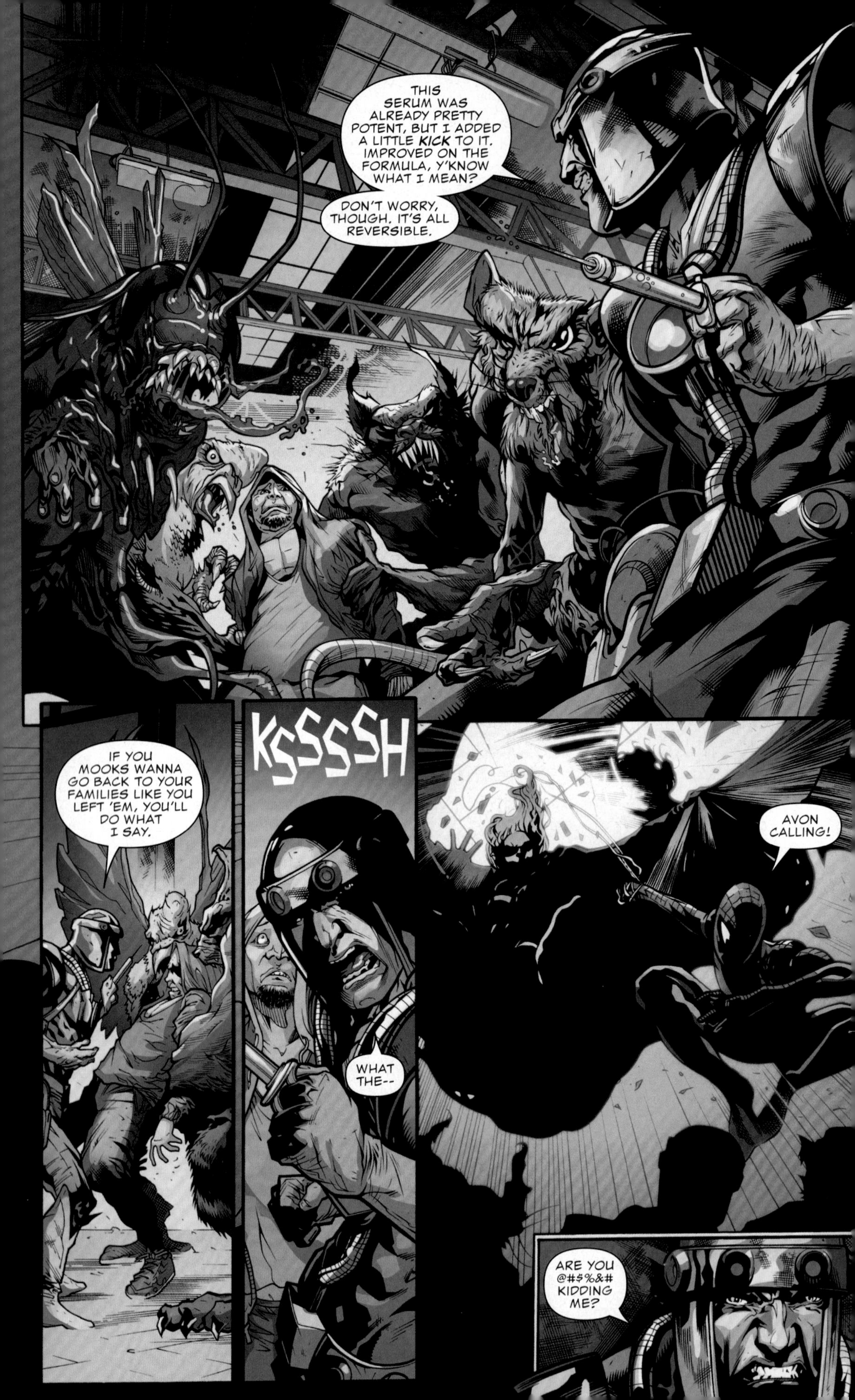
THIS SERUM WAS ALREADY PRETTY POTENT, BUT I ADDED A LITTLE KICK TO IT. IMPROVED ON THE FORMULA, Y'KNOW WHAT I MEAN?
DON'T WORRY, THOUGH. IT'S ALL REVERSIBLE.
IF YOU MOOKS WANNA GO BACK TO YOUR FAMILIES LIKE YOU LEFT 'EM, YOU'LL DO WHAT I SAY.
KSSSSH
WHAT THE--
AVON CALLING!
ARE YOU @#$%&# KIDDING ME?

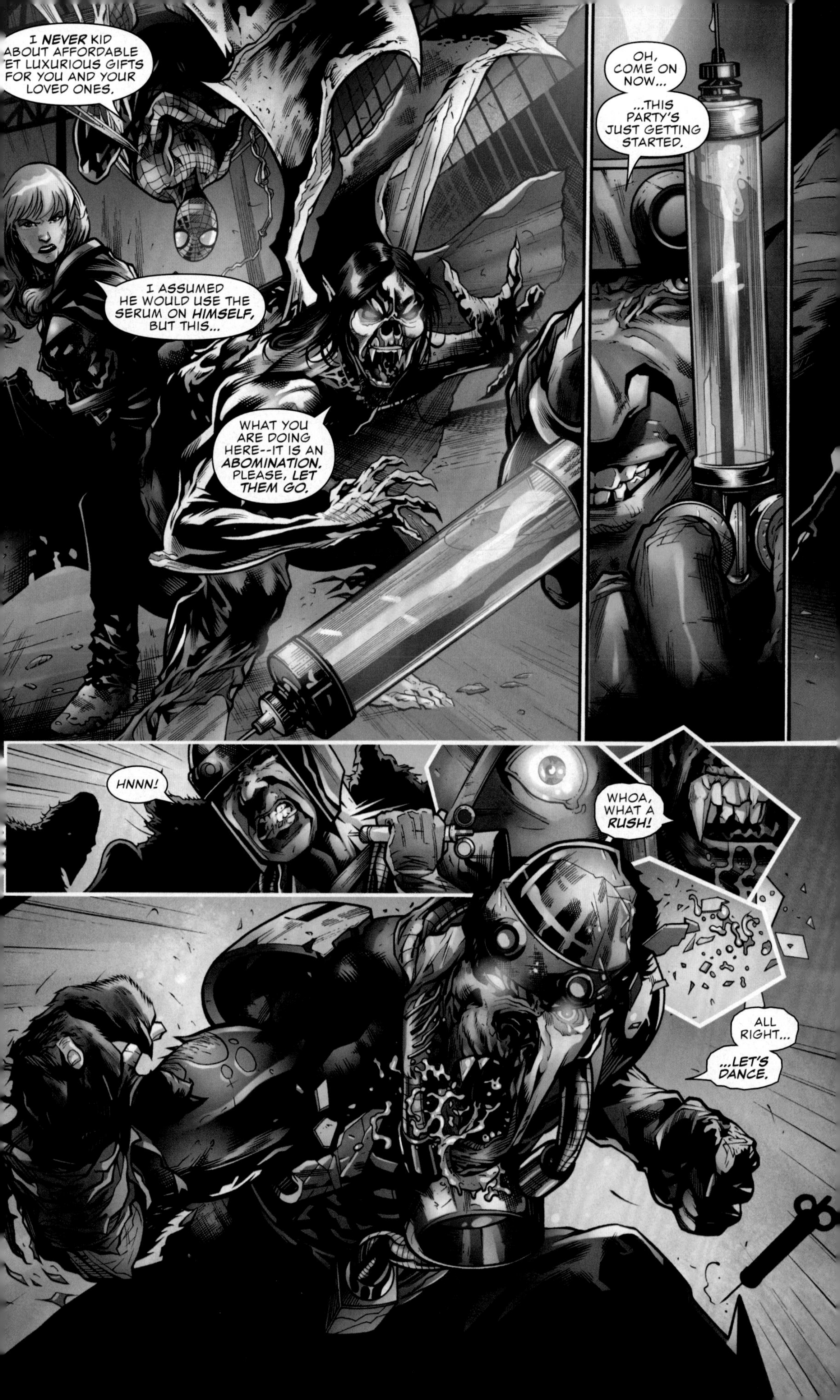
I NEVER KID ABOUT AFFORDABLE YET LUXURIOUS GIFTS FOR YOU AND YOUR LOVED ONES.
I ASSUMED HE WOULD USE THE SERUM ON HIMSELF, BUT THIS...
WHAT YOU ARE DOING HERE--IT IS AN ABOMINATION. PLEASE, LET THEM GO.
OH, COME ON NOW...
...THIS PARTY'S JUST GETTING STARTED.
HNNN!
WHOA, WHAT A RUSH!
ALL RIGHT...
...LET'S DANCE.

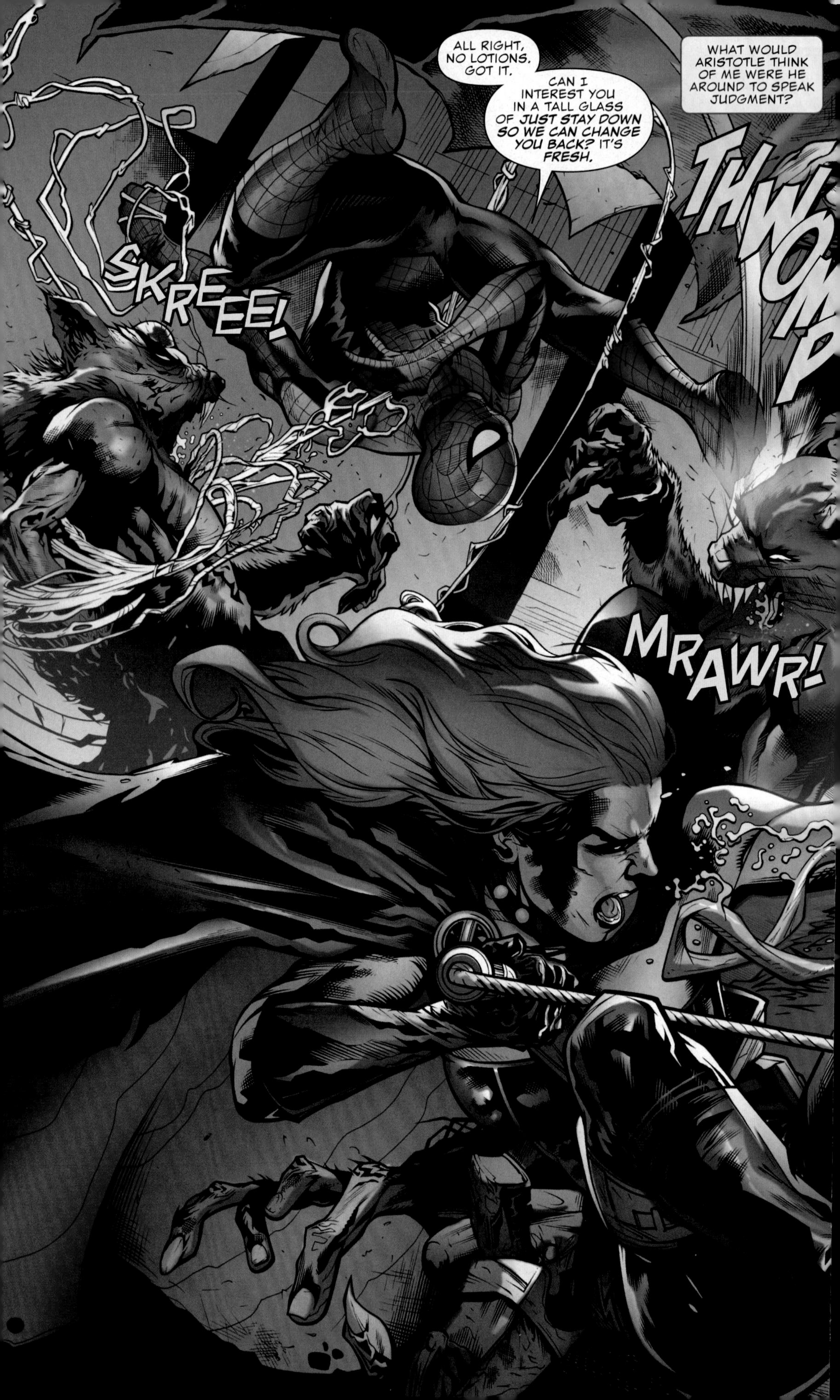
ALL RIGHT, NO LOTIONS. GOT IT.
CAN I INTEREST YOU IN A TALL GLASS OF JUST STAY DOWN SO WE CAN CHANGE YOU BACK? IT'S FRESH.
WHAT WOULD ARISTOTLE THINK OF ME WERE HE AROUND TO SPEAK JUDGMENT?
SKREEEE!
THWOMP
MRAWR!

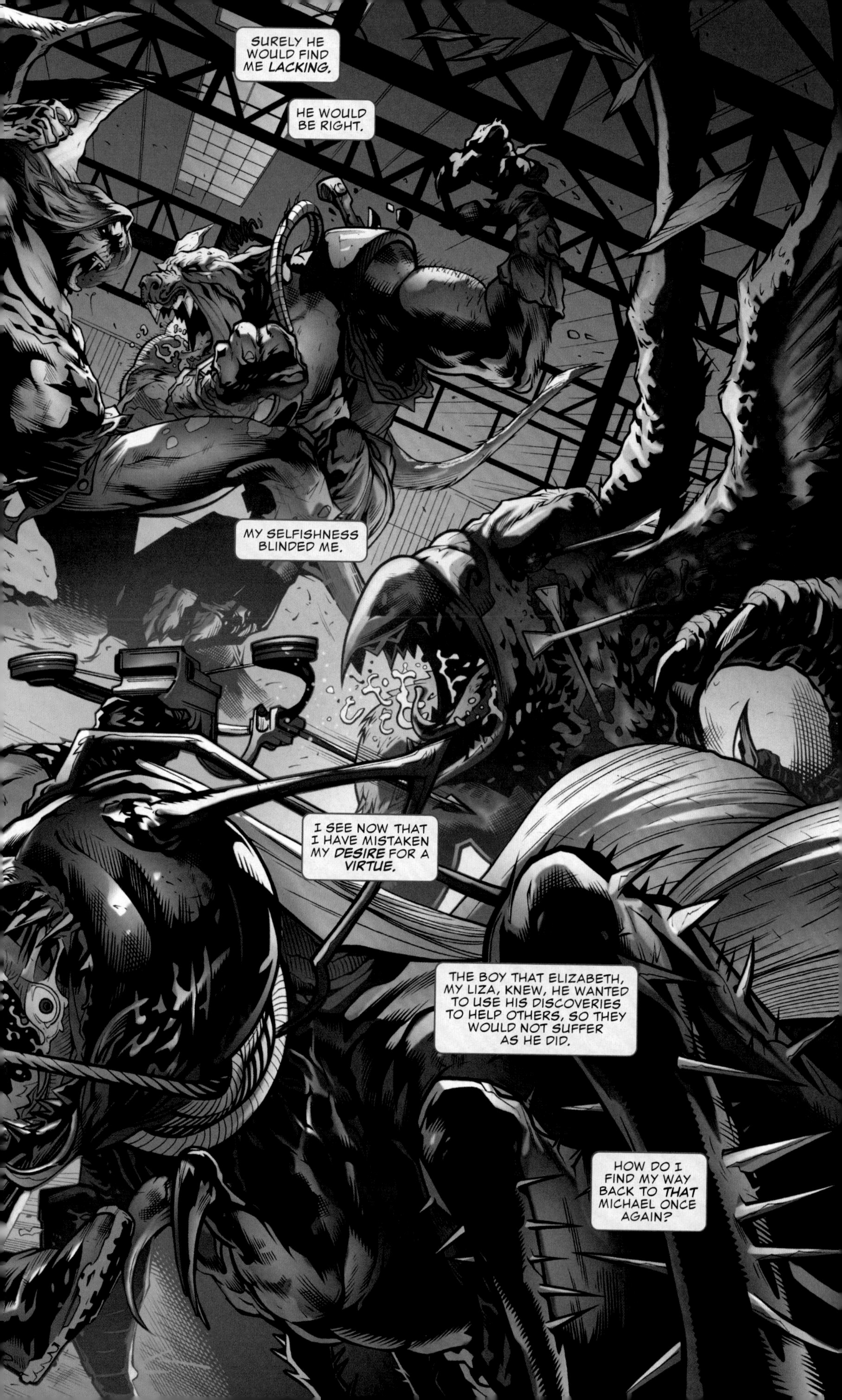
SURELY HE WOULD FIND ME LACKING.
HE WOULD BE RIGHT.
MY SELFISHNESS BLINDED ME.
I SEE NOW THAT I HAVE MISTAKEN MY DESIRE FOR A VIRTUE.
THE BOY THAT ELIZABETH, MY LIZA, KNEW, HE WANTED TO USE HIS DISCOVERIES TO HELP OTHERS, SO THEY WOULD NOT SUFFER AS HE DID.
HOW DO I FIND MY WAY BACK TO THAT MICHAEL ONCE AGAIN?

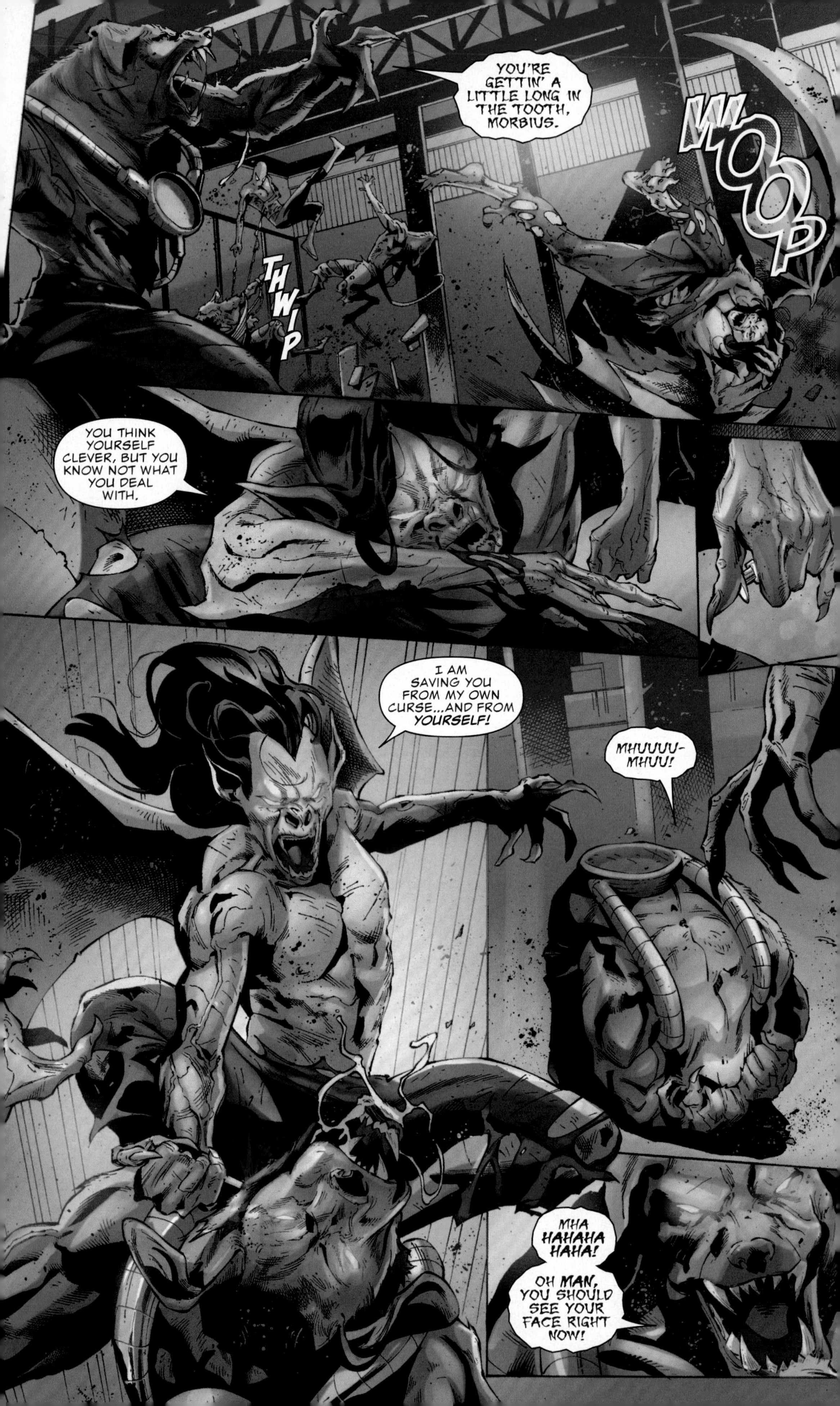
YOU'RE GETTIN' A LITTLE LONG IN THE TOOTH, MORBIUS.
WOOOP
THWIP
YOU THINK YOURSELF CLEVER, BUT YOU KNOW NOT WHAT YOU DEAL WITH.
I AM SAVING YOU FROM MY OWN CURSE...AND FROM YOURSELF!
MHUUUU-MHUU!
MHA HAHAHA HAHA!
OH MAN, YOU SHOULD SEE YOUR FACE RIGHT NOW!

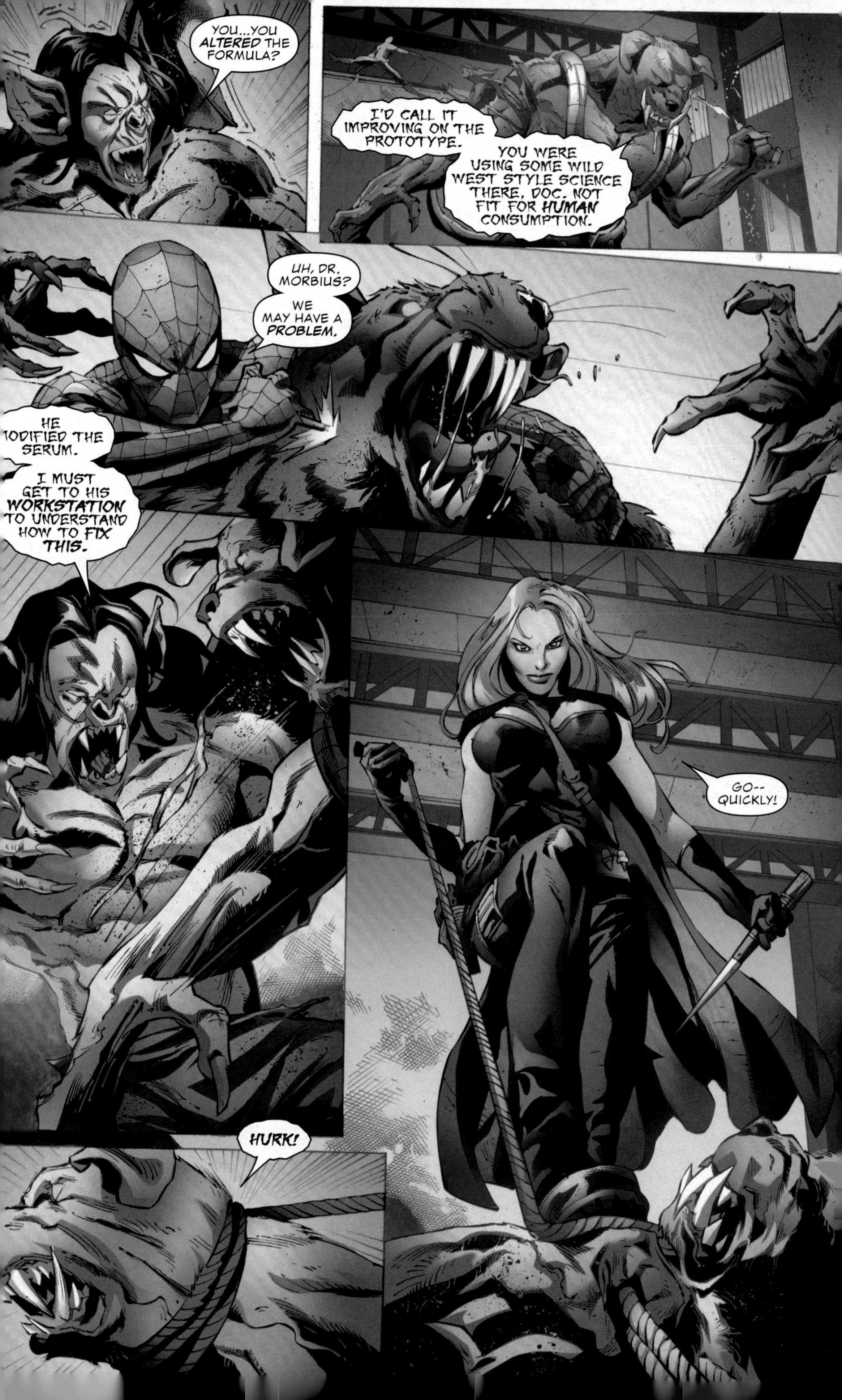

YOU...YOU *ALTERED* THE FORMULA?
I'D CALL IT IMPROVING ON THE PROTOTYPE.
YOU WERE USING SOME WILD WEST STYLE SCIENCE THERE, DOC. NOT FIT FOR *HUMAN* CONSUMPTION.
UH, DR. MORBIUS?
WE MAY HAVE A *PROBLEM.*
HE MODIFIED THE SERUM.
I MUST GET TO HIS **WORKSTATION** TO UNDERSTAND HOW TO **FIX THIS.**
GO-- QUICKLY!
HURK!

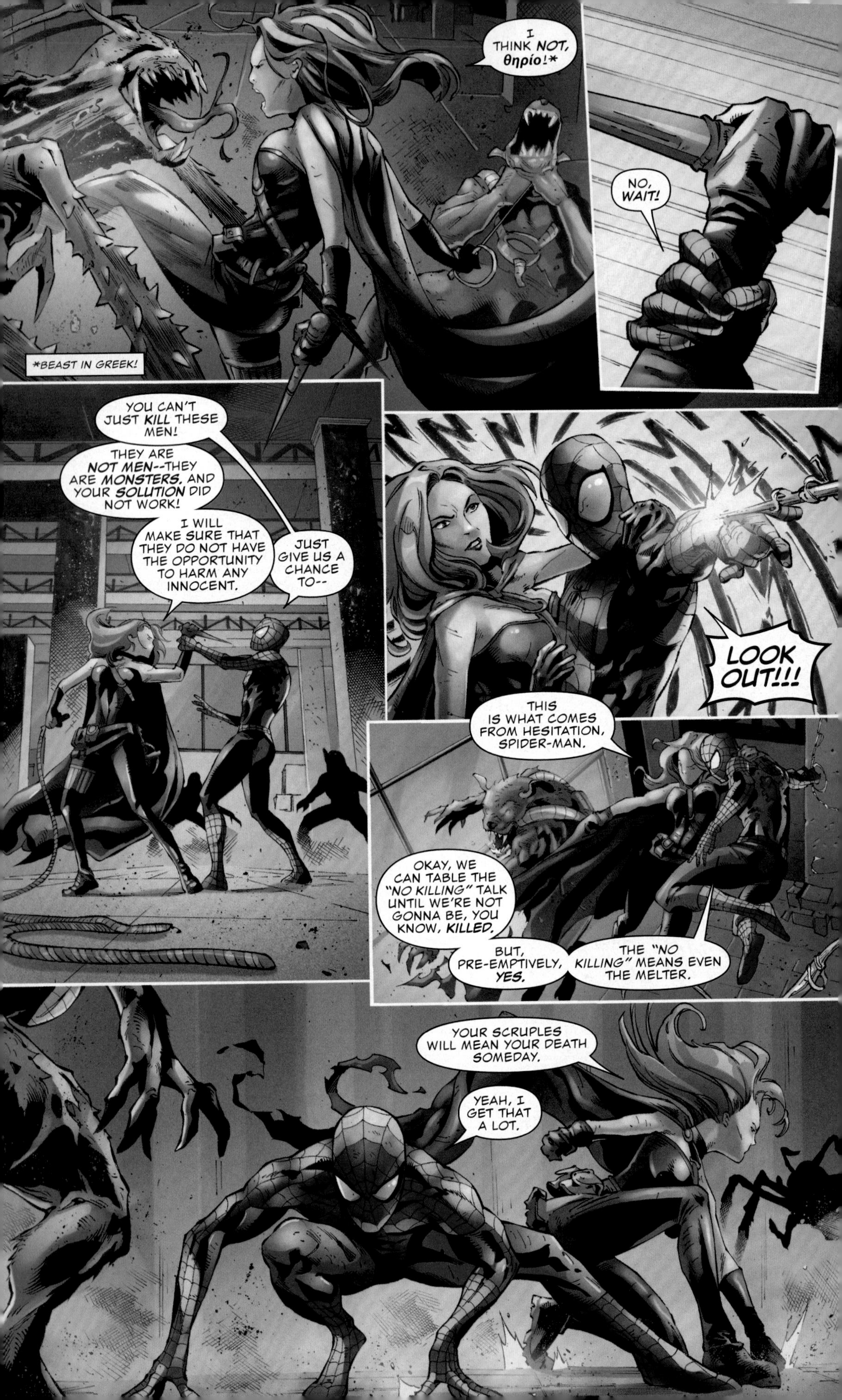

I THINK NOT, θηρίο!*
*BEAST IN GREEK!
NO, WAIT!
YOU CAN'T JUST KILL THESE MEN!
THEY ARE NOT MEN--THEY ARE MONSTERS. AND YOUR SOLUTION DID NOT WORK!
I WILL MAKE SURE THAT THEY DO NOT HAVE THE OPPORTUNITY TO HARM ANY INNOCENT.
JUST GIVE US A CHANCE TO--
LOOK OUT!!!
THIS IS WHAT COMES FROM HESITATION, SPIDER-MAN.
OKAY, WE CAN TABLE THE "NO KILLING" TALK UNTIL WE'RE NOT GONNA BE, YOU KNOW, KILLED.
THE "NO KILLING" MEANS EVEN THE MELTER.
BUT, PRE-EMPTIVELY, YES.
YOUR SCRUPLES WILL MEAN YOUR DEATH SOMEDAY.
YEAH, I GET THAT A LOT.

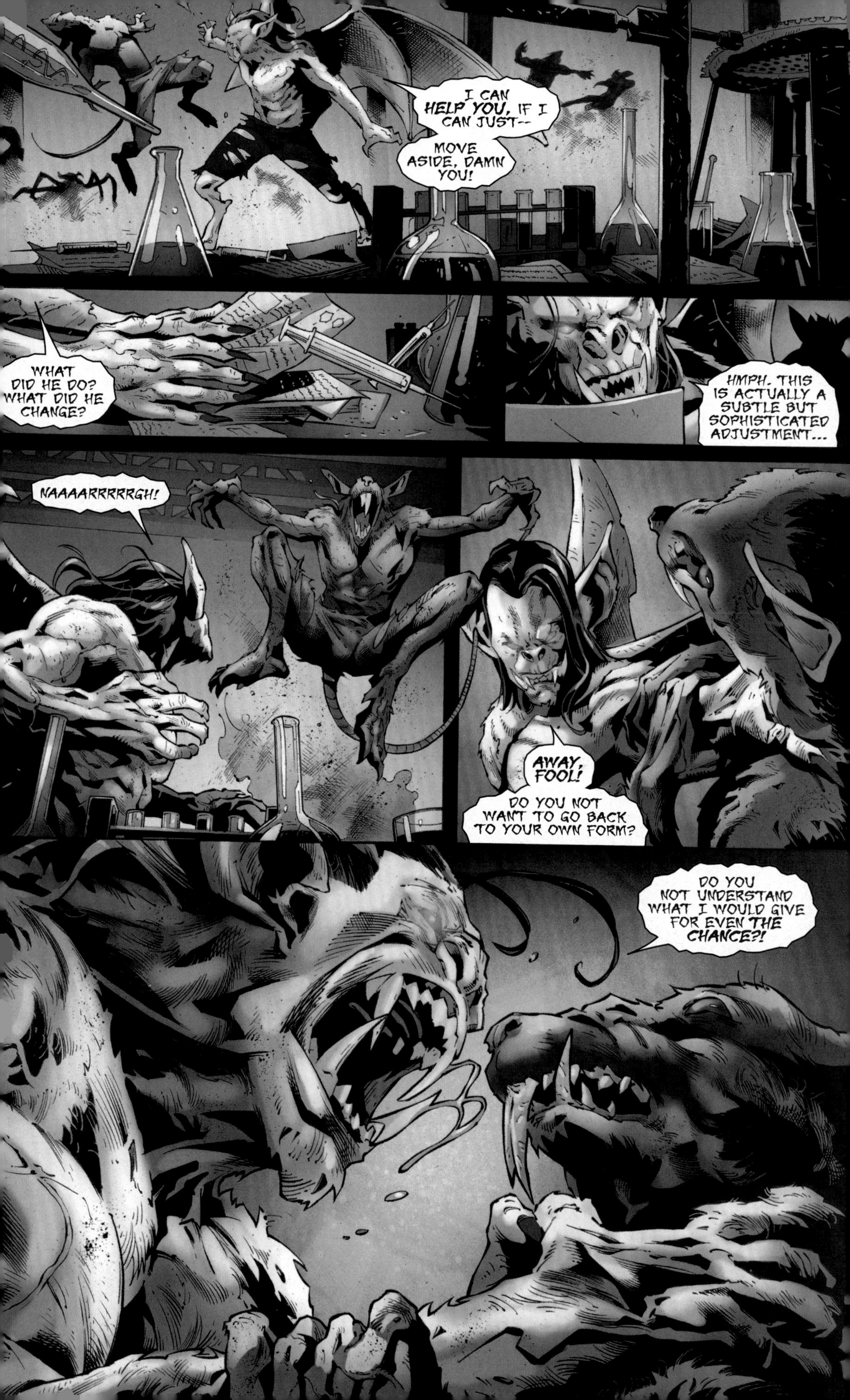
I CAN HELP YOU, IF I CAN JUST--
MOVE ASIDE, DAMN YOU!
WHAT DID HE DO? WHAT DID HE CHANGE?
HMPH. THIS IS ACTUALLY A SUBTLE BUT SOPHISTICATED ADJUSTMENT...
NAAAARRRRRGH!
AWAY, FOOL!
DO YOU NOT WANT TO GO BACK TO YOUR OWN FORM?
DO YOU NOT UNDERSTAND WHAT I WOULD GIVE FOR EVEN THE CHANCE?!

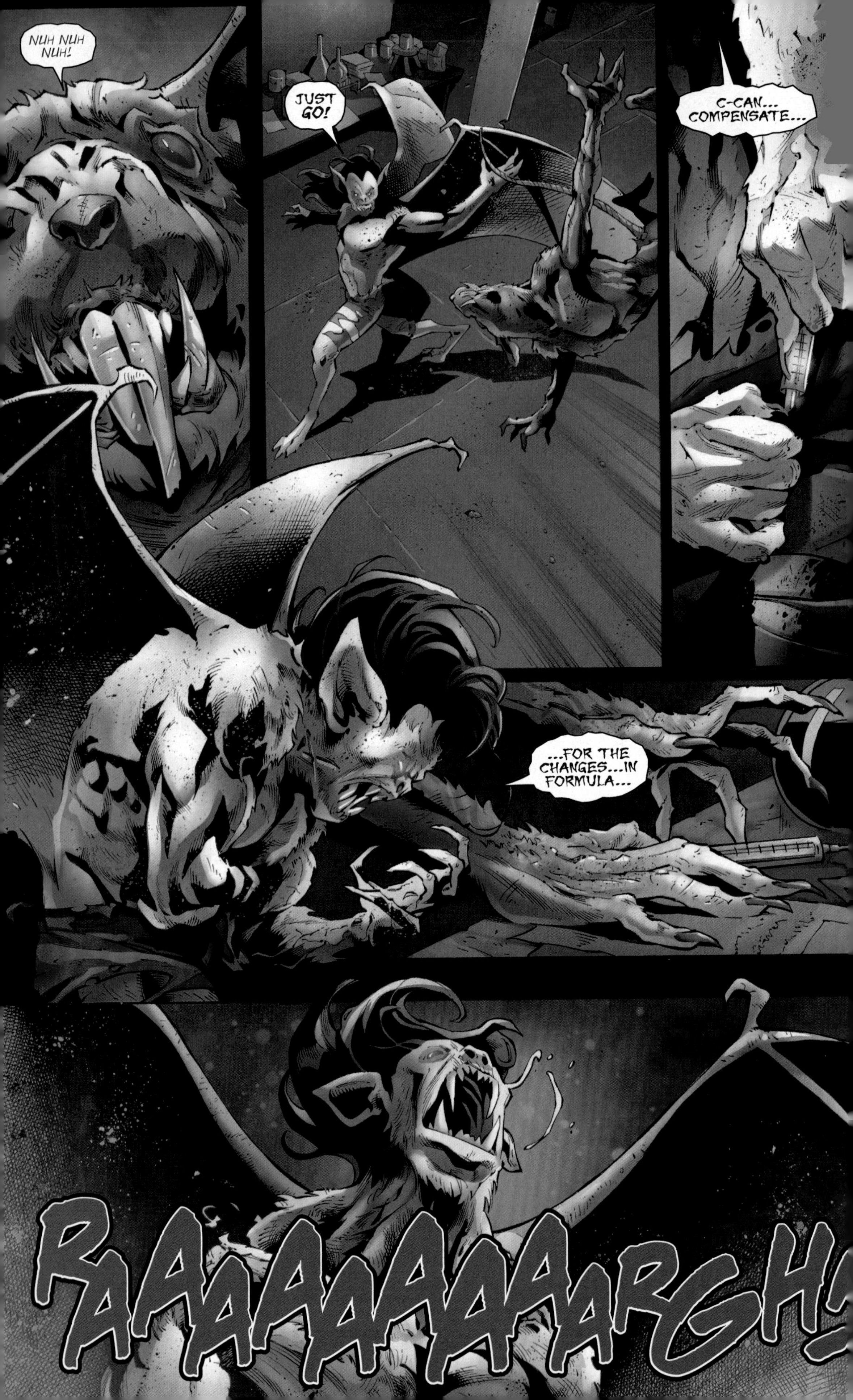
NUH NUH NUH!
JUST GO!
C-CAN... COMPENSATE...
...FOR THE CHANGES...IN FORMULA...
RAAAAAAAARGH!

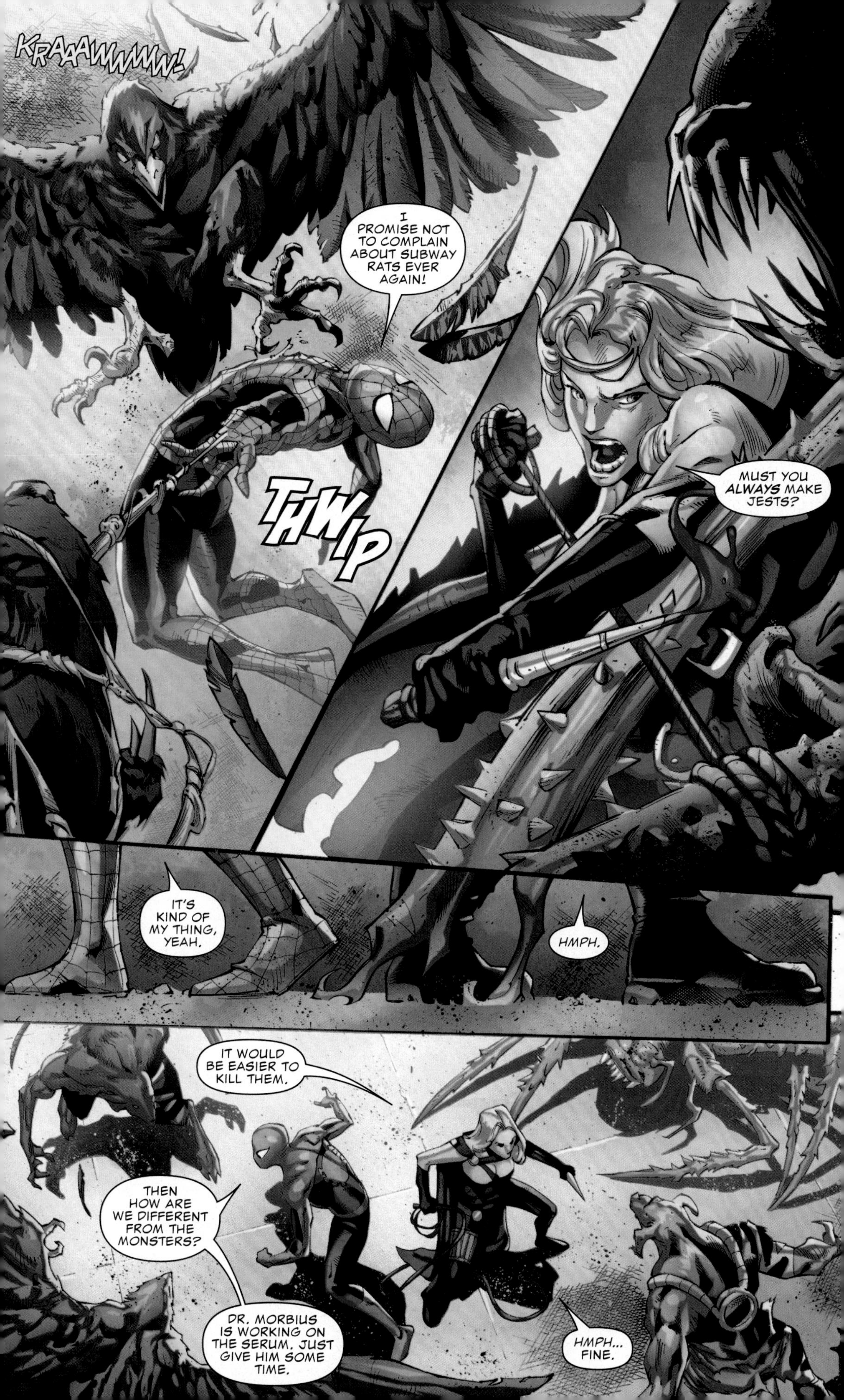
KRAAAWWWW!
I PROMISE NOT TO COMPLAIN ABOUT SUBWAY RATS EVER AGAIN!
THWIP
MUST YOU ALWAYS MAKE JESTS?
IT'S KIND OF MY THING, YEAH.
HMPH.
IT WOULD BE EASIER TO KILL THEM.
THEN HOW ARE WE DIFFERENT FROM THE MONSTERS?
DR. MORBIUS IS WORKING ON THE SERUM. JUST GIVE HIM SOME TIME.
HMPH... FINE.

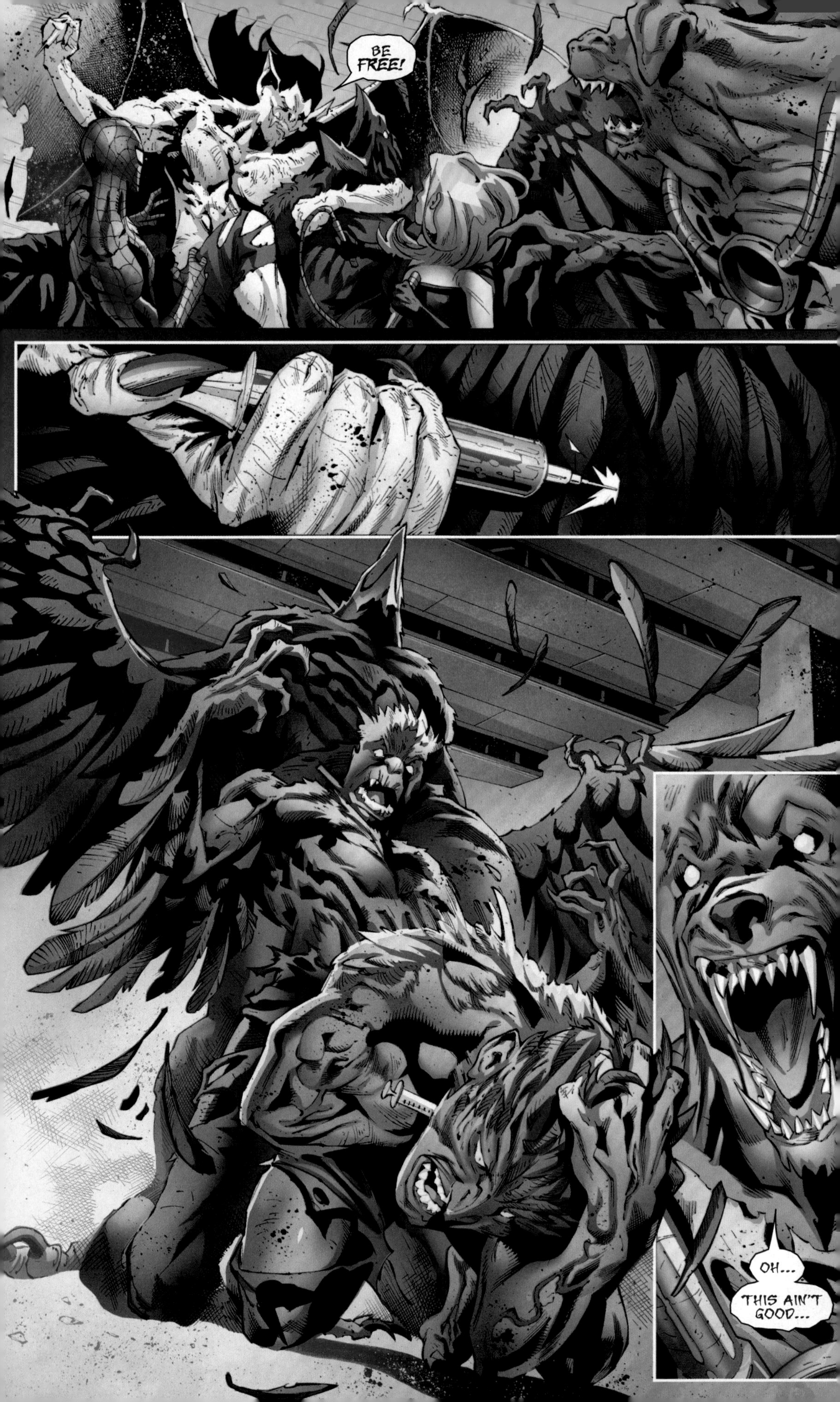
BE FREE!
OH...
THIS AIN'T GOOD...

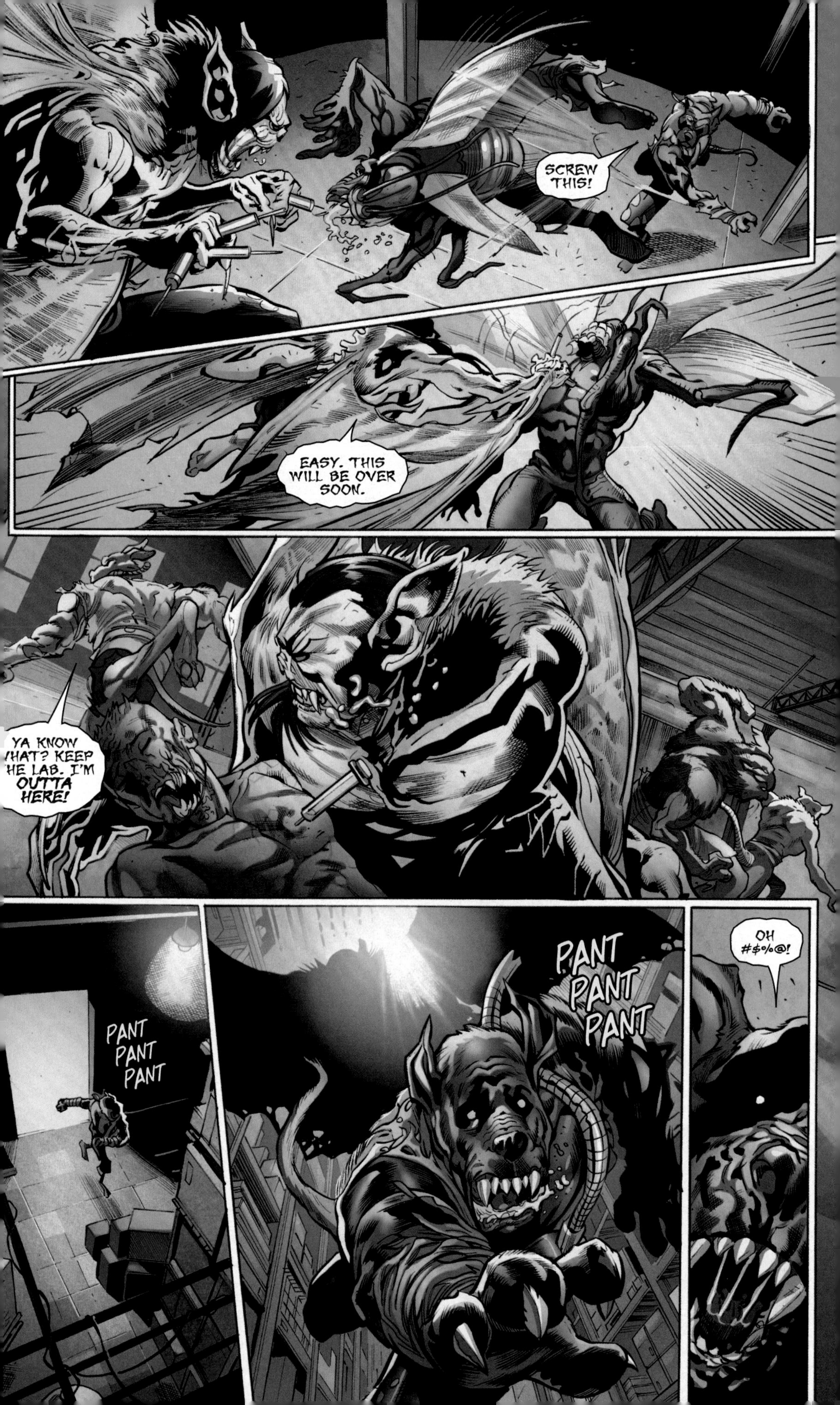
SCREW THIS!
EASY. THIS WILL BE OVER SOON.
YA KNOW WHAT? KEEP THE LAB. I'M OUTTA HERE!
PANT PANT PANT
PANT PANT PANT
OH #$%@!

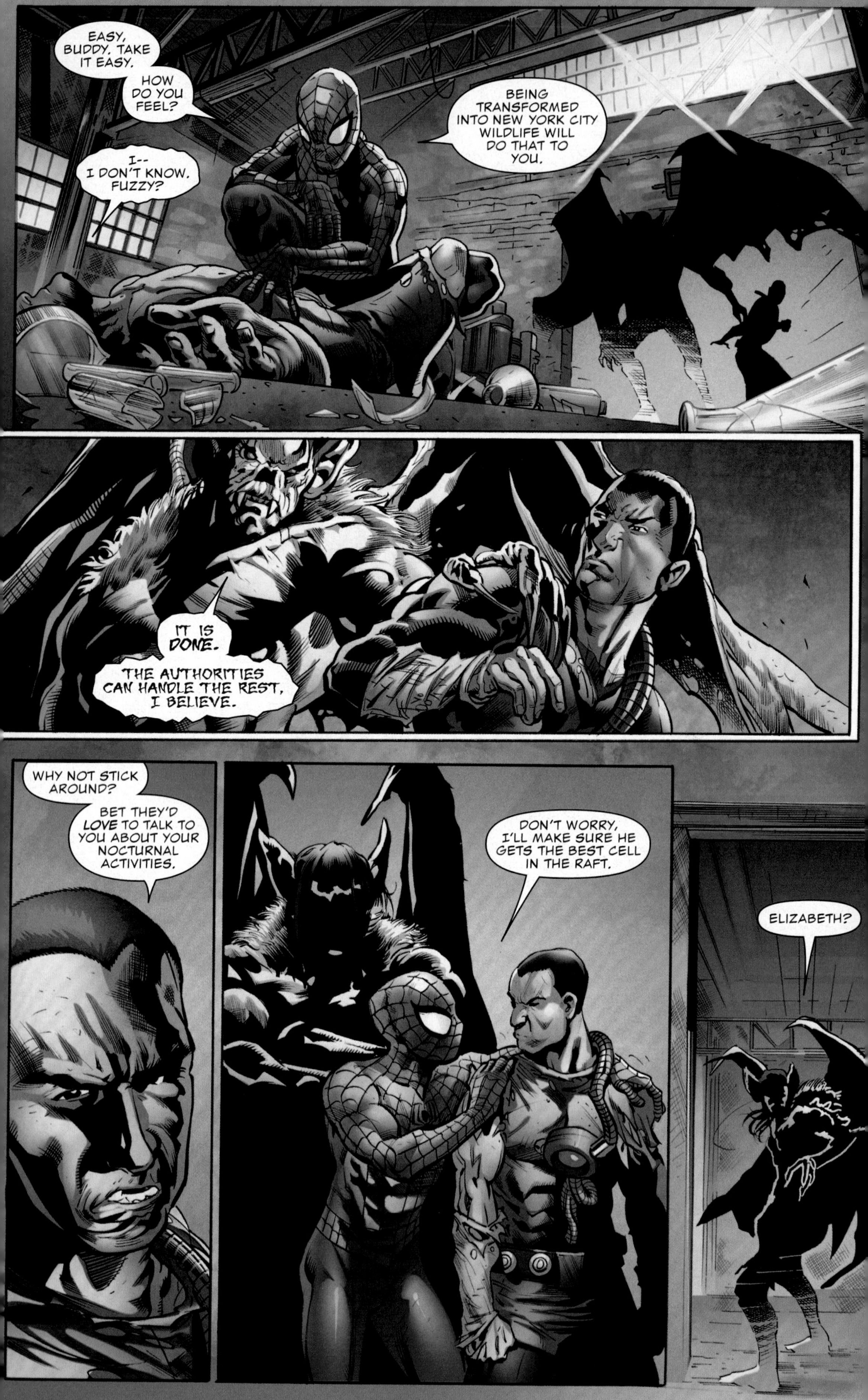
EASY, BUDDY. TAKE IT EASY.
HOW DO YOU FEEL?
I-- I DON'T KNOW. FUZZY?
BEING TRANSFORMED INTO NEW YORK CITY WILDLIFE WILL DO THAT TO YOU.
IT IS DONE.
THE AUTHORITIES CAN HANDLE THE REST, I BELIEVE.
WHY NOT STICK AROUND?
BET THEY'D LOVE TO TALK TO YOU ABOUT YOUR NOCTURNAL ACTIVITIES.
DON'T WORRY, I'LL MAKE SURE HE GETS THE BEST CELL IN THE RAFT.
ELIZABETH?

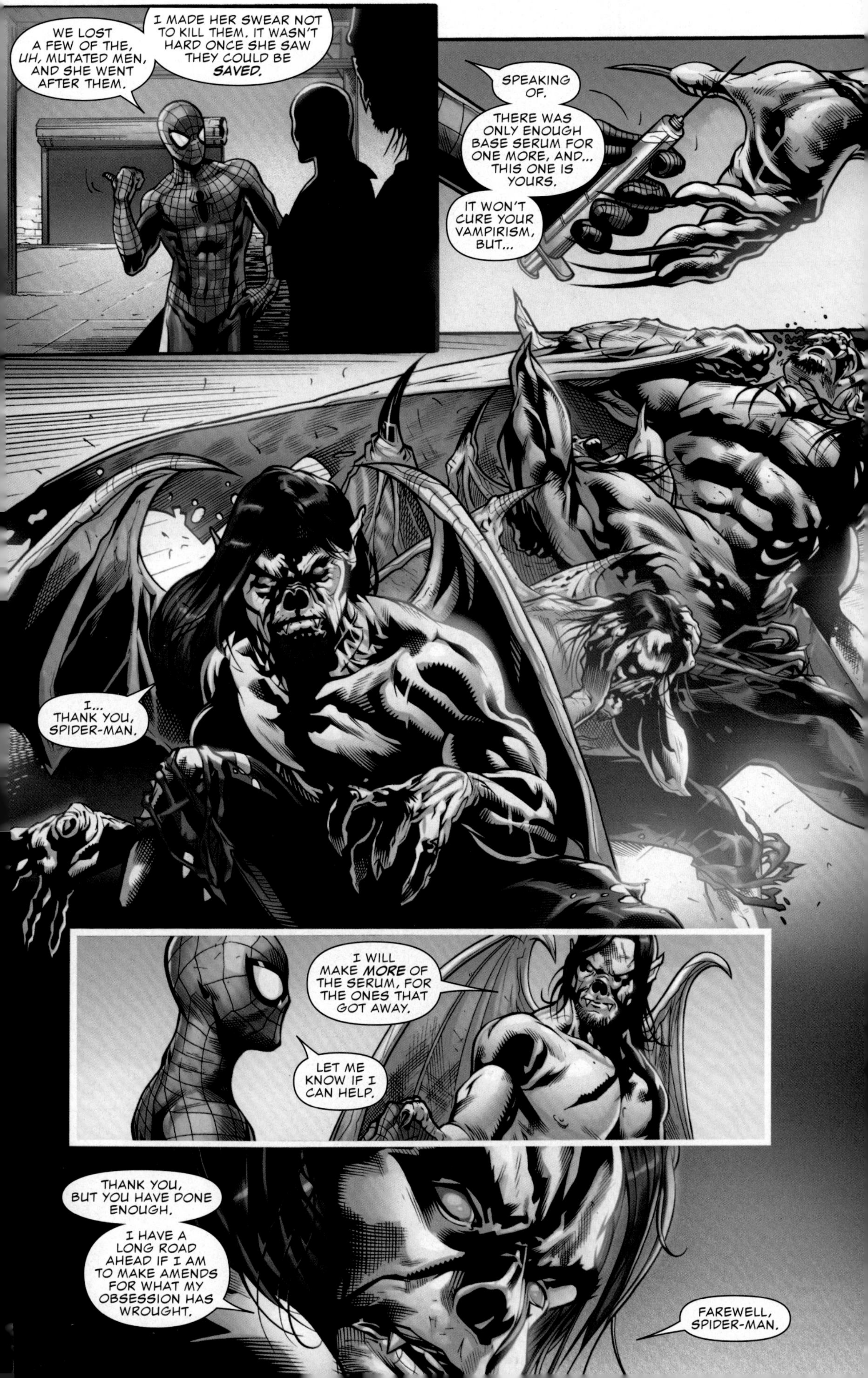
WE LOST A FEW OF THE, UH, MUTATED MEN, AND SHE WENT AFTER THEM.
I MADE HER SWEAR NOT TO KILL THEM. IT WASN'T HARD ONCE SHE SAW THEY COULD BE SAVED.
SPEAKING OF.
THERE WAS ONLY ENOUGH BASE SERUM FOR ONE MORE, AND... THIS ONE IS YOURS.
IT WON'T CURE YOUR VAMPIRISM, BUT...
I... THANK YOU, SPIDER-MAN.
I WILL MAKE MORE OF THE SERUM, FOR THE ONES THAT GOT AWAY.
LET ME KNOW IF I CAN HELP.
THANK YOU, BUT YOU HAVE DONE ENOUGH.
I HAVE A LONG ROAD AHEAD IF I AM TO MAKE AMENDS FOR WHAT MY OBSESSION HAS WROUGHT.
FAREWELL, SPIDER-MAN.

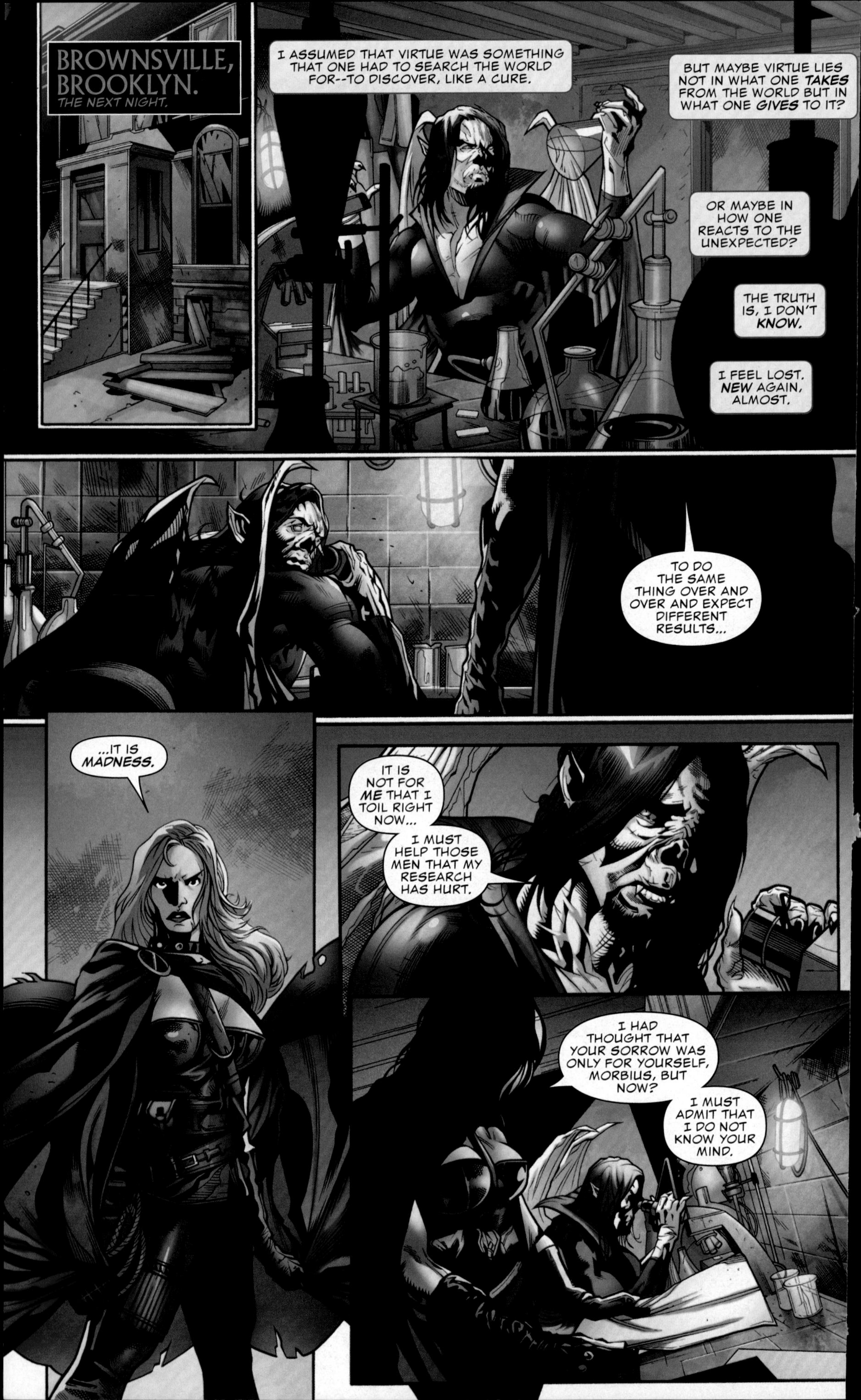
BROWNSVILLE, BROOKLYN.
THE NEXT NIGHT.
I ASSUMED THAT VIRTUE WAS SOMETHING THAT ONE HAD TO SEARCH THE WORLD FOR--TO DISCOVER, LIKE A CURE.
BUT MAYBE VIRTUE LIES NOT IN WHAT ONE TAKES FROM THE WORLD BUT IN WHAT ONE GIVES TO IT?
OR MAYBE IN HOW ONE REACTS TO THE UNEXPECTED?
THE TRUTH IS, I DON'T KNOW.
I FEEL LOST. NEW AGAIN, ALMOST.
TO DO THE SAME THING OVER AND OVER AND EXPECT DIFFERENT RESULTS...
...IT IS MADNESS.
IT IS NOT FOR ME THAT I TOIL RIGHT NOW...
I MUST HELP THOSE MEN THAT MY RESEARCH HAS HURT.
I HAD THOUGHT THAT YOUR SORROW WAS ONLY FOR YOURSELF, MORBIUS, BUT NOW?
I MUST ADMIT THAT I DO NOT KNOW YOUR MIND.

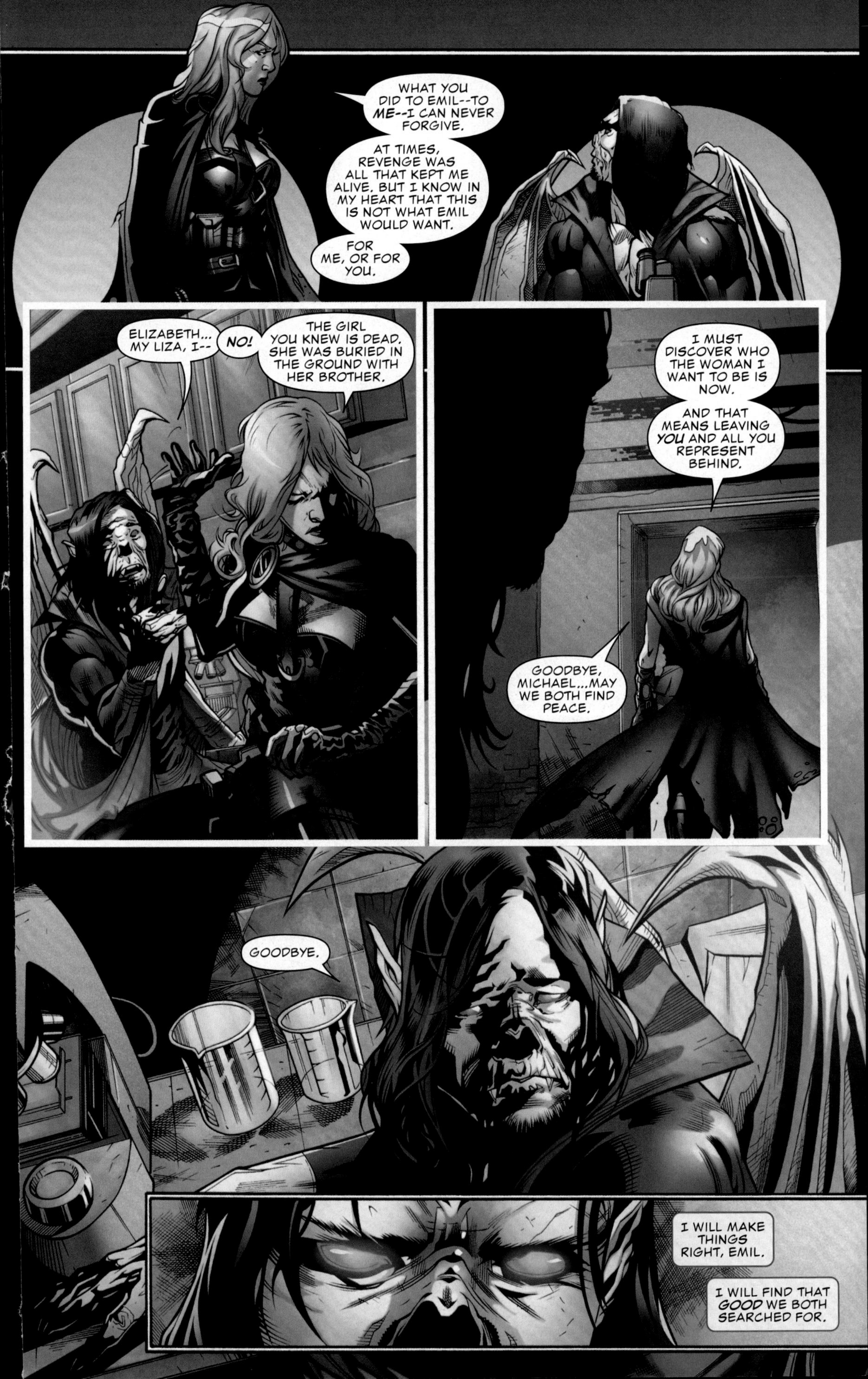
WHAT YOU DID TO EMIL--TO ME--I CAN NEVER FORGIVE.
AT TIMES, REVENGE WAS ALL THAT KEPT ME ALIVE. BUT I KNOW IN MY HEART THAT THIS IS NOT WHAT EMIL WOULD WANT.
FOR ME, OR FOR YOU.
ELIZABETH... MY LIZA, I--
NO!
THE GIRL YOU KNEW IS DEAD. SHE WAS BURIED IN THE GROUND WITH HER BROTHER.
I MUST DISCOVER WHO THE WOMAN I WANT TO BE IS NOW.
AND THAT MEANS LEAVING YOU AND ALL YOU REPRESENT BEHIND.
GOODBYE, MICHAEL...MAY WE BOTH FIND PEACE.
GOODBYE.
I WILL MAKE THINGS RIGHT, EMIL.
I WILL FIND THAT GOOD WE BOTH SEARCHED FOR.

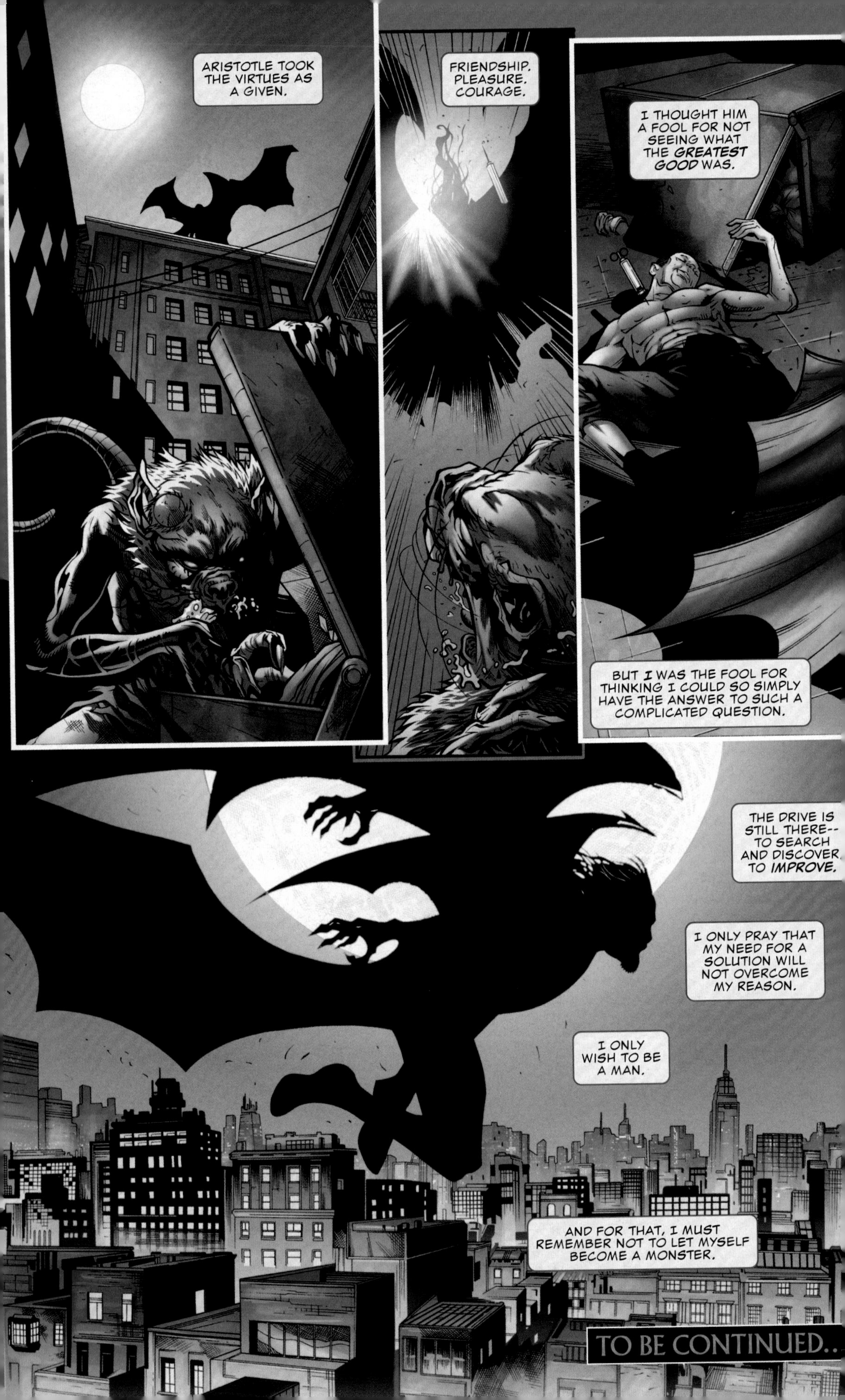
ARISTOTLE TOOK THE VIRTUES AS A GIVEN.
FRIENDSHIP. PLEASURE. COURAGE.
I THOUGHT HIM A FOOL FOR NOT SEEING WHAT THE *GREATEST GOOD* WAS.
BUT *I* WAS THE FOOL FOR THINKING I COULD SO SIMPLY HAVE THE ANSWER TO SUCH A COMPLICATED QUESTION.
THE DRIVE IS STILL THERE-- TO SEARCH AND DISCOVER. TO *IMPROVE.*
I ONLY PRAY THAT MY NEED FOR A SOLUTION WILL NOT OVERCOME MY REASON.
I ONLY WISH TO BE A MAN.
AND FOR THAT, I MUST REMEMBER NOT TO LET MYSELF BECOME A MONSTER.
TO BE CONTINUED...

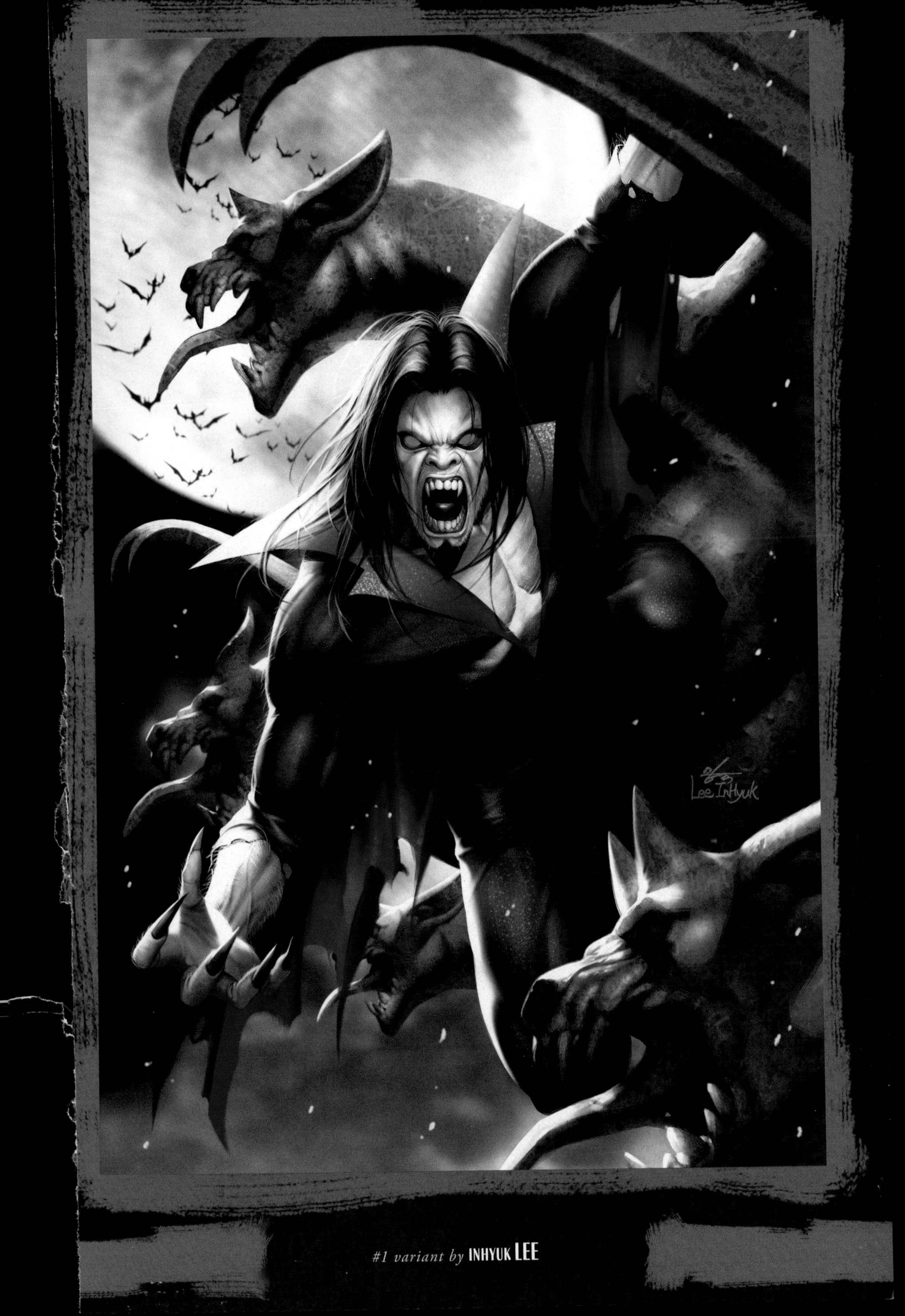
Lee InHyuk

#1 variant by **INHYUK LEE**

#1-5 connecting variants by **JUAN JOSÉ RYP** *&* **BRIAN REBER**

#1 2nd printing variant by **MARCELO FERREIRA**

#2 variant by E. M. GIST

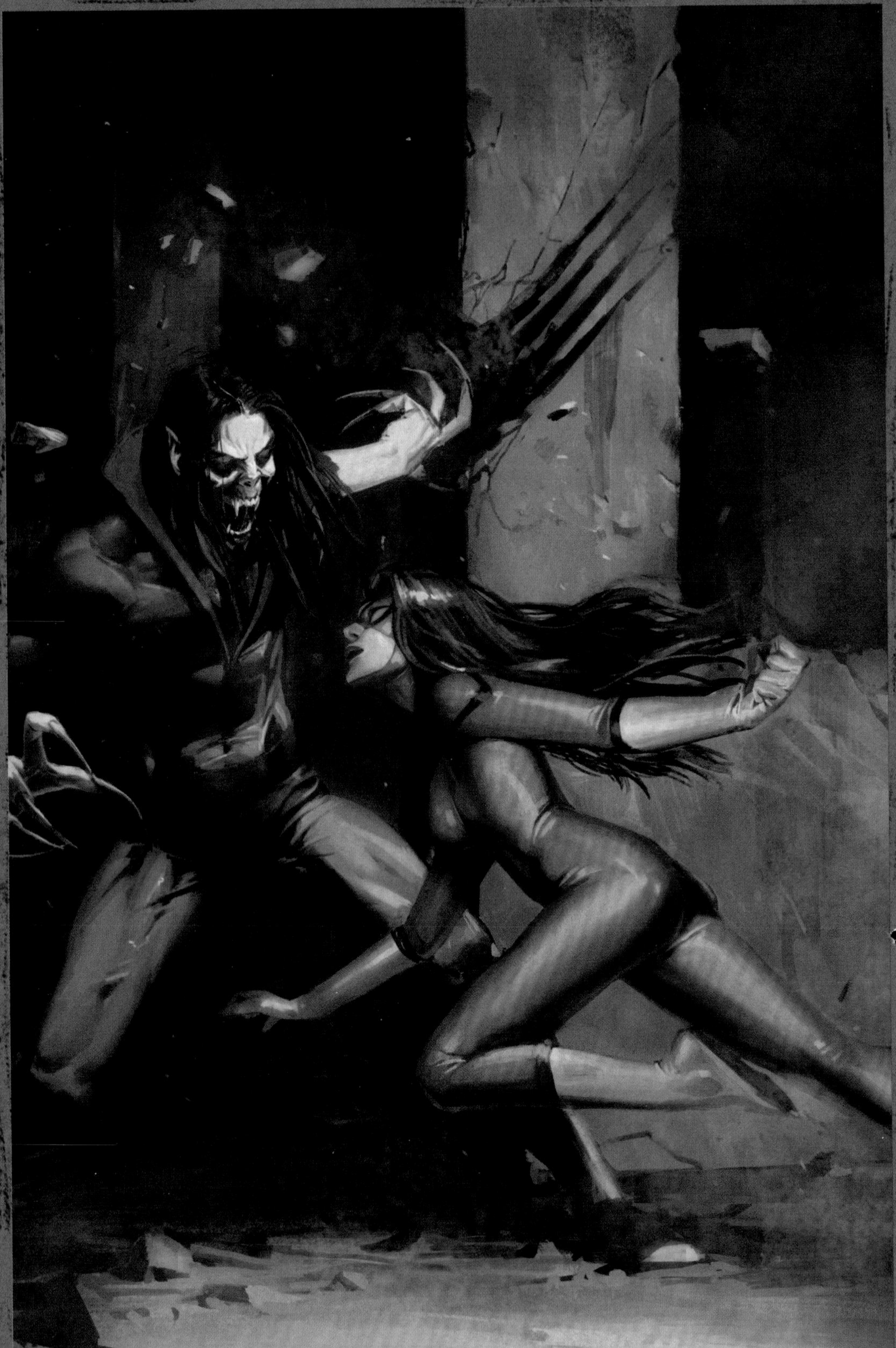

#5 Spider-Woman variant by **PYEONG-JUN PARK**

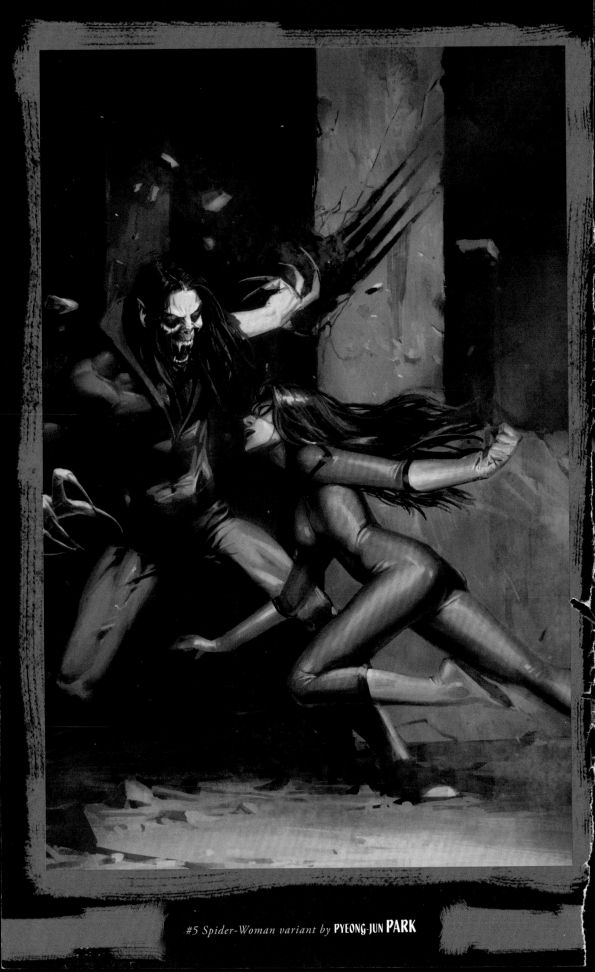